HIGH SCHOOL TECH CURRICULUM

Book 1

Grades 9-12

High School Technology Curriculum Book 1: Teacher Manual

2024

Visit the companion website at Ask a Tech Teacher for more resources to teach technology

ALL MATERIAL IN THIS BOOK IS PROTECTED BY THE INTELLECTUAL PROPERTY LAWS OF THE USA.

No part of this work can be reproduced or used in any form or by any means—graphic, electronic, or mechanical, including photocopying, recording, taping, Web distribution or information storage and retrieval systems—without the prior written permission of the publisher

For permission to use material from this text or product, contact us by email at: info@structuredlearning.net

978-1-942101-49-9

Structured Learning LLC. © All Rights Reserved

Introduction

The educational paradigm has changed. Technology, once optional, is now granular to college and career preparation, blended into educational standards that expect students to:

- **evaluate print and digital media**
- **gather information** from print/digital sources
- integrate and evaluate **information presented in diverse media** and formats
- **interpret information** visually, orally, quantitatively
- make **strategic use of digital media**
- use **print/digital glossaries/dictionaries**
- use information from **images and words in print/digital** text
- communicate with a **variety of media**
- **use text features and search tools** (e.g., key words, sidebars, **hyperlinks**) to locate information

But how do educators teach the technology that allows students to achieve these standards?

This **High School Technology Curriculum** is a great start. It provides critical tech knowledge and skills that will make a difference in student learning and life. Lessons are designed to be self-paced, platform-agnostic, aligned with core subjects, and themed to the topics important to high school students.

The volumes are project-based with wide-ranging opportunities for students to show their knowledge in the manner best fit to their communication style.

Each volume is stand-alone with a particular focus to help you choose which is best for your needs:

Book 1: *Reviews the tech skills required for college and career.*

Book 1 (this book) is a perfect choice to establish comprehensive tech skills as students prepare for independent use and understanding in college or career. Depending upon how well-versed students are in technology, they move faster or slower through lessons, but with the confidence that they are learning critical skills.

> ❋ ❋ ❋
>
> "New technologies have broadened and expanded the role that speaking and listening play in acquiring and sharing knowledge and have tightened their link to other forms of communication. Digital texts confront students with the potential for continually updated content and dynamically changing combinations of words, graphics, images, hyperlinks, and embedded video and audio."
> —CCSS
>
> ❋ ❋ ❋
>
> "Use of technology differentiates for student learning styles by providing an alternative method of achieving conceptual understanding, procedural skill and fluency, and applying this knowledge to authentic circumstances."
> —CCSS
>
> ❋ ❋ ❋

Book 2: *Applies learned skills to popular tech projects (not available yet)*

Book 2 is a perfect choice for students who have a solid background in tech skills and are interested in using it in projects like coding, robotics, writing ebooks, and others that apply to classes and interests. The overarching goal of Book 2 and 3 is to teach students to be problem solvers and independent thinkers prepared for whatever they face in the future.

Book 3: *Applies learned skills to more advanced projects (not available yet)*

Book 3 is a perfect choice for students who have a solid background in applying tech skills to projects and are looking for more advanced opportunities in Word certification, SketchUp, Engineering, Alice, and other tech-intensive topics. The overarching goal of Book 2 and 3 is to teach students to be problem solvers and independent thinkers so they are prepared for whatever their future holds.

What's in this Curriculum?

Lessons in these three volumes (this is the first of three—Book 2 and 3 are sold separately) may focus on coding, debate, engineering, financial literacy, Genius Hour, Google Earth, image editing, infographics, Internet searches, math, presentations, Photoshop, robotics, SketchUp, spreadsheets, visual learning, webtools, word processing, writing ebooks, and more. All books include three foundational topics that are considered critical to student technology success:

- keyboarding
- digital citizenship
- problem-solving

Included in each is 1) a Scope and Sequence which catalogues what is covered and in which volume, and 2) short articles on the curriculum's pedagogic foundation.

Each weekly lesson includes:

- assessment strategies
- class exit ticket
- Common Core and ISTE alignment
- differentiation strategies
- educational applications
- essential question and big idea
- examples, rubrics, images, printables
- materials and preparation required
- problem solving for the project
- steps to accomplish goals
- time required
- vocabulary used
- warm-ups

All except the 'steps to accomplish goals' can quickly be viewed on the first and last page of each lesson, providing a snapshot of what will be happening without digging through lots of pages. *Figures 1a-b* are screenshots from a sample lesson showing where these are in the lesson (zoom in if needed):

Figure 1a-b—What's included in each lesson

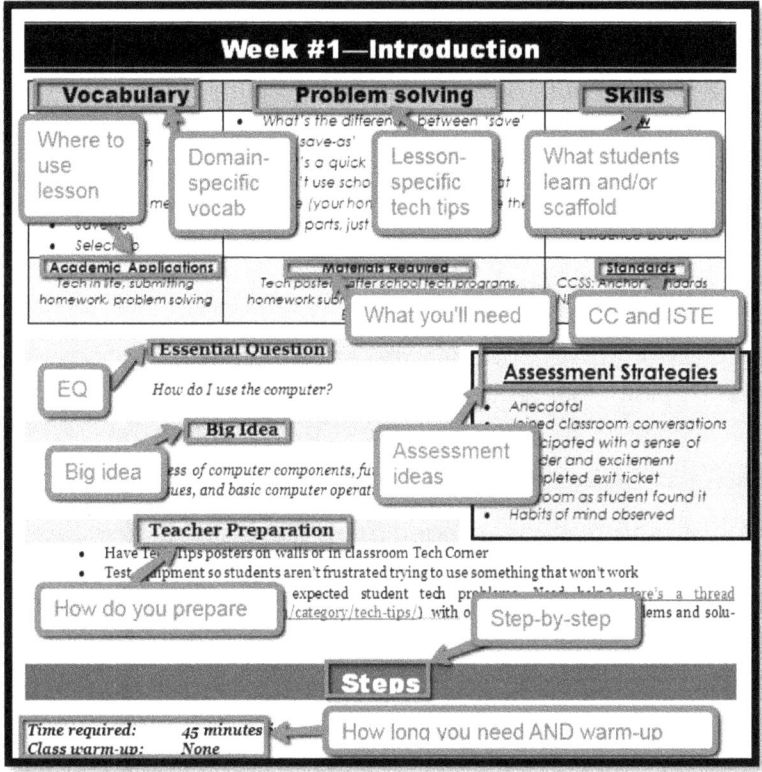

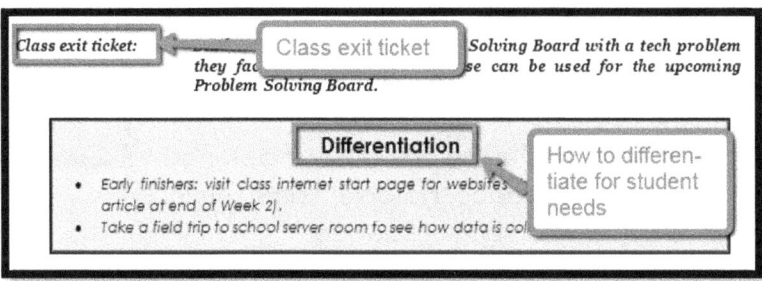

How to Use This Book

This is the teacher manual for Book 1, 2, or 3 of the high school technology curriculum. Use it by itself to guide teaching or in conjunction with the companion student workbooks (sold separately at Structured Learning LLC). If there is a skill students don't know, take time to teach it. If it is a skill students have already learned (such as beginning word processing), expect students to transfer that knowledge to this class.

Here are hints on using this volume:

- Don't expect to finish all lessons in a year. Pick what works best for your unique group.
- You don't have to teach the lessons in any particular order, as you did if you used the K-5 technology curriculum. As in middle school, students learn based on themes.
- A lesson requires one week—two-to-three classes.
- There are five curricular themes—*Math, Productivity, Search and Research, Speaking and Listening, and Writing*. Pick one that applies to your students. Work through the lessons. Or, rather than working on a theme, mix and match lessons—pick what you want to cover.
- The first theme—*Integrated into all*—denotes lessons integrated into all other lessons.
- Lessons you'll want to complete regardless of the themes selected are:

    - #1   Introduction
    - #2   Digital Tools
    - #3   Digital Citizenship
    - #4   Keyboarding
    - #5   Problem Solving
    - #23   Webtools

- Personalize each lesson to your needs with 'Academic Applications'. These are suggestions for blending learning into your grade-level curriculum.
- Here are popular reasons to invest in student digital workbooks (sold separately):

    - *Full-color projects at student fingertips, with examples and directions (licensing varies based on plan).*
    - *EWorkbooks can be annotated.*
    - *Students can work at their own pace, spiraling forward or back as needed.*

Figure 1—Student Wkbks

- Some lessons offer several activities that meet goals outlined in the Essential Question and Big Idea. Pick what works for your students.
- *'Teacher Preparation'* often includes chatting with the grade-level team to tie into their inquiry and/or offer targeted websites for early-finishers.
- Check off completed items on the line preceding the step so you know what's finished. Use Adobe, Notable, Kami, Lumin, or any annotation tool that works on your device.
- Icons are used to denote the following activity:

    - video
    - collaboration
    - an article for you
    - workbook material

- Lessons expect students to develop 'habits of mind'. You can read more about Art Costa and Bena Kallick's discussion of these principles on their website *Habits of Mind*, in *Figure 3 (zoom in if needed)*, and in the article at the end of Lesson #1. In a sentence: Habits of Mind ask students to engage in their learning, not simply memorize.

Figure 3—Habits of Mind

- Use as much tech as possible in your class. Make it adaptive, authentic, and agile. Encourage students to do the same whether it's a smartphone timing a quiz, a video posted to the class website, or an audio file. If you treat tech as a tool in daily activities, so will students.
- Always use lesson vocabulary. Students gain authentic understanding by your example.
- Expect students to back up their work. This can be to a flash drive, by emailing the document to themselves, or saving to a secondary location.
- Expect students to direct their own learning. You are a facilitator not lecturer. Learning is accomplished by success and failure.
- Expect students to be risk takers. Don't rush to solve their problems. Ask them to think how it was done in the past. Focus on problem-solving listed in the lesson but embrace all. This trains critical thinking and troubleshooting when you aren't there to help.
- Encourage student-directed differentiation. If the Big Idea and Essential Question can be completed in ways other than what is listed, embrace those.
- Every effort is made to accommodate a variety of digital devices. If the activity is impossible in a particular digital device (i.e., software doesn't run in Chromebooks), adapt the **Big Idea and Essential Question**—the skill taught and its application to inquiry—to your circumstances.
- **Need more help?** Email admin@structuredlearning.net or askatechteacher@gmail.com.

Here are useful pieces to extend this volume. You can check the publisher's website:

- *Student workbooks—allow students to be self-paced (sold separately)*
- *Digital Citizenship curriculum—if this is a school focus (sold separately)*
- *Keyboarding Curriculum—if this is a school focus (sold separately)*
- *Ask a Tech Teacher.com—free lesson plans, tech tips, websites, and lots of teacher resources.*

High School Technology Curriculum Book 1: Teacher Manual

Who Needs This Book?

You are the Tech Specialist, Coordinator for Instructional Technology, IT Coordinator, Technology Facilitator or Director, Technology Specialist, or tech teacher—tasked with preparing students for class tech needs. You have the drive to do this no matter roadblocks.

You are a homeschooler. You're not comfortable with technology but you're committed to providing the tools your children need to succeed. Just as important: Your children WANT to learn with these tools!

Use this book to prepare students for learning and life. To build **Tomorrow's Student** requires integration of technology with learning. We show you how.

Figure 2--Tomorrow's Student

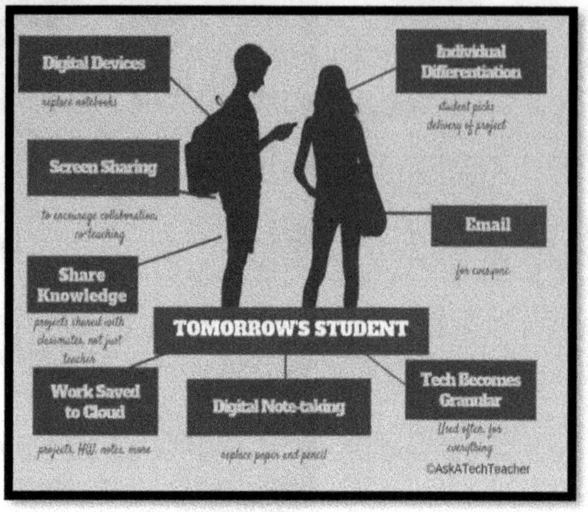

Copyrights

You have a single-user license of this book. That means you may reproduce copies of material in this text for classroom use only. Reproduction of the entire book (or an entire lesson) is strictly prohibited. No part of this publication may be transmitted, stored on an accessible server, or recorded in any form without written permission from the publisher.

About the Authors

Ask a Tech Teacher *is a group of technology teachers who run an award-winning resource blog. Here they provide free materials, advice, lesson plans, pedagogical conversation, website reviews, and more to all who drop by. The free newsletters and articles help thousands of teachers, homeschoolers, and those serious about finding the best way to maneuver the minefields of technology in education.*

*Throughout this text, we refer to Common Core State Standards and a license granted to "...copy, publish, distribute, and display the Common Core State Standards for purposes that support the CCSS Initiative. Copyright 2010. National Governors Association Center for Best Practices and Council of Chief State School Officers. All rights reserved.

Table of Contents

How to use this book
Programs used
Scope and Sequence
Certificate

Lessons

1. Introduction
2. Digital Tools in the Classroom
3. Digital Citizenship
4. Keyboarding
5. Problem Solving
6. Screenshots, Screencasts, Videos
7. Word Processing Summative
8. Writing with Comics, Twitter, More
9. Desktop Publishing I
10. Desktop Publishing II
11. Spreadsheets I
12. Spreadsheets II
13. Financial Literacy
14. Internet Search and Research
15. Presentation Boards
16. Slideshow Summative
17. Slideshows: Presentations
18. Infographics
19. Google Earth Lit Trip
20. Online Image Legalities
21. Image Editing I
22. Image Editing II
23. Webtools
24. Webtools: Presentations
25. Genius Hour I
26. Genius Hour II
27. Coding I
28. Coding II
29. Write an Ebook
30. Publish an Ebook
31. The Debate: Research
32. The Debate: Presentation

Arranged by theme

Integrated into all

#2	Digital Tools in the Classroom
#3	Digital Citizenship
#4	Keyboarding
#5	Problem Solving

Productivity

#4	Keyboarding
#6	Screencasts, Screenshots, Videos
#7	Word Processing Summative
#8	Writing with Comics, Twitter, More
#9-10	Desktop Publishing
#11-12	Spreadsheets

	#15	*Presentation Boards*
	#18	*Infographics*
	#19	*Google Earth Lit Trip*
	#21-22	*Image Editing*
	#23	*Webtools*
	#29	*Write an Ebook*
	#31	*The Debate*

Speaking and Listening

	#6	*Screencasts, Screencasts, Videos*
	#15	*Presentation Boards*
	#17	*Slideshows: Presentations*
	#24	*Webtools: Presentations*
	#25-26	*Genius Hour*
	#32	*The Debate: Presentation*

Math

	#11-12	*Spreadsheets*
	#13	*Financial Literacy*
	#27-28	*Coding*

Writing

	#8	*Writing with Comics, Twitter, More*
	#18	*Infographics*
	#19	*Google Earth Lit Trip*
	#29	*Write an Ebook*
	#30	*Publish an Ebook*

Search and Research

	#3	*Digital Citizenship*
	#14	*Internet Search and Research*
	#20	*Online Image Legalities*
	#23	*Webtools*
	#25-26	*Genius Hour*
	#31	*The Debate: Research*

Articles

Article 1—Habits of Mind vs. CC vs. IB 28
Article 2—Class Warm-ups and Exit Tickets 30
Article 3—4 Things Every Teacher Must Teach and How 31
Article 7—Which Internet Start Page is Best 57
Article 8—13 Ways Blogs Teach Common Core 59
Article 9—Paper-free Classroom 61
Article 10—11 Ways X/Twitter improves education 68
Article 11—Will texting destroy writing skills? 71

Article 12—Digital Rights and Responsibilities *72*
Article 13—5 Ways to make classroom keyboarding fun *97*
Article 14—How to Prepare Students for PARCC/SBA Tests *99*
Article 15—How to Teach Students to Solve Problems *108*
Article 16—Teach Critical Thinking *110*
Article 17—Plagiarism *205*

Table of Images

Figure 1a-b—What's included in each lesson *8*
Figure 2—Student Wkbks *9*
Figure 3—Habits of Mind *10*
Figure 4--Tomorrow's Student *11*
Figure 5—Class rules *26*
Figure 6—Mouse skills *35*
Figure 7a-d—Digital devices Quiz *35*
Figure 8a-b—Parts of iPad, Chromebook *35*
Figure 9a-c—Digital annotation tools *36*
Figure 10a-c—Avatars *37*
Figure 11a-b—Backchannel devices *38*
Figure 12a-c—Student blogs *38*
Figure 13a—Blogging rules; 13b—rubric *39*
Figure 14—Class Internet start page *40*
Figure 15a-c—Class start page examples *41*
Figure 16a-b—Notetaking tools *41*
Figure 17—Collaborative notes in Google Spreadsheets *42*
Figure 18a-b –Digital notetaking tools *42*
Figure 19a-b—Digital portfolio examples *43*
Figure 20—Dropbox *43*
Figure 21—Email Etiquette *44*
Figure 22a—Evidence Board; 22b—Badge *45*
Figure 23—Google Apps *45*
Figure 24a—Screenshot; 24b—screencast *46*
Figure 25—Student website rubric *47*
Figure 26—Personal responsibility quote *65*
Figure 27—Digital law—rephrased *67*
Figure 28—Netiquette Rules *68*
Figure 29—Why learn to keyboard *76*
Figure 30a-b—Keyboarding posture *76*
Figure 31—Keyboarding hand position *77*
Figure 32—Shortkeys *79*
Figure 33a-d—Project-based learning and keyboarding *79*
Figure 34a-d—Shortkeys for iPads, Chromebooks, PCs, and Internet *80*
Figure 35a-b—Blank keyboard quiz for PC and Chromebook *81*
Figure 36—Problem-solving quotes *103*
Figure 37—How to solve a problem *104*
Figure 38—Common tech problems *104*
Figure 39a-b—Problem-solving Board sign-ups *105*
Figure 40—Problem-solving Board rubric *105*

Figure 41a-b—Samples of screenshots 114
Figure 42a-b—Annotation Tools 115
Figure 43—Sequencing in a screenshot 115
Figure 44—Sample screencast 116
Figure 45a-d—Word processing examples from elementary and middle school 120
Figure 46—Compare-contrast: Productivity tools 120
Figure 47—Toolbar, menu bar 121
Figure 48—Tools on toolbars 121
Figure 49a-c—Examples of outlines in word processing programs 122
Figure 50a—MS Word; 50b—Google Docs 123
Figure 51a-c—Comic samples 128
Figure 52—Decoding a comic strip 129
Figure 53—Twitter novel sample 130
Figure 54—Serialized novel by Conrad 132
Figure 55a-e—DTP project samples 135
Figure 56—Compare-contrast digital tools—incomplete 135
Figure 57—Compare-contrast digital tools—complete 136
Figure 58a—Newsletter in Publisher; 58b—in Google Docs; 58c—online tool 137
Figure 59a-c—Newsletter 137
Figure 60a-c—DTP examples 138
Figure 61a-d—Magazine cover examples 139
Figure 62a-b—Magazine table of contents 140
Figure 63a-c—Magazine internal pages 140
Figure 64—Magazine timeline 140
Figure 65a-d—Magazine compare-contrast 141
Figure 66a-b—Magazine graphic organizers 141
Figure 67a—Magazine primary source; 67b—The End 142
Figure 68a-b—Curating articles 142
Figure 69a-e—DTP project samples 147
Figure 70—Compare-contrast digital tools—complete 147
Figure 71a-d—DTP flier examples 148
Figure 72a-b—Posters in DTP 148
Figure 73a-d—Online tools to create fliers 149
Figure 74a-c—Calendar samples 149
Figure 75a-b—Two formulas 154
Figure 76a-c—Spreadsheet projects 154
Figure 77—Compare spreadsheets to other tools 155
Figure 78a-b—Formula unpacked 155
Figure 79—Spreadsheet project 156
Figure 80—AutoMath 157
Figure 81a-c—Tables, charts, and graphs 158
Figure 82—Graph data 159
Figure 83—Chart formatted for easier reading 160
Figure 84a-b: Graph options in Excel and Google Spreadsheet 160
Figure 85a-b: Two types of graphs 160
Figure 86—What are the parts of a website? 170
Figure 87a-b—Presentation Board sign-ups 174
Figure 88—Common problems and solutions 174
Figure 89a—Google Form; 89b—answers 175
Figure 90—Domain-specific vocabulary 176
Figure 91a-c—Virtual wall options 176
Figure 92—Definitions from Google.com 177

High School Technology Curriculum Book 1: Teacher Manual

Figure 93—Google Earth placemark 178
Figure 94—Presentation tool vs. word processing 181
Figure 95a-c Sample slideshows from earlier grades 181
Figure 96a-c—Slideshows in various digital tools 181
Figure 97a-c—Slideshow covers in various slideshow programs 182
Figure 98a-c—Table of Contents 182
Figure 99a-b—Introduction in two digital tools 182
Figure 100a—Topic and subpoints; 100b-c—graphic organizer 183
Figure 101a-b—About the author 183
Figure 102—Slideshow rubric 183
Figure 103a-c—Graphic organizers examples 192
Figure 104a-c—Sample infographics 193
Figure 105a-b—Infographic in varied webtools 194
Figure 106a-c—Google Earth projects 196
Figure 107a—Google Earth placemark; 107b—sample GE tour 196
Figure 108a—Placemark with image; 108b—with overlay 197
Figure 109—Measure distances in GE 198
Figure 110a-b—Student drawing used without permission 200
Figure 111—Copyright protections on browsers 201
Figure 112—Two copyrighted images 202
Figure 113—Digital law—rephrased 203
Figure 114—Real or a hoax? 203
Figure 115a-b: Add or remove pieces from a photo 203
Figure 116a-c—Real or hoax pictures? 204
Figure 117—Row graphic for image editing 210
Figure 118—Edit image with word processing tool 210
Figure 119a-b—Before and after PS auto-correct 213
Figure 120a-c: 3 ways to crop 213
Figure 121a-c—Cropping an image into a new background 213
Figure 122a-b—Cloning within a picture 214
Figure 123a and 123b-- Cloning 215
Figure 124—Background layers 216
Figure 125a-b: Drill through background layers 217
Figure 126a-b—Filters 217
Figure 127a-c: Changing hue and saturation 218
Figure 128a is the original; 128b is desaturated; 128c is painted back to original 218
Figure 129a is desaturated; 129b has part painted back to original picture 219
Figure 130a-b—Car color changed with hue-saturation 219
Figure 131a—Quadrant colors; 131b—sepia toned 220
Figure 132—Paint dialogue box 221
Figure 133a—Image editing brushes; 133b-c— completed drawings 221
Figure 134a-c—Cast shadows 222
Figure 135a-b—Sample collages 223
Figure 136—Genius Hour planning sheet 232
Figure 137—Find your passion 234
Figure 138a-b—What programming feels like vs. what it is 240
Figure 139a-e—Coding from previous years 240

Table of Assessments

Assessment 1--Parts of the Computer 49
Assessment 2--Hardware: Parts of the Smartphone 50
Assessment 3—Chromebook parts 52
Assessment 4—Student blogging agreement 53
Assessment 5—Blog grading rubric 54
Assessment 6—Website grading rubric 55
Assessment 7—Digital portfolio rubric 56
Assessment 8—Keyboarding quiz 82
Assessment 9—Important Keys 83
Assessment 10—Blank keyboard quiz 84
Assessment 11—Chromebook blank keyboard quiz 86
Assessment 12—Keyboarding Challenge 96
Assessment 13—Problem solving authentic data 106
Assessment 14—Problem-solving Board 107
Assessment 15—Problem-solving Presentation Assessment 108
Assessment 16—Compare-contrast productivity tools 121
Assessment 17—Word processing summative 124
Assessment 18—Newsletter rubric 144
Assessment 19—Magazine rubric 145
Assessment 20—Flier grading rubric 151
Assessment 21—Calendar grading rubric 152
Assessment 22—Spreadsheet summative 161
Assessment 23—Spreadsheet summative 163
Assessment 24—Presentation Board assessments 178
Assessment 25—Slideshow storyboard 186
Assessment 26—Slideshow presentation rubric 187
Assessment 27—Slideshow presentation rubric 189
Assessment 28—GE Lit Tour rubric 198
Assessment 29—Photoshop Tennis 224
Assessment 30—Webtool presentation 228
Assessment 31—Genius Hour rubric 238
Assessment 32—Debate evaluation 256

GRADES 9-12 TECH SCOPE AND SEQUENCE©

Aligned with ISTE (International Society for Technology in Education) and Common Core State Standards
Check each skill off with I (Introduced), W (Working on), or M (Mastered)
Organized by ISTE Standards 1-7

	Empowered Learner	**Bk1**	**Bk2**	**Bk3**
	Use technology and digital media strategically and capably (CCSS C&CR profile)	W	M	M
	Familiar with strengths and limitations of various tech tools and mediums and can select and use those best suited to communication goals (CCSS C&CR Profile)	W	M	M
	Strategize personal learning			
	Understand how inquiry contributes to creative and empowered learning	W	W	M
	Understand how technology contributes to classroom and personal learning	W	M	M
	Understand how higher order thinking skills are buttressed by technology	W	M	M
	Select between available options, choosing one best suited to learning	W	M	M
	Compare-contrast available tools, determining which is best suited to need	W	M	M
	Know digital tools available and how to use (i.e., calendars, blogs, annotation)	M	M	M
	Be responsive to varied needs of task-audience-purpose	M	M	M
	Interact, collaborate, publish with peers employing a variety of digital media	W	M	M
	Develop cultural understanding by engaging with learners of other cultures	W	M	M
	Seek feedback to demonstrate learning			
	Add comments to class blogs, forums, discussion boards, webtools	M	M	M
	Work in groups collaboratively and productively	M	M	M
	Transfer knowledge			
	Scaffold learning year-to-year and lesson-to-lesson	M	M	M
	Transfer understanding of one digital tool or device to others	M	M	M
	Use familiar tech tools (like Google Earth's ruler) to solve real-world problems	M	M	M
	Hardware			
	Know parts of digital devices and how to connect them	M	M	M
	Can troubleshoot hardware	M	M	M
	Operating Systems (PC, Mac, Chromebook, iPads)			
	Know how to find files, add more, and save to network file folder and/or cloud	M	M	M
	Know how to drag-drop (or copy-paste) within a doc and between folders	M	M	M
	Know how to use tool tips (hover over icon) and right-click menus	M	M	M
	Can troubleshoot operating systems	M	M	M
	Online Tech for Classroom Management			
	Understand school technology	W	M	M
	Understand Cloud for transferring school work to home	M	M	M
	Know how to annotate a PDF or online document	W	M	M
	Know how to share out classwork (including homework)	I	W	M
	Know how to use online vocabulary decoding tools quickly and efficiently	M	M	M
	Keyboarding			

	Know how to practice keyboarding on internet sites and software	M	M	M
	Strive to achieve grade-appropriate keyboarding speed and accuracy goal	M	M	M
	Practice touch typing	M	M	M
	Compose at keyboard by creating classroom-based projects	M	M	M
	Understand speed difference between handwriting and keyboarding	M	M	M
	Select shortkeys instead of toolbar tools when appropriate	M	M	M
	Use correct posture, elbows at sides	M	M	M
	Know parts of keyboard—keys, numbers, F keys, arrows, Esc	W	M	M
	Word Processing			
	Know when to use a word processing program, both software and online tools	W	M	M
	Use classroom principles of grammar, spelling when word processing on computer	M	M	M
	Know basic page layout—heading, title, body, footer	W	M	M
	Know how to use the thesaurus	M	M	M
	Know how to format a document—i.e., add header, footer, border, cover page, embedded link	W	M	M
	Can troubleshoot word processing	W	M	M
	Google Earth			
	Display familiarity with tools for moving around world	M	M	M
	Run a tour of placemarks around the planet	W	M	M
2	**Digital Citizen**			
	Gather information from print and digital sources, assess credibility, integrate information while avoiding plagiarism. (CCSS C&CR Writing Anchor Standards)	I	W	M
	Internet privacy and safety			
	Know how to configure privacy settings	I	W	M
	Understand cyberbullying, use of passwords	M	M	M
	Understand digital footprint and online presence	I	W	M
	Understand how online entities track student activity online	I	W	M
	Understand the appropriate use of the 'digital neighborhood'	M	M	M
	Legal use of online materials			
	Discuss copyright, fair use, intellectual property, rights/obligations of digital world	W	M	M
	Discuss plagiarism and how to cite sources	W	M	M
	Digital Netiquette			
	Understand etiquette in the digital neighborhood	M	M	M
	Digital Citizenship			
	Understand what a 'digital citizen' is	M	M	M
	Exhibit a positive attitude toward technology that supports collaboration and learning	M	M	M
	Demonstrate personal responsibility for lifelong learning	M	M	M
	Exhibit leadership for digital citizenship—set the standard for classmates	M	M	M
	Interactions online			
	Address digital commerce	I	W	M
	Use safe, responsible and ethical behavior on the internet	M	M	M
	Discuss social media	I	W	M
	Discuss digital rights and responsibilities	M	M	M

	Recognize irresponsible and unsafe practices on the internet	I	W	M
	Know how online comments follow same rules as speaking and listening	I	W	M
3 Knowledge Constructor				
	Use the internet to build strong content knowledge (CCSS C&CR profile)	M	M	M
	Use technology to publish writing and collaborate with others (CCRA.W.6)	M	M	M
	Use technology and digital media strategically and capably (CCSS C&CR profile)	M	M	M
	Comprehend as well as critique. (CCSS C&CR profile)	W	M	M
	Value evidence (CCSS C&CR profile)	W	M	M
	Compare-contrast documents across varied digital media (CCSS Anchor Standards)	W	M	M
	Gather relevant information from multiple digital sources (CCRA.W.8)	W	M	M
	Assess credibility of digital sources used for research (CCSS Anchor Standards)	W	M	M
	Integrate and evaluate information from diverse media (CCRA.R.7)	W	M	M
	Make strategic use of digital media to express information (CCRA.SL.5)	W	M	M
	Use electronic menus and links to locate key facts (RI/)	W	M	M
Effective online research strategies				
	Use screenshots to collect information	W	M	M
	Locate, organize, analyze, evaluate, synthesize information from many sources	M	M	M
	Evaluate and select information sources and digital tools based on task	W	M	M
	Know how to search efficiently, limit search as needed, and use Ctrl+F	I	W	M
	Know how to effectively use LMS systems and the Cloud	I	W	M
Technology as knowledge curator				
	Evaluate the accuracy, perspective, relevancy of information, media, data resources	I	W	M
	Curate information from digital resources using a variety of tools and methods that demonstrate meaningful connections or conclusions (such as outlines, mindmaps).	I	W	M
	Present information in a manner suited to task, audience, and purpose (i.e., infographics, graphic organizers, Google Earth)	M	M	M
	Build knowledge by exploring real-world issues, developing ideas, and pursuing solutions using online learning programs	M	M	M
Online collaborative environments				
	Use blogs for journaling and tracking project progress	W	M	M
	Incorporate text, images, widgets to better communicate ideas	W	M	M
	Know how to use Discussion boards and forums	I	W	M
4 Innovative Designer				
	Respond to demands of audience, task, purpose, discipline (CCSS C&CR profile)	M	M	M
	Use glossaries or dictionaries to clarify meaning (CCSS.L.K.4)	M	M	M
	Gather, comprehend, evaluate, synthesize, and report on information in order to answer questions or solve problems, (CCSS Key Design Consideration)	W	M	M
	Draw on information from multiple print or digital sources, demonstrating the ability to locate an answer to a question quickly or solve a problem efficiently (CCSS. RI.5)	I	W	M
	Reason abstractly and quantitatively (CCSS. Math.Practice.MP2)	M	M	M
	Use appropriate tools strategically (CCSS. Math.Practice.MP5)	M	M	M
	Attend to precision (CCSS. Math.Practice.MP6)	M	M	M
Design Process				
	Use planning tools such as mindmaps to organize ideas and solve problems	I	W	M

	Use presentation tools like graphic organizers, Infographics, screencasts, trailers to share topical ideas and solve authentic problems in a variety of creative ways	I	W	M
	Use templates and patterns to create new designs (like shapes, letters)	M	M	M
	Select and use digital tools (such as comics) to plan and manage a design process that considers design constraints and calculated risk	M	M	M
	Develop, test and refine prototypes as part of a cyclical design process	W	M	M
	Able to tolerate ambiguity, with a capacity to work with open-ended problems.	M	M	M
	Use established patterns and design processes in solving common tech problems	M	M	M
	Recognize the part 'failure' plays in solving problems	M	M	M
	Decision Making			
	Identify and define authentic problems and questions for investigation	M	M	M
	Collect, analyze data to identify solutions and make informed decisions	M	M	M
	Able to debug programs using sequencing, if-then thinking, logic, or other strategies	M	M	M
	Able to evaluate which program is right for which task	M	M	M
	Slideshows			
	Know when and how to use presentation tools as software and online tools	W	M	M
	Understand how to deliver a professional presentation	W	M	M
	Can troubleshoot presentation tools	M	M	M
	Graphics			
	Use drawing software and web-based tools efficiently	M	M	M
	Know how to create and annotate screenshots to share information	M	M	M
	Desktop publishing			
	Can identify parts of the desktop publishing screen	W	M	M
	Know when to use a desktop publishing program to share information	W	M	M
	Know how to plan a publication	I	W	M
	Can troubleshoot publishing tools	W	M	M
	Screencasts, Videos			
	Know how to create screencasts, videos, and trailers to share information	I	W	M
	Know how to upload screencasts, videos, and trailers to easily-accessible locations for peers	I	W	M
	Know how to use the design process to prepare screencasts	I	W	M
5	**Computational Thinker**			
	Gather, comprehend, evaluate, synthesize, and report on information to conduct research, answer questions, solve problems, (CCSS Key Design Consideration)	M	M	M
	Draw on information from multiple sources, demonstrating the ability to locate an answer to a question quickly or to solve a problem efficiently (CCSS. RI.5)	M	M	M
	Make sense of problems and persevere in solving them (CCSS. Math.Practice.MP1)	M	M	M
	Reason abstractly and quantitatively (CCSS. Math.Practice.MP2)	M	M	M
	Construct viable arguments and critique the reasoning of others (CCSS. Math.Practice.MP3)	M	M	M
	Model with mathematics (CCSS. Math.Practice.MP4)	M	M	M
	Use appropriate tools strategically (CCSS. Math.Practice.MP5)	M	M	M
	Attend to precision (CCSS. Math.Practice.MP6)	M	M	M
	Look for and make use of structure (CCSS. Math.Practice.MP7)	M	M	M

High School Technology Curriculum Book 1: Teacher Manual

	Look for and express regularity in repeated reasoning (CCSS. Math.Practice.MP8)	M	M	M
	Critical Thinking			
	Understand how to identify, define authentic problems, questions	M	M	M
	Know how to use digital tools including calendars, blogs, websites, annotation tools	M	M	M
	Always attempt to solve a problem before asking for teacher assistance	M	M	M
	Know how to research and develop an argument (such as for a debate)	I	W	M
	Know how to use programs not yet learned	M	M	M
	Know why a particular digital tool is suited to a specific need	M	M	M
	Know how to analyze data digitally and use in problem-solving and decision-making.	I	W	M
	Problem solving			
	Identify, define, and solve authentic problems, questions for investigation	M	M	M
	Know how to access work from anywhere in the school	M	M	M
	Know how to solve common hardware problems	M	M	M
	Know what to do if computer doesn't work	I	W	M
	Can trouble shoot a non-working program	I	W	M
	Can break problems into component parts, extract key information, and develop descriptive models to understand complex systems or facilitate problem-solving.	I	W	W
	Programming			
	Understand technology contributes to higher-order thinking	W	M	M
	Understand the cause-effect relationship inherent in actions	W	M	M
	Eagerly experiment with programming tools	M	M	M
	Understand how automation works; use algorithmic thinking to develop a sequence of steps to create solutions. (i.e., timelines, brainstorming)	W	W	W
	Able to debug programs using sequencing, if-then thinking, logic, or other strategies	W	W	W
	Robotics			
	Contribute to project teams to produce original works or solve problems		I	W
	Build, program, debug a robot		I	W
	Trouble shoot simple problems		I	W
	Use sensors to monitor the environment and able to measure distances with robots		I	W
	Spreadsheets			
	Process and sort data, report results by collecting data and reporting it	I	W	M
	Know how to publish spreadsheet through a widget to blog and/or website	I	W	M
	Can troubleshoot spreadsheets	I	W	W
6	**Creative Communicator**			
	Use technology and digital media strategically and capably (CCSS C&CR profile)	W	M	M
	Use technology to produce and publish writing and collaborate with others (ELA-LITERACY.CCRA.W.6)	M	M	M
	Explore digital tools to produce and publish writing (CCSS.ELA-Literacy.W)	M	M	M
	Explore digital tools to collaborate with peers (CCSS.ELA-Literacy.W)	M	M	M
	Use multimedia to aid comprehension (CCSS.ELA-Literacy.W)	W	M	M
	Ask and answer questions from information presented (CCSS.ELA-Literacy.SL)	M	M	M
	Include audio recordings and multimedia to enhance ideas (CCSS.ELA-Literacy.SL)	W	M	M

	Integrate and evaluate information presented in diverse media and formats, including visually, quantitatively, and orally (CCSS.ELA-LITERACY.CCRA.SL.2)	M	M	M
	Use multimedia to organize ideas, concepts, info (CCSS.ELA-Literacy.WHST)	M	M	M
Blogs				
	Interact, collaborate, publish with peers employing a variety of digital media	W	M	M
	Develop cultural understanding and global awareness by engaging other cultures	W	M	M
Digital Tools				
	Communicate ideas effectively to audiences using a variety of formats including visual organizers, infographics, comics, Twitter (where appropriate), and more	W	M	M
	Use web-based communication tools to share unique and individual ideas	W	M	M
	Learn a variety of tools that address varied communication styles (from written to visual to video) by teaching them to classmates	W	M	M
	Know how to use models and simulations to explore complex systems and issues	W	M	M
	Develop cultural understanding by engaging with learners of other cultures	M	M	M
Digital Storytelling, Debate				
	Work collaboratively to develop a persuasive argument (such as for a debate)	M	M	M
	Participate in a virtual field trip that tells the story of a student's experience	M	M	M
Speaking and Listening				
	Engage in impromptu speaking such as the Evidence Board	I	W	W
	Present well-prepared presentations such as slideshows or debate, knowing how to use multimedia props	W	M	M
	Engage in short presentations such as the Presentation Boards	I	W	M
	Interact, collaborate, publish with peers or others employing digital media	W	M	M
7 Global Collaborator				
	Understand other perspectives and cultures. (CCSS C&CR profile)	M	M	M
	Respond to the varying demands of audience, task, purpose, discipline. (CCSS C&CR Profile)	M	M	M
	Use digital tools to connect with learners from a variety of backgrounds and cultures, engaging with them to broaden mutual understanding and learning	M	M	M
	Explore local and global issues and use technologies to investigate solutions	M	M	M
Collaborate with Others				
	Use collaborative technologies to work with peers, experts or community members, to examine issues and problems from multiple viewpoints.	I	W	M
	Contribute constructively to project teams to work effectively toward a common goal.	I	W	M
	Use blogs, forums, Discussion Boards to collaborate and share	I	W	M
	Work in groups to teach technology skills to others	I	W	M

Askatechteacher©

Lesson #1—Introduction

Vocabulary	Problem solving	Skills
<ul><li>Back-up</li><li>Digital</li><li>Digital citizen</li><li>Hardware</li><li>Landscape</li><li>Orientation</li><li>Portrait</li><li>Right-click menu</li><li>Select-do</li><li>Technology</li><li>Webtool</li></ul>	<ul><li>What's the difference between 'save' and 'save-as'</li><li>What's a quick way to ** (shortkey)</li><li>How do I annotate student workbook (addressed in Digital Tools lesson)</li><li>I don't have a flash drive (does the school have spares?)</li><li>Why worry about my online actions if they're anonymous?</li><li>I can't do my keyboarding at home (come to afterschool keyboarding)</li></ul>	Keyboarding Digital citizenship Problem solving Hardware Digital devices Online grades
Academic Applications General	**Materials Required** Student workbooks (if using), list of class rules from last year, class syllabus,	**Standards** CCSS: various NETS: 1a, 1b

Essential Question

How do I share with classmates?

Big Idea

Students use tech to enhance their education

Teacher Preparation

- Integrate domain-specific vocabulary into lesson.
- Have info on afterschool Keyboard Club and Help.
- Something happen you weren't prepared for? Show students how you fix it without a meltdown and with a positive attitude.

Assessment Strategies

- Annotated workbook (if using)
- Completed exit ticket
- Joined classroom conversations
- [tried to] solve own problems
- Decisions followed class rules
- Left room as s/he found it
- Higher order thinking: analysis, evaluation, synthesis
- Habits of mind observed

Steps

Time required: **45 minutes**
Class warm-up: **None** *(for pedagogy of warm-ups, see article at end of lesson)*

_____ Required skill level: Enthusiasm and passion for technology.

_____ Tour classroom to familiarize students with room. Where are the tech devices that will assist them? Printer? Class announcements? Evidence Board and Presentation sign-up sheets (if you're doing these activities)? What else?

_____ What does 'technology' mean at your school? Do students understand 'tech in education'? How have they used it?

_____ Discuss focus of this year's tech: Students will use tech to support education goals like:

- *deciding what program works best for what inquiry*
- *learning to use tools they have never seen*
- *self-assess knowledge, insuring they got what they need*

_____Success is predicated on student enthusiasm for learning, transfer of knowledge, and evidence of problem-solving skills. Students will often 'pick which program works best' or 'devise a plan to accomplish goals' or 'teach themselves'.

_____Discuss student tech background, what they know and want to know, difficulties they see taking this class. Discuss your expectations.

_____Domain-specific language will be taught two ways:

- *Students use correct 'geek speak' words during class, as do you. New tech words will be added to a (virtual) wall or a similar collection spot. These will be included in Speak Like a Geek (if following this activity).*
- *When students find a word they don't understand, decode it—use class dictionary tool, ask friends, in context, or ask the teacher. Don't skip over it.*

_____Review class syllabus via Table of Contents and Scope and Sequence .

_____Review class rules (see *Figure 5* and full-size sample at end of lesson). Collect more from students that will make class productive, efficient, and fair for all students, such as:

- *No food or drink around devices.*
- *Respect work of others and yourself.*
- *Don't touch neighbor's device.*
- *No excuses—don't blame people or computer.*
- *When collaborating, build on others' ideas.*

Figure 3—Class rules

_____If using workbooks, students can write their rules suggestions right onto the PDF.

_____Students will learn to be good digital citizens (see Lesson on *Digital Citizenship*).

_____Let students know you are open to alternative tools for class projects. For example, if you suggest Wordle, a student can request Tagxedo. The change will be approved if the tool meets class guidelines, essential question, and/or big idea. Expect student to use **evidence** to build their case, **compare-contrast** their tool to yours, and **draw logical conclusions**.

_____Offer an **after-school Keyboarding Club** two days a week to accommodate students who can't do their tech work at home. Limit it to 45 minutes.

_____Offer **after-school help** on Keyboarding Club days for students who need assistance with a tech skill or a project involving tech. Request student volunteers to assist classmates. Collaborate with your school's volunteer program if available.

_____Discuss correct keyboarding posture. Keyboarding is important whenever student sits at digital device—at home, library, friend's house, lab, and classroom. If you are starting the year with the *Keyboarding* lesson, skip this in the Introduction.

_____Let students know that they will use a wide range of webtools (more on this in another Lesson). Additionally, students will be expected to independently learn to use those that suit their particular needs.

_____Let students know you will expect them to try to solve tech problems before requesting assistance (more on this in another Lesson).

_____Show how to check grades online.

_____Discuss student responsibility to make up missed classes. Show where you post lesson plans and videos (if these are available).

_____Discuss passwords and privacy. Do not share log-ins with anyone. Have students save log in info wherever it is secure. More on this in another lesson.

_____Discuss backing up student work. How does that happen at your school? If students use flash drives, review how to use them.

Class exit ticket: *Tweet on class X/Twitter account about this intro.*

Differentiation

- Have a student familiar with your class run this less.
- Instead of going through all of this information, create a video and/or screen-cast.

NOTES:

Computer Lab Manners and Responsibilities

Assignments / Homework

- Check class website each day.
- Read and respond to communications at least once a day.
- If an assignment is not completed in class, turn it in remotely from home by 6:00 pm the same day with no penalty.
- Late assignments are 10% off for each day late.

Behavior in the Lab

- Keep an open mind that *something new will be learned* each day.
- Have clean hands; keyboards are shared by everyone.
- No food or drinks allowed in lab
- When helping other students, don't take over their computer.

Posting Online

- Always enter subject of email
- Start each email with a greeting. (e.g. Hi Mrs. *** or Dear Mr. ***)
- Use correct punctuation.
- Proofread email and check spelling every time.
- Show insight and intelligence when responding to a class discussion or commenting on a post.
- CC anyone mentioned in an email. That's polite
- Don't share private information in emails. They aren't secure!
- Don't be rude in emails. They aren't private.
- Don't use capitals—THIS IS SHOUTING

Article 1—Habits of Mind vs. CC vs. IB

Habits of Mind vs. Common core vs. IB

Pedagogic experts have spent an enormous amount of time attempting to unravel the definition of 'educated'. It used to be the 3 R's—reading, writing, and 'rithmetic. The problem with that metric is that, in the fullness of time, those who excelled in the three areas weren't necessarily the ones who succeeded. As long ago as the early 1900's, Teddy Roosevelt warned:

""C students rule the world."

It's the kids without their nose in a book that notice the world around them, make connections, and learn natively. They excel at activities that aren't the result of a GPA and an Ivy League college. Their motivation is often failure and taking the wrong path again and again. As Thomas Edison said:

""I have not failed. I've just found 10,000 ways that won't work."

Microsoft founder, Bill Gates, and Albert Einstein are poster children for that approach. Both became change agents in their fields despite following a non-traditional path.

In the face of mounting evidence, education experts accepted a prescriptive fact: student success is not measured by milestones like 'took a foreign language in fifth grade' or 'passed Algebra in high school' but by how s/he thinks. One curated list of cerebral skills that has become an education buzz word is Arthur L. Costa and Bena Kallick's list of sixteen what they call Habits of Mind (Copyright ©2000):

1. *Persisting*
2. *Managing impulsivity*
3. *Listening with Understanding and Empathy*
4. *Thinking Flexibly*
5. *Thinking about Thinking*
6. *Striving for Accuracy*
7. *Questioning and Posing Problems*
8. *Applying Past Knowledge to New Situations*
9. *Thinking and Communicating with Clarity and Precision*
10. *Gathering Data through All Senses*
11. *Creating, Imagining, Innovating*
12. *Responding with Wonderment and Awe*
13. *Taking Responsible Risks*
14. *Finding Humor*
15. *Thinking Interdependently*
16. *Remaining Open to Continuous Learning*

Together, these promote strategic reasoning, insightfulness, perseverance, creativity and craftsmanship.

But they're not new. They share the same goals with at least three other widely-used education systems: 1) Common Core (as close as America gets to national standards), 2) the International Baccalaureate (IB) program (a well-regarded international curriculum, much more popular outside the US than within), and 3) good ol' common sense. Below, I've listed each Habit of Mind with a brief explanation of what that means (in italics). I then point out connections to

Common Core, the IB Program, and the common sense your grandma shared with you. The result is a compelling argument that education is less a data download and more a fitness program for our brains.

Persisting

Stick with a problem, even when it's difficult and seems hopeless.

Winston Churchill said, "Never, never, in nothing great or small, large or petty, never give in..." The same decade, Albert Einstein said:

> *"It's not that I'm so smart, it's just that I stay with problems longer."*

The Common Core is not a curriculum, rather a collection of forty-one overarching Standards in reading, writing, language, math, and speaking/listening that shape a student's quest for college and career. Sprinkled throughout are fundamental traits that go beyond the 3R's and delve deeply into the ability of a student to think. The math standards require students learn to 'persevere in solving problems'.

The IB Program has twelve attitudes that are fundamental to every learner: *appreciation, empathy, commitment, enthusiasm, confidence, independence, cooperation, integrity, creativity, respect, curiosity, and tolerance.* Students exhibiting the attitude of commitment persist in their own learning, persevere no matter the difficulties.

Managing Impulsivity

Consider options. Think before speaking.

Among his endless words of wisdom, Benjamin Franklin said:

> *"It is easier to suppress the first desire than to satisfy all that follow it."*

Common Core Standards tell us to 'Use appropriate tools strategically'.

Besides the twelve attitudes listed above, the IB Program names ten traits that profile a learner: *inquirer, knowledgeable, thinker, communicator, principle, open-minded, caring, a risk-taker, balanced, and reflective.* Students who are reflective give thoughtful consideration before acting.

For the rest of the article, visit Ask a Tech Teacher

Article 2—Class Warm-ups and Exit Tickets

Class Warm-ups and Exit Tickets

Warm-ups are given at the beginning of class to measure what students remember from prior lessons or know about a subject before jumping into a unit. They inform teachers how to optimize time by teaching what students need to learn, not wasting time on what students already know. They are a couple of minutes, can be delivered via a Discussion Board, blog comments, a Google Form, or many other methods. Exit tickets are similar, but assess what students learned **during** the lesson. In this way, teachers know if they should review material, find a different approach to teaching a topic, or students are ready to move on. Like Warm-ups, Exit tickets are a few minutes, and delivered in a wide variety of creative methods.

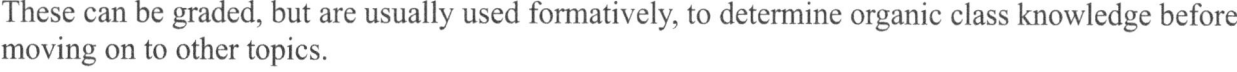

Here are a few examples:

Polls

Polls are quick ways to assess student understanding of the goal of your daily teaching. It measures student learning as much as lesson effectiveness. Polls are fast—three-five minutes—are anonymously graded and shared immediately with students. It lets everyone know if the big idea of the lesson is understood and if the essential questions have been answered.

These can be graded, but are usually used formatively, to determine organic class knowledge before moving on to other topics.

Tools: Google Forms
Time: a few minutes
Method: Formative assessment

Virtual Wall

Ask students a question and have them add their answer to a virtual wall.

Virtual walls are also great ideas for reviewing a subject prior to a summative assessment. Have each student post an important idea they got from the unit with significant required details.

Tools: Padlet, Linoit
Time: a few minutes
Method: Formative assessment

Article 3—4 Things Every Teacher Must Teach and How

4 Things Every Teacher Must Teach and How

Teaching technology is not sharing a new subject, like Spanish or math. It's exploring an education tool, knowing how to use computers, iPads, the Internet, and other digital devices to serve learning goals. Sure, there are classes that teach MS Word and C++, but for most schools, technology is employed strategically and capably to achieve all colors of education.

Which gets me to the four subjects every teacher must teach, whether s/he's a math teacher, science, literacy, or technology. In today's education world, all of us teach—

- *vocabulary*
- *keyboarding*
- *digital citizenship*
- *research*

They used to be taught in isolation—*Fridays at 8:20, we learn vocabulary*—but not anymore. Now they must be blended into all subjects like ingredients in a cake, the result—college or career for the 21st century student. Four subjects that must be taught—and thanks to technology, CAN be with ease. Let me explain.

Vocabulary

Common Core requires that:

> *Students constantly build the transferable vocabulary they need to access grade level complex texts. This can be done effectively by spiraling like content in increasingly complex texts.*

Does that sound difficult? Think back to how you conquered vocabulary. As an adult, you rarely meet words you can't understand—unless you're chatting with William F. Buckley—and if you do, you decode it by analyzing prefixes, suffixes, roots, context. Failing that, e-dictionaries are available on all digital devices.

Teach your students to do the same:

- first: try to decode the word using affixes, root, context
- second: research meaning

You might think that will grind the academic process to a halt, but truth, in age-appropriate texts, there are likely less than five unknown words per page. What you don't want to do is have students write down words for later investigation. That becomes a chore, cerebral excitement leeched like heat to a night desert sky. Much better to stop, decode, and move on.

As students work on a project in my classes, I see neighbors ask for help with a mysterious word (students are welcome to chat during class about academic topics), screens light up as students use the online dictionary to discover meaning, and words appear on the class screen as part of the backchannel X/Twitter stream. Seconds later, a definition will appear—someone's contribution. If it's wrong, invariably a student will correct it. Rarely, I jump in.

Don't believe this works? Try it out.

Keyboarding

For years, I taught keyboarding as a separate activity. We warmed up class with 10-15 minutes of keyboarding augmented by 45 minutes a week of keyboard homework. I've revised my thinking. Since keyboarding benefits all classes, I make all teachers—including the librarian—my partners in this effort. I go into classrooms and show students the broad strokes of keyboarding posture, good habits, skills that will enable them to type fast and accurately enough to eventually—maybe third or fourth grade—use the keyboard without slowing down their thinking. That's a big deal and worth repeating—

To be organic, students must be able to keyboard without thinking of their fingers, fast enough that they keep up with their thoughts.

That's about 25 words per minute. *Really?* Yes really. Sure, we think fast, but ruminating over a class question, essay, report is much [much] slower. 25-35 words per minute suffice.

I start students with mouse and keyboard familiarity, introduce the concept of hands and fingers next, and speed and accuracy after that, focusing on:

- good posture
- hands on home row (by 3rd grade)
- elbows at sides
- paper (if using one) to the side of keyboard
- eyes on screen
- no flying fingers or hands
- paced rhythm

Parents, too, are my partners. I communicate the same requirements to them with the hope they'll reinforce these at home. A reminder that assessments are often online gets their attention.

Digital Citizenship

It's frightening how much time students spend in an online world they consider safe, following links like blind streets to places most parent wouldn't take their child. Just as students have learned how to survive in a physical community of strangers, they must now learn to do the same in a digital neighborhood. Parents and teachers can't be everywhere and hiding children from danger doesn't teach them survival skills, so we must teach them how to live in this wild new online world.

For more, visit this article on Ask a Tech teacher

Lesson #2—Digital Tools in the Classroom

Vocabulary	Problem solving	Skills
• Annotation • Backchannel • Benchmark • Digital citizen • Digital portfolio • Digital tools • Domain-specific • Geek • Hashtag • Linkback • PDF • Portal • Template	▪ I'm too young for Twitter (class account) ▪ Avatar didn't show in my wiki page (ask a neighbor how they did it) ▪ My work disappeared! (Google Apps automatically saves—pull up revision) ▪ Teacher is busy and I need help (ask for peer support) ▪ Just give me a handout (Sorry, we learn through experience and collaboration) ▪ I'm not fast enough decoding vocabulary (keep at it—it gets easier) ▪ I forgot my Evidence for the Evidence Board (write it down for the next time)	Blogging Backchannel Digital notetaking Hardware parts Avatars Annotating PDFs Class calendar Internet start page Digital portfolios Email Evidence Board Decoding vocab
Academic Applications Writing, research, online safety	**Materials Required** Back channel, hardware assessments, Student accounts, Evidence badges for Evidence board, training videos, student workbooks (if using)	**Standards** CCSS: WHST.9-10.7-9 NETS: 1b, 4b

Essential Question

How do I use technology to pursue education?

Big Idea

Students are aware of how tech enhances educational goals

Teacher Preparation

- Know which tasks weren't completed last class and whether they are necessary to move forward.
- Have copies of blogging agreement (if necessary) available to review and sign.
- Something happen you weren't prepared for? Show how you fix it with a positive attitude.
- Have student hardware assessments (if needed).
- Integrate domain-specific tech vocabulary into lesson.
- Know whether you need extra time to complete lesson.
- Make sure all student accounts are active.

Assessment Strategies

- Annotated workbook (if using)
- Completed warm-up, exit ticket
- Joined classroom conversations
- [tried to] solve own problems
- Decisions followed class rules
- Left room as s/he found it
- Higher order thinking: analysis, evaluation, synthesis
- Habits of mind observed

Steps

Time required: 90 minutes
Class warm-up: Test digital tool accounts while waiting for class to start

_____ Have neighbors check each other's mouse hold (see *Figure 6—zoom in if needed)*:

Figure 6—Mouse skills

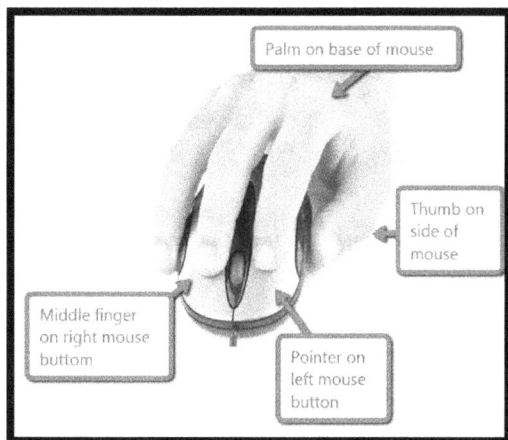

_____Review digital device hardware used in your school. Students should know the basic parts and whether they're input or output. There are assessments at the end of this Lesson. *Figures 8a-b* are completed worksheets (zoom in if necessary). These can be filled out in student workbooks or as formative assessments during class time.

Figure 7a-d—Digital devices Quiz

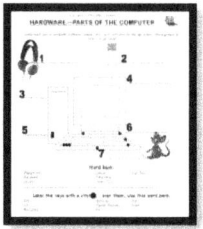 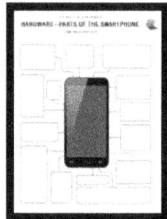  

_____If necessary, review with students. For example, if you use iPads, ask where the headphones are on this device? Or the mouse? How about the USB Port (trick question: there isn't one)? Ask students where the microphone is on a PC or Chromebook. How about a charging dock?

Figure 8a-b—Parts of iPad, Chromebook

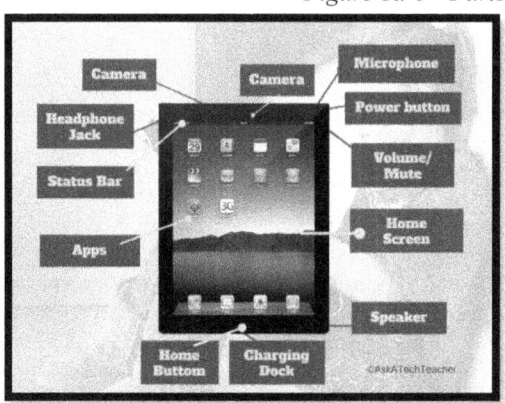 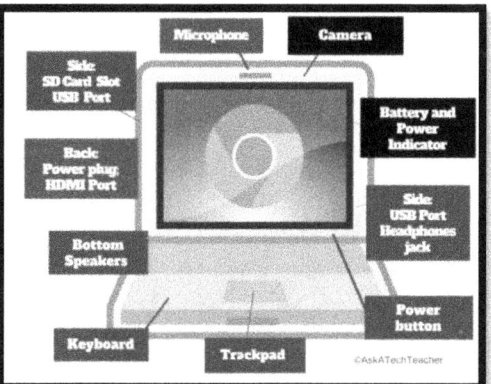

_____Discuss how understanding hardware helps to solve tech problems.

_____The following tools are discussed in this Lesson. Pick those that your students use and add others you have that aren't mentioned:

- *annotation tool*
- *avatars*
- *backchannel devices*
- *blogs*
- *class calendar*
- *class Internet start page*
- *class website*
- *digital notetaking*
- *digital portfolios*
- *drop box*
- *email*
- *Evidence Board*
- *Google Apps*
- *student websites*
- *student workbooks*
- *vocabulary decoding tools*

_____Adapt them to your digital devices (Chromebooks, PCs, Mac, iPads, or other).
_____Introduce, demo, and test. Dig deeper when necessary.

Student workbooks

_____If using student PDF workbooks that align with this volume, introduce them now. Show how to open in their digital device, find rubrics and project samples, and annotate. Students can see full-color images, circle back to review concepts or forward to preview upcoming lessons.

Annotation Tool

_____If using student workbooks, show students how to annotate their copy with the notetaking tool used in your school such as iAnnotate (*Figure 9a*), Notability (*Figure 9b*), or Adobe Acrobat (free—*Figure 9c*).

Figure 9a-c—Digital annotation tools

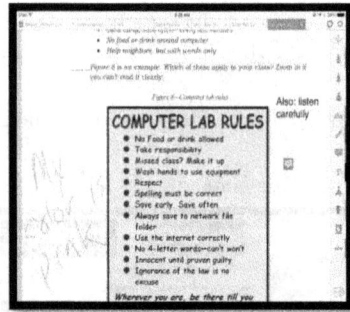 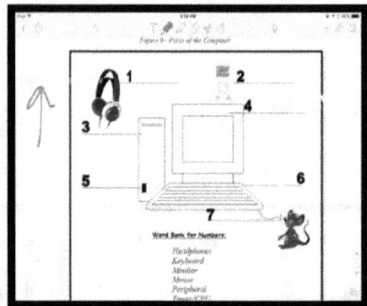 

_____If students share the PDF with other students (for example, it's installed on a class digital device that multiple classes visit), show how to select a color that's different from other students.
_____Discuss screenshots. If students annotate a page (say, a rubric) in their workbook, they send you a screenshot. Depending upon your digital device, you'll use a screenshot tool like one of these:

- **Windows:** *the Snipping Tool*
- **Chromebook:** *hold down the control key and press the window switcher key*
- **Mac:** *Command Shift 3 to do a full screenshot and Command Shift 4 to take a partial*

- **iPad**: *hold Home button and power button at same time*
- **Online**: *a screenshot tool*

Avatars

_____Students create a profile picture with an avatar creator like (Google for websites or visit Ask a Tech Teacher resource pages for Avatars):

Figure 10a-c—Avatars

_____These can be used in student blogs, websites, or any other digital platform that requires a profile picture. Use them to reinforce a discussion of digital privacy and safety.

Backchannel Devices

_____The 'backchannel' is communication not from the presenter. It encourages students to share their thoughts and ideas, even questions, during a lesson. Typically, the comments show up on the class screen, shared with all classmates, likely anonymously. Students read and respond. Teacher easily sees when students get/don't get a topic s/he is covering.

_____Popular backchannel options are:

- *Padlet — a virtual wall where students comment and respond; Figure 11a*
- *X/Twitter — a virtual comment stream organized by hashtags; private or public*

Figure 11a-b—Backchannel devices

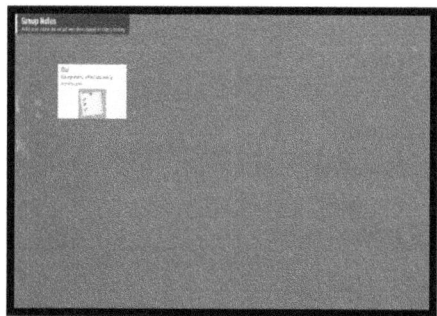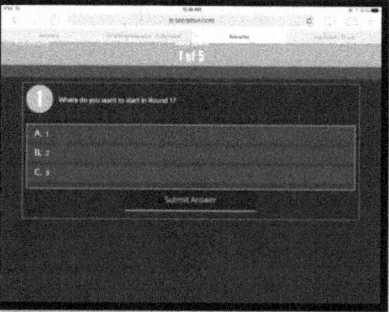

_____Why use backchannels? So you:

- *know what engages students and extend those ideas*
- *hear from shy students who need a classroom voice*
- *allow chatty students to ask as much as they want without dominating the class*

Blogs

_____Blogs are collections of short online articles that share ideas and garner feedback. With high school students, you are particularly interested in their facility to:

- o engage effectively in collaborative discussions with diverse partners
- o build on others' ideas
- o express their own ideas clearly

_____If you're a Common Core school, review *"13 Ways Blogs Teach Common Core"* at the end of the lesson.

_____In *Figures 12a-c*, notice how blogs incorporate text and images to discuss a topic:

Figure 12a-c—Student blogs

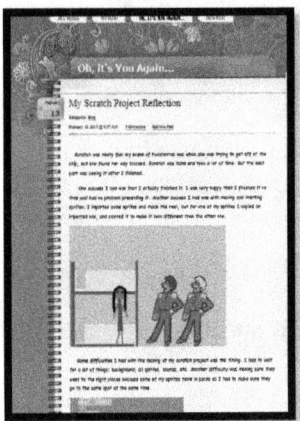 

_____Blogs teach writing skills, how to use evidence in arguments (in both posts and comments), and perspective-taking. They are student-directed but you approve posts and comments until students get used to the rules that apply to online conversations.

_____Blog design reflects student personalities with colors, fonts, and widgets. What students include will help you better understand their interests, how they learn, and how to reach them academically.

_____In general, student blogs require:

- titles that pull reader in
- tone/voice that fits this type of writing and intended audience
- working link(s) to evidence that supports statements
- at least one media to support each article (picture, video, sound)
- understanding of target audience
- understanding of purpose—how is it different from tweets? Essays? Poetry?
- citations—authors name, permission, linkbacks, copyright where required
- occasional teamwork

_____Before beginning, students sign an agreement similar to *Blogging Rules (Figure 13a*—full size at end of lesson). Ask them to discuss the agreement with parents and bring it to school before the next class. If you're using workbooks, students can sign the copy in there, take a screenshot, and email that to you.

Figure 13a—Blogging rules; 13b—rubric

Blogging Rules
(adapted from Academy of Discovery wiki)

1. I will not give out any information more personal than my first name
2. I will not plagiarize; instead I will expand on others' ideas and give credit where it is due.
3. I will use language appropriate for school.
4. I will always respect my fellow students and their writing.
5. I will only post pieces that I am comfortable with everyone seeing.
6. I will use constructive/productive/purposeful criticism, supporting any idea, comment, or critique I have with evidence.
7. I will take blogging seriously, posting only comments and ideas that are meaningful and that contribute to the overall conversation.
8. I will take my time when I write, using formal language (not text lingo), and I will try to spell everything correctly.
9. I will not bully others in my blog posts or in my comments.
10. I will only post comments on posts that I have fully read, rather than just skimmed.
11. I will not reveal anyone else's identity in my comments or posts.

Any infraction of the Blogging Rules may result in loss of blogging privileges and an alternative assignment will be required.

Student Signature _____ Date _____

CRITERIA	Exemplary	Proficient	Partially	Incomplete	POINTS
Relevance of Content to Students and Parents	9 points • Content has useful information. • Content is clear, concise; points reader to up to date resources. • Blog is updated frequently	6 points • Content points readers to quality resources, is informative • Resources are clearly described so readers can navigate easily	3 points • Content points to unrelated information. • Resources are not clearly described so readers cannot navigate easily	0 points • Resources pointed to are inaccurate, misleading or inappropriate • Annotations are missing, do not describe what is found	
Use of Media	6 points • Media enhance content and interest. • Creativity enhances content	4 points • Most media enhance content • Most files show creativity	2 points • Some media don't enhance content. • Some use of creativity is evident to enhance content.	0 points • Media are inappropriate or detract from content.	
Fair Use Guidelines	6 points Fair use guidelines are followed with proper citations.	4 points Fair use guidelines are frequently followed, most material is cited.	2 points Sometimes fair use guidelines are followed with some citations.	0 points Fair use guidelines not followed. Material is improperly cited	
Links	3 points All links are active and functioning.	2 points Most links are active	1 point Some links are not active.	0 points Many links are not active.	
Layout and Text Elements	3 points • Fonts are easy-to-read • Use of bullets, italics, bold, enhances readability. • Consistent format throughout	2 points • Sometimes fonts, size, bullets, italics, bold, detract from readability. • Minor formatting inconsistencies exist	1 point Text is difficult to read due to formatting	0 points • Text is difficult to read with misuse of fonts, size, bullets, italics, bold • Many formatting tools are misused	
Writing Mechanics	3 points No grammar, capitalization, punctuation, spelling errors	2 points Few grammar, capitalization, punctuation, and spelling errors	1 point 4+ errors in grammar, capitalization, punctuation, and spelling	0 points More than 6 grammar/spelling/punctuation errors	
				TOTAL POINTS	6/36

_____ Students can create blogs in WordPress, Blogger, or a favorite you prefer.

_____ Discuss blogging netiquette—like email etiquette:

- *be polite*
- *use good grammar and spelling*
- *don't write anything everyone shouldn't read (school blogs are private but get students used to the oxymoron of privacy and the Internet)*

_____ Remind students to practice good keyboarding as they type the entry.

_____ Once a month, students post an article that discusses an inquiry topic. Then, visit and comment on five classmate blogs.

_____ Set account so you approve comments before they go live. If you find inappropriate messages, chat with students about how nasty comments shut down the conversation.

_____ Occasionally throughout the year, use the Student Blogs Rubric *(Figure 13b*—full size assessment at end of lesson) to assess student progress.

Class Calendar

_____ Class calendars can run through Google Apps or another tool that works for your student group. Show students how to access it and how it's updated to reflect class activities.

_____ If students are going to oversee updating, demonstrate this.

_____ If using Google Apps, students can embed the calendar into blogs or websites.

_____ For Google Calendar training, visit Google's comprehensive calendar training.

Class Internet Start Page

_____A *start page* is a webpage that opens with the Internet. It organizes critical content in a single location and curates links students will use.

Figure 14—Class Internet start page

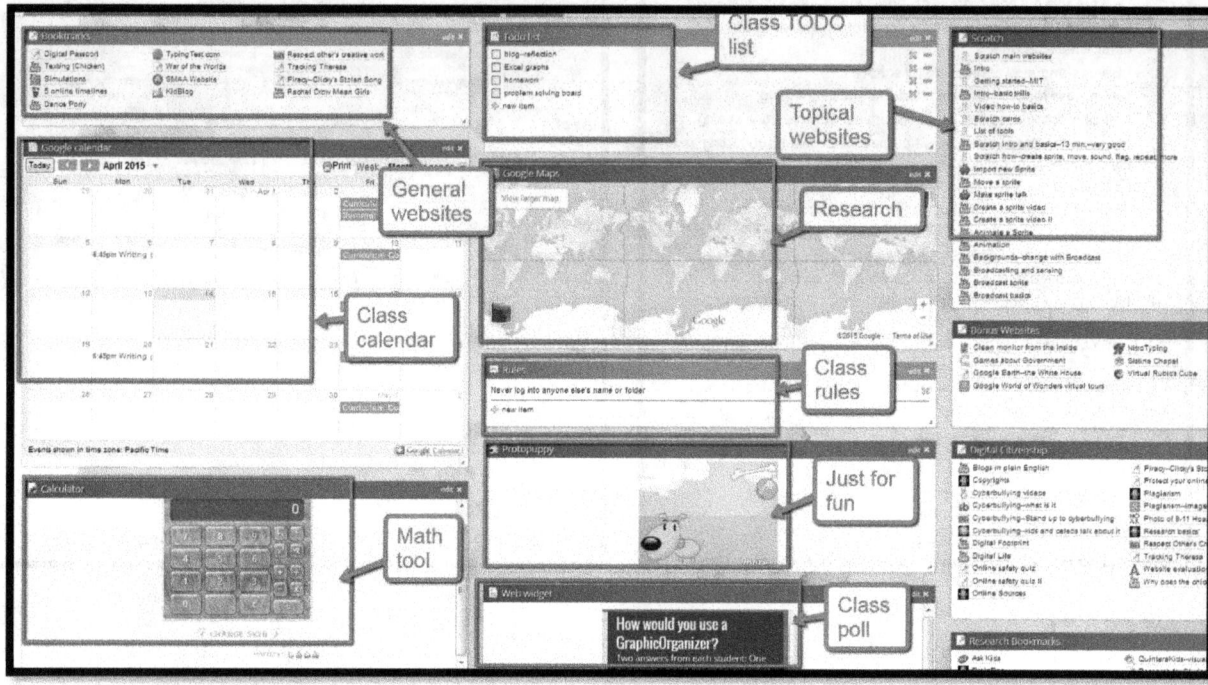

_____Include what students visit daily (i.e., guidelines, calendar, 'to do' list, typing websites, research locations, and calculator) as well as links specific to current project.

_____Mine also includes pictures of interest, RSS feeds, weather, a graffiti wall, and a class pet. Yours will be different.

_____Suggestions: Protopage.com *(Figure 14)*, Ighome, a collection site like Symbaloo *(Figure 15a)*, Portaportal *(Figure 15b)*, LiveBinders *(Figure 15c)*, Diigo account, or class Evernote account (Google for website addresses):

Figure 15a-c—Class start page examples

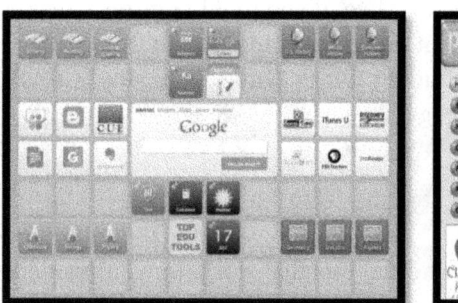 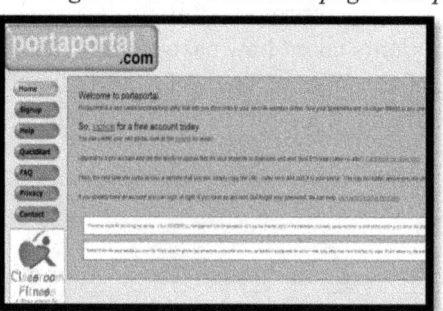 

_____Remind students that any time they visit the Internet, they must do so safely and legally. If you didn't discuss digital citizenship yet, take time right now to review it.

Class website

_____Class websites serve as a general resource collection location for class information.
_____Create this using the same tool that students will use for their student blog or website.

Digital Notetaking

_____Why take notes (from Common Core):

- *determine central ideas*
- *provide accurate summary*
- *identify key steps*
- *cite text evidence to support analysis*
- *analyze structure used to organize text*
- *analyze author's purpose*

_____Here are five digital notetaking methods for students:

- *Word processing program (for any digital device) – Figure 16a*
- *Notability (for iPads) – Figure 16b*

Figure 16a-b—Notetaking tools

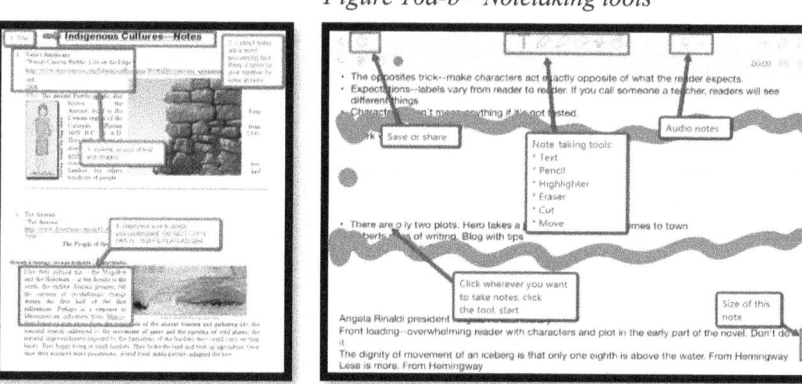

- *Google Apps – (for any digital device) – Figure 17*

Figure 17—Collaborative notes in Google Spreadsheets

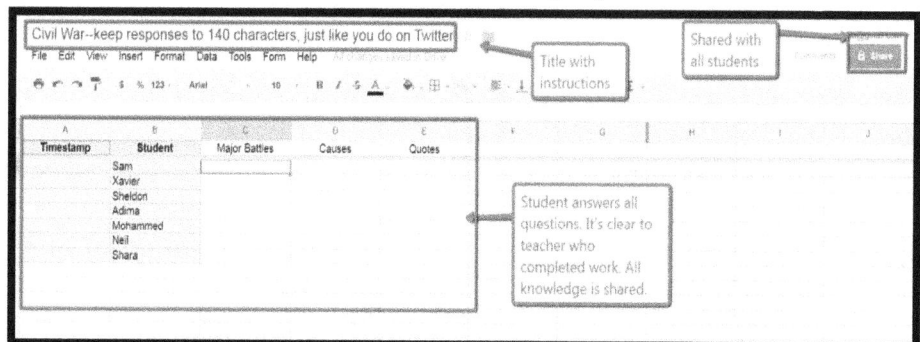

- *Evernote/OneNote (for most digital devices) — Figure 18a*
- *Twitter (for most digital devices) — Figure 18b*

Figure 18a-b — Digital notetaking tools

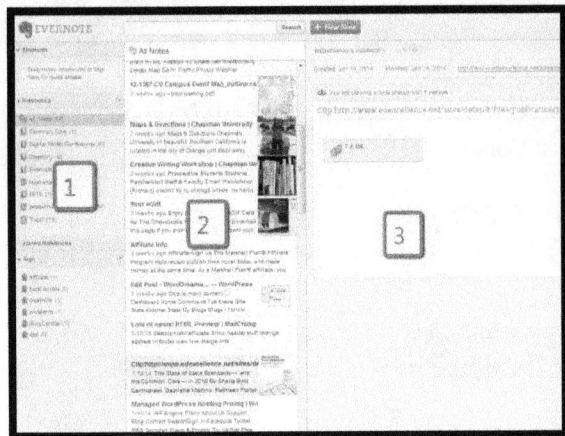
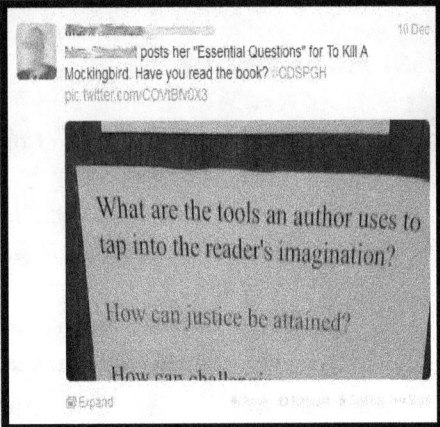

Digital portfolios

_____Discuss how Digital Portfolios are used to (also known as digital lockers or digital binders):

- *store work (in Cloud) required in other classes or at home*
- *interact, collaborate, and publish with peers, experts, or others*
- *edit or review work in multiple locations*
- *submit class assignments*

_____There are a variety of approaches that satisfy some or all of the above uses: 1) folders on school network, 2) fee-based programs, 3) cloud-based storage like Dropbox or Google Apps, and 4) online collaborative sites like PBWorks.com (Google for websites).
_____Occasionally, use *Assessment* at end of this lesson to review student progress.

Figure 19a-b—Digital portfolio examples

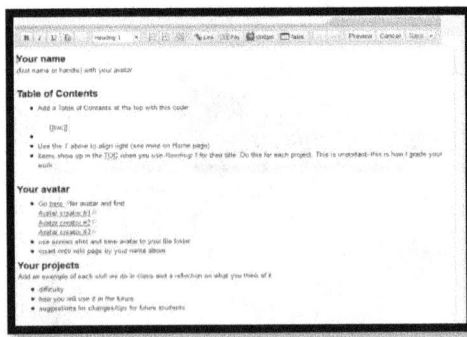
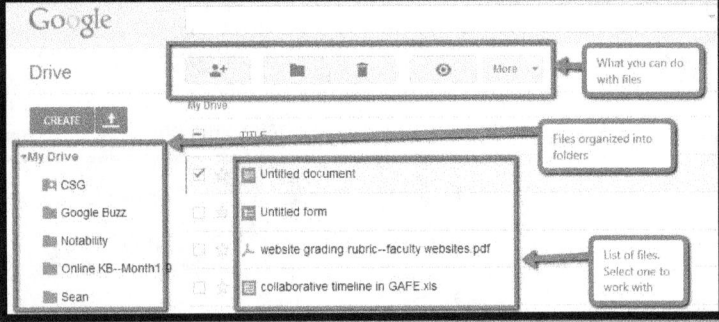

Dropbox

_____If your school has this option, review it with students. If you don't, show students how they will be expected to submit classwork and/or homework.

_____An assignment drop box can be created through the school Learning Management System (LMS), email, Google Apps (through 'share' function)—even a Discussion Board.
_____If you have Google Apps (but not Google Classroom), create a drop box like *Figure 20*:

- *Each student creates a folder called 'Homework' that is shared with you.*
- *To submit work, copy it to that folder so the teacher can view.*

Figure 20—Dropbox

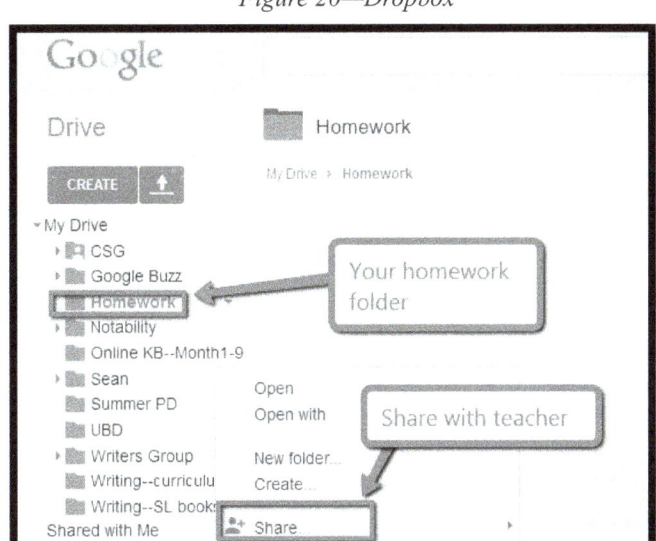

Email

_____Use web-based account such as Gmail (comes with GAFE and Google Classrooms).
_____Review **email** etiquette (*Figure 21*—full-size poster at end of lesson):

Figure 4—Email Etiquette

- *Use proper writing conventions.*
- *CC anyone mentioned.*
- *Make 'Subject line' topic of email.*
- *Answer swiftly.*
- *Re-read before sending.*
- *Don't use all caps—THIS IS SHOUTING.*
- *Don't attach unnecessary files.*
- *Don't overuse high priority.*
- *Don't email confidential information.*
- *Don't email offensive remarks.*
- *Don't forward chain letters or spam.*
- *Don't open attachments from strangers.*

_____Clarify 'high priority' 'BCC', and 'CC'.
_____If you have GAFE or Google Classroom (with Gmail activated), review how to use email. Show

students how to control settings so they don't get spam.

_____Let students (and parents) know that the email program used at home may not match the instructions you provided. Ask parents to show their children how to use the home-based email.

_____Why is correct grammar/spelling important in email and not so much in texting? Hint: Consider Common Core—*Produce clear and coherent writing in which development, organization, and style are appropriate to **task, purpose, and audience**.*

_____Discuss 'spam'. What is it? Why is it sent? What should students do when it shows up in email?

_____Discuss how email can be used to back-up important documents (by emailing a copy to themselves or creating a draft email with doc attached and stored in 'Draft' file).

_____When students get an email, follow this checklist:

- Do you know sender?
- Is email legitimate? For example, does the 'voice' sound like sender?
- Is sender asking for personal information? Legitimate sources never do.
- Is there an attachment? If so, don't open it.

Evidence Board

_____The Evidence Board (*Figure 22a*) is a bulletin board that celebrates student transfer of knowledge from tech class to home, friends, or other educational endeavors.

Figure 22a—Evidence Board; 22b—Badge

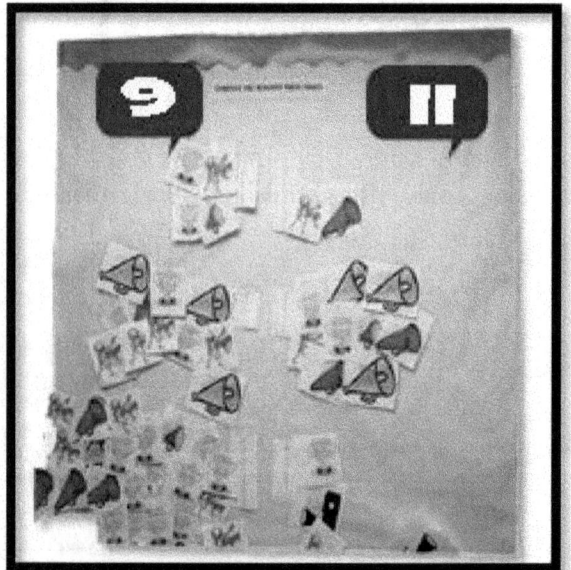

_____About once a month, students share how they use tech skills outside of your class. They will make a ten-second presentation to class, fill out a badge (like *Figure 22b*), and post it on the Evidence Board by their class. By year end, you want this collection to encircle the room.

Google Apps

_____To access Google Apps requires a Google account and starts at Google Drive. *Figure 23* is an example of what the Google Drive might look like:

Figure 23—Google Apps

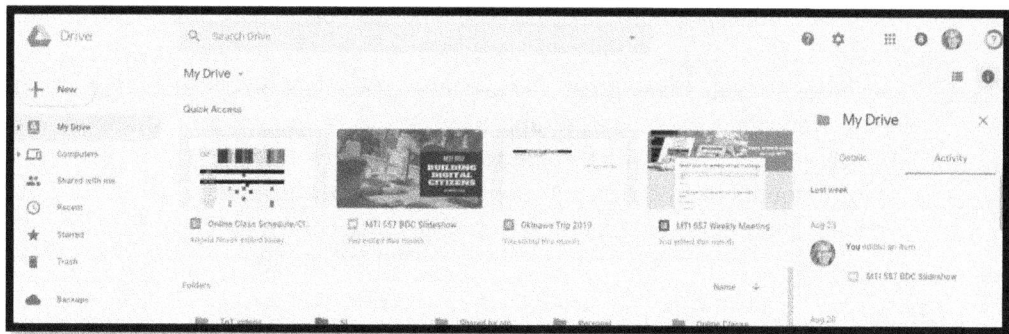

_____There are many resources available for teaching how to use Google Apps. Check this list on Ask a Tech Teacher's Google resource pages.

_____Give students time to explore Google Drive before moving on.

_____The most popular Google Drive apps—and the ones students will use the most—are:

- *Google Docs—for word processing projects*
- *Google Slides—for slideshow presentations*
- *Google Spreadsheets—for the analysis of data using spreadsheets*
- *Google Forms (if available)*
- *Google Draw*

_____Review any of these you determine students should know.

Screenshots and Screencasts

_____Students will use screenshot tools, apps, or add-ons (depending upon your digital device), as well as screencasts (videos), to record information from their screen. More on this in the lesson on *Screenshots and Screencasts*.

Figure 24a—Screenshot; 24b—screencast

 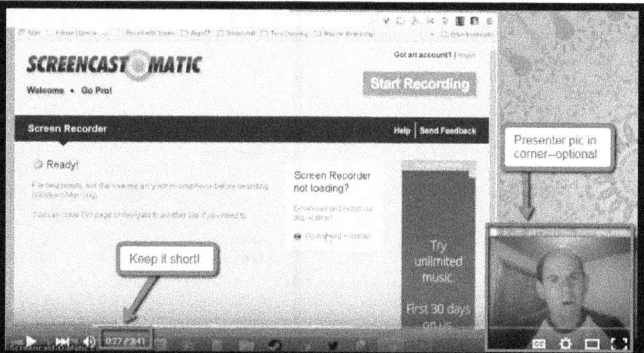

Student website

_____Most teachers will select either student blogs or websites, depending upon their goal:

- *Blogs are more interactive and time-sensitive.*
- *Websites more fully cover a topic and new posts don't push older out of the way.*

_____Like blogs, websites are a great way to encourage reflection, organization, logical thinking, and are a perfect place to embed sharable projects, i.e., Tagxedos and Animotos.

_____Websites are available with Google accounts. Or free websites can be created at Weebly, Wix, or blog accounts like WordPress (Google for website addresses).

_____Websites should reflect student personalities with colors, fonts, and layout.

_____In general:

- *Website and article titles pull reader in.*
- *Articles review the topic, provide evidence with supporting links.*
- *Tone/voice fits this type of writing and intended audience.*
- *Links connect to evidence and links work.*
- *At least one media is provided to support each article (picture, video, sound).*
- *Writing purpose is clear; citations are included as needed.*
- *Occasional teamwork is exhibited.*

_____Occasionally (several times a grading period), assess websites based on the criteria in *Figure 25* (full size assessment at end of lesson):

Figure 25—Student website rubric

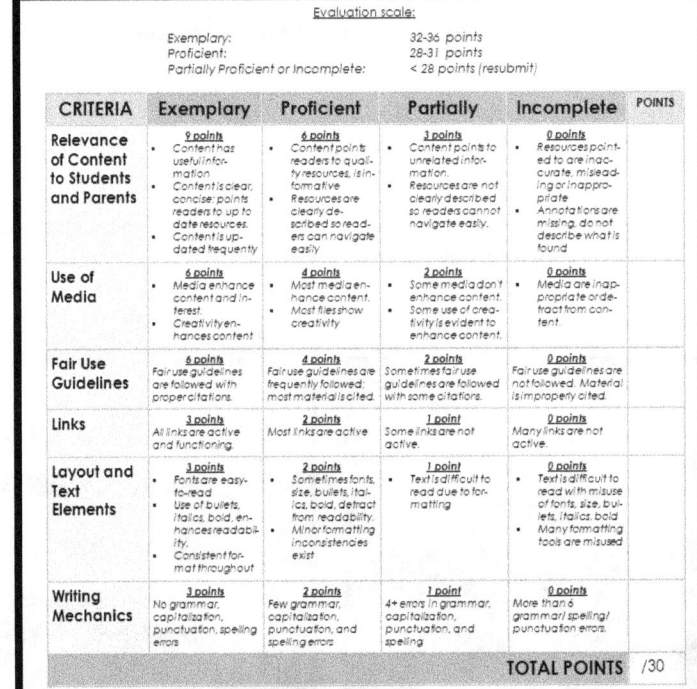

Vocabulary Decoding Tools

_____Show students how to access the native apps or webtools on their digital devices that can be used to decode unknown vocabulary. Depending upon the device, these will be on the homepage, _____the browser toolbar, a shortkey, or a right click. Show students how to quickly look up words from any of their classes rather than skipping over content that includes the word. Let them practice with several of the words in this lesson's *Vocabulary* list.

_____If relevant, review Common Core's three tiers of vocabulary. How does this apply to them?

_____Decoding options include:

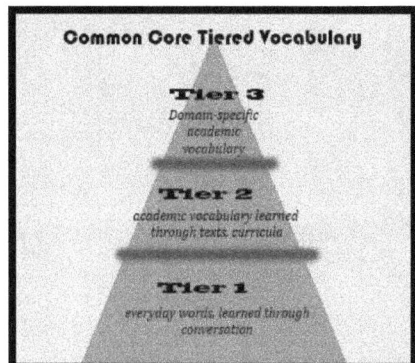

- *Right click on word*
- *Access an online dictionary*
- *Double-click the word on a webpage (if you have an app).*

_____A note: Every chance you get, use technology to facilitate teaching. Lead by example. Students will see you use tech quickly and facilely and follow your good example. They want to use tech. Don't discourage them!

Class exit ticket: *Students send a well-constructed email to a classmate (if students have email accounts) and reply to one they receive appropriately.*

Differentiation

- *Explore inside computer.*
- *Click here for how to use Padlet*
- *See article at end of Lesson on* **Internet Start Pages**.
- *What's Evernote? Watch this video*
- *Many digital tools promote a paper-free classroom. See the article,* **It's Time to Make Your Classroom Paper-free**, *at the end of this lesson,*
- *For more Google Apps, try these:*

    - *Scholar: Research and analyze sources from books, websites, other*
    - *SketchUp: Create and explore 3D Models*
    - *Translate: Free online translation tool for any text*

Assessment 1--Parts of the Computer

HARDWARE—PARTS OF THE COMPUTER

Student name: _____

Name each part of computer hardware system. Label it as INPUT or OUTPUT.
Spelling must be correct.

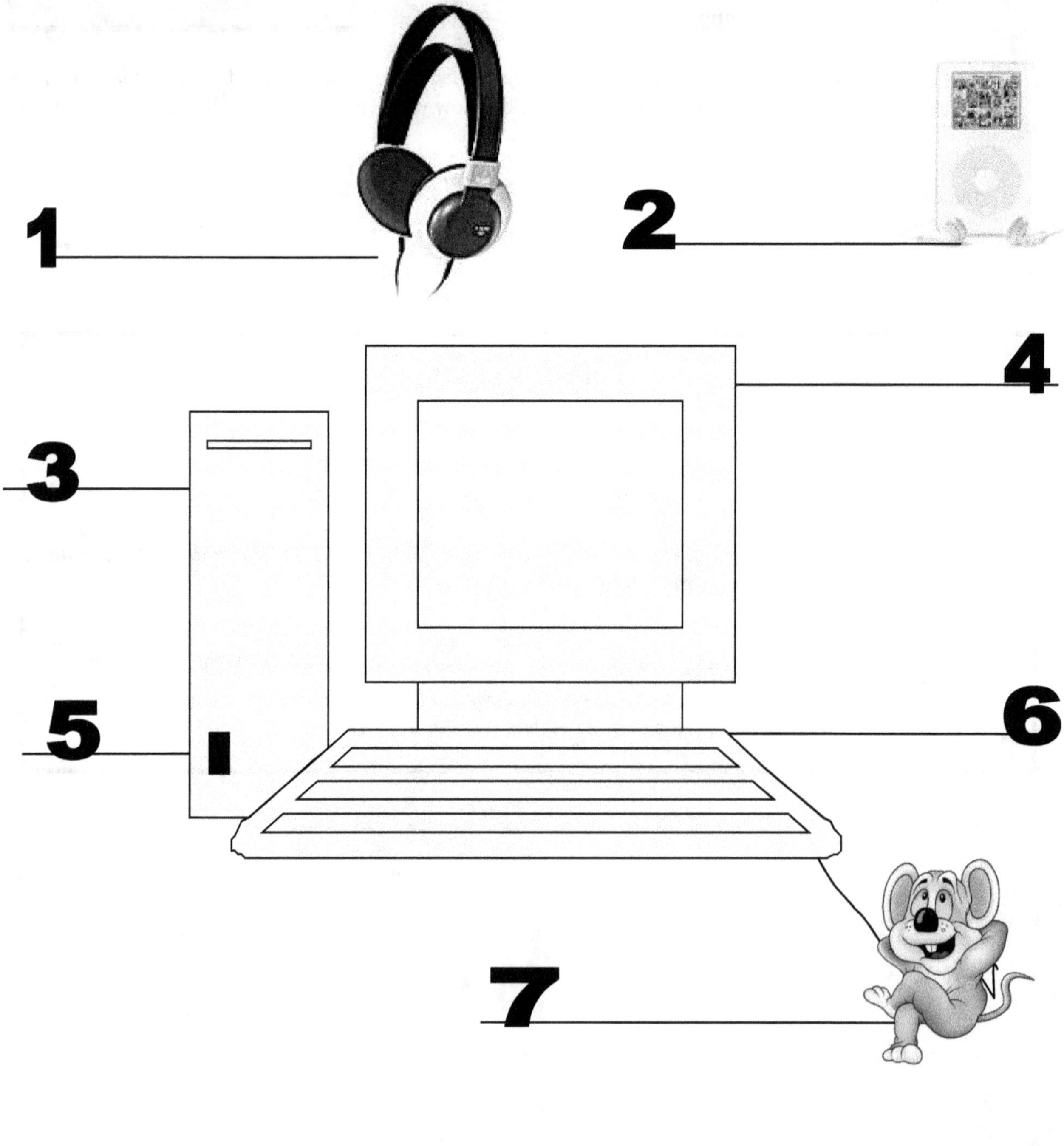

1 _____

2 _____

3 _____

4 _____

5 _____

6 _____

7 _____

Assessment 2--Hardware: Parts of the Smartphone

HARDWARE—PARTS OF THE SMARTPHONE

Adapt this to your needs

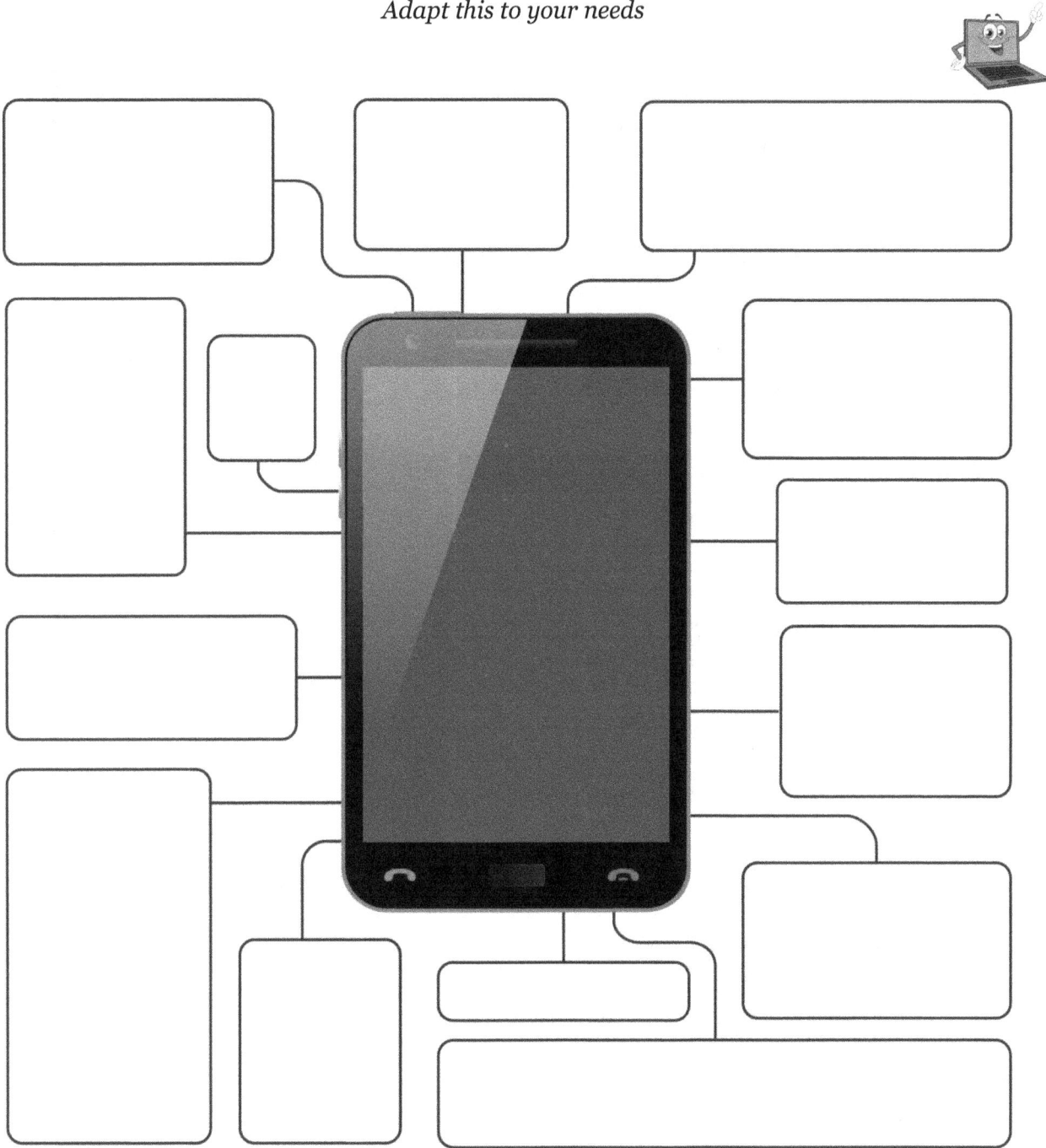

High School Technology Curriculum Book 1: Teacher Manual

Assessment 3aAssessment Assessment --Parts of an iPad

Parts of an iPad

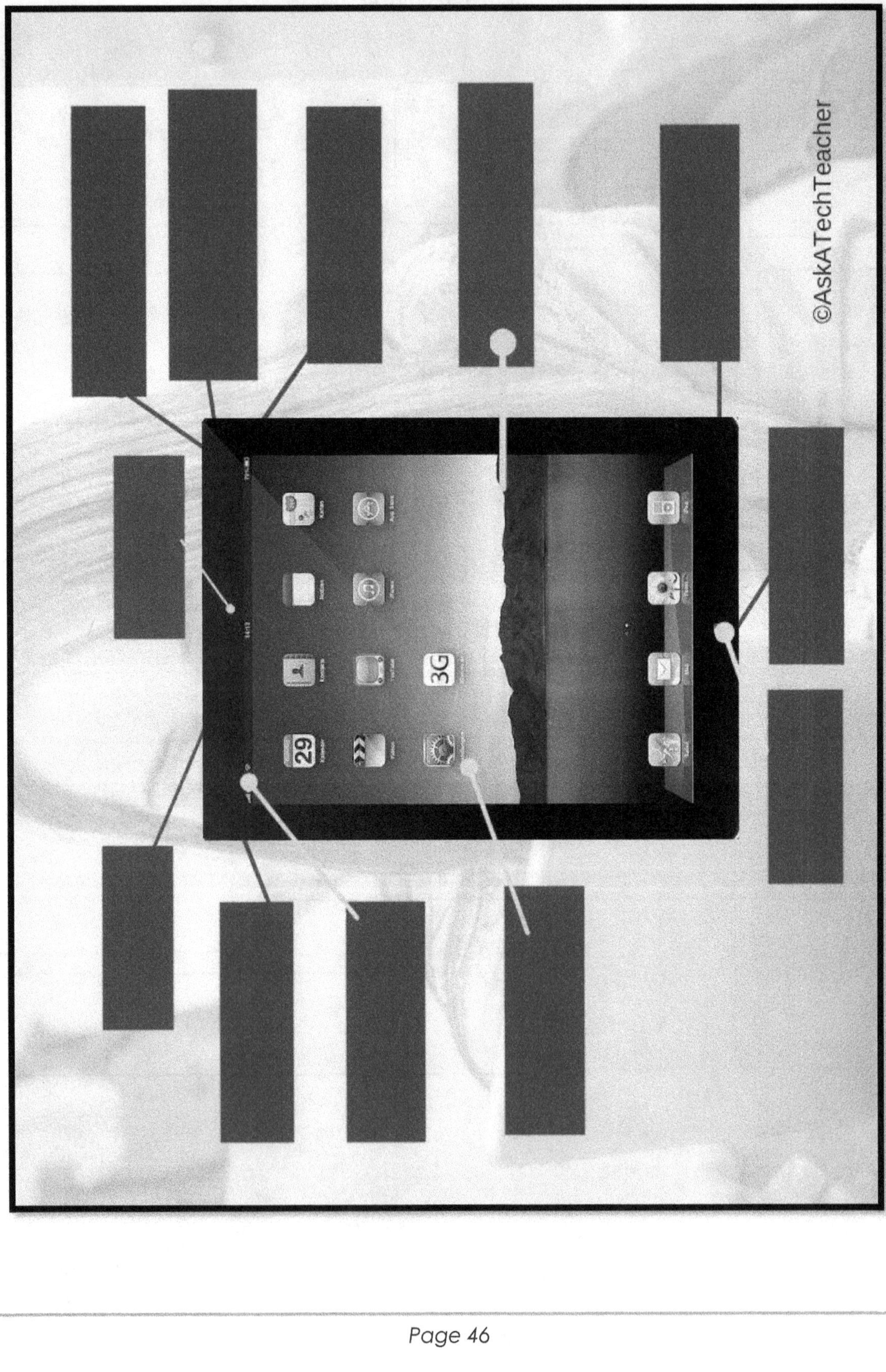

Assessment 3b—Chromebook parts

Parts of a Chromebook

Assessment 4—Student blogging agreement

Blogging Rules

(adapted from Academy of Discovery)

1. I will not give out any information more personal than my first name
2. I will not plagiarize; instead I will expand on others' ideas and give credit where it is due.
3. I will use language appropriate for school.
4. I will always respect my fellow students and their writing.
5. I will only post pieces that I am comfortable with everyone seeing.
6. I will use constructive/productive/purposeful criticism, supporting any idea, comment, or critique I have with evidence.
7. I will take blogging seriously, posting only comments and ideas that are meaningful and that contribute to the overall conversation.
8. I will take my time when I write, using formal language (not text lingo), and I will try to spell everything correctly.
9. I will not bully others in my blog posts or in my comments.
10. I will only post comments on posts that I have fully read, rather than just skimmed.
11. I will not reveal anyone else's identity in my comments or posts.

Any infraction of the Blogging Rules may result in loss of blogging privileges and an alternative assignment will be required.

Student Signature _____ Date _____

Assessment 5—Blog grading rubric

Student Blog Rubric

Adapted from University of Wisconsin-Stout

Evaluation scale:

Exemplary:	32-36 points
Proficient:	28-31 points
Partially Proficient or Incomplete:	< 28 points (resubmit)

CRITERIA	Exemplary	Proficient	Partially	Incomplete	PTS
Relevance of Content to Students and Parents	**9 points** • Content has useful information • Content is clear, concise; points readers to up to date resources. • Blog is updated frequently	**6 points** • Content points readers to quality resources, is informative • Resources are clearly described so readers can navigate easily	**3 points** • Content points to unrelated information. • Resources are not clearly described so readers cannot navigate easily.	**0 points** • Resources pointed to are inaccurate, misleading or inappropriate • Annotations are missing, do not describe what is found	
Use of Media	**6 points** • Media enhance content and interest. • Creativity enhances content	**4 points** • Most media enhance content. • Most files show creativity	**2 points** • Some media irrelevant. • Some creativity evident to enhance content.	**0 points** • Media are inappropriate or detract from content.	
Fair Use Guidelines	**6 points** Fair use guidelines are followed with proper citations.	**4 points** Fair use guidelines are frequently followed; most material is cited.	**2 points** Sometimes fair use guidelines are followed with some citations.	**0 points** Fair use guidelines not followed. Material improperly cited.	
Links	**3 points** All links are active and functioning.	**2 points** Most links are active	**1 point** Some links are not active.	**0 points** Many links are not active.	
Layout and Text Elements	**3 points** • Fonts are easy-to-read • Use of bullets, italics, bold, enhances readability. • Consistent format throughout	**2 points** • Sometimes fonts, size, bullets, italics, bold, detract from readability. • Minor formatting inconsistencies exist	**1 point** • Text is difficult to read due to formatting	**0 points** • Text is difficult to read with misuse of fonts, size, bullets, italics, bold • Many formatting tools are misused	
Writing Mechanics	**3 points** No grammar, capitalization, punctuation, spelling errors	**2 points** Few grammar, capitalization, punctuation, and spelling errors	**1 point** 4+ errors in grammar, capitalization, punctuation, and spelling	**0 points** More than 6 grammar/ spelling/ punctuation errors.	
				TOTAL POINTS	/30

Assessment 6—Website grading rubric

Student Website Rubric

Adapted from University of Wisconsin-Stout

Evaluation scale:

Exemplary:	32-36 points
Proficient:	28-31 points
Partially Proficient or Incomplete:	< 28 points (resubmit)

CRITERIA	Exemplary	Proficient	Partially	Incomplete	PTS
Relevance of Content to Students and Parents	**9 points** • Content has useful information • Content is clear, concise; points readers to up to date resources. • Content is updated frequently	**6 points** • Content points readers to quality resources, is informative • Resources are clearly described so readers can navigate easily	**3 points** • Content points to unrelated information. • Resources are not clearly described so readers cannot navigate easily.	**0 points** • Resources pointed to are inaccurate, misleading or inappropriate • Annotations are missing, do not describe what is found	
Use of Media	**6 points** • Media enhance content and interest. • Creativity enhances content	**4 points** • Most media enhance content. • Most files show creativity	**2 points** • Some media don't enhance content. • Some use of creativity is evident to enhance content.	**0 points** • Media are inappropriate or detract from content.	
Fair Use Guidelines	**6 points** Fair use guidelines are followed with proper citations.	**4 points** Fair use guidelines are frequently followed; most material is cited.	**2 points** Sometimes fair use guidelines are followed with some citations.	**0 points** Fair use guidelines are not followed. Material is improperly cited.	
Links	**3 points** All links are active and functioning.	**2 points** Most links are active	**1 point** Some links are not active.	**0 points** Many links are not active.	
Layout and Text Elements	**3 points** • Fonts are easy-to-read • Use of bullets, italics, bold, enhances readability. • Consistent format throughout	**2 points** • Sometimes fonts, size, bullets, italics, bold, detract from readability. • Minor formatting inconsistencies exist	**1 point** • Text is difficult to read due to formatting	**0 points** • Text is difficult to read with misuse of fonts, size, bullets, italics, bold • Many formatting tools are misused	
Writing Mechanics	**3 points** No grammar, capitalization, punctuation, spelling errors	**2 points** Few grammar, capitalization, punctuation, and spelling errors	**1 point** 4+ errors in grammar, capitalization, punctuation, and spelling	**0 points** More than 6 grammar/ spelling/ punctuation errors.	
				TOTAL POINTS	/30

Assessment 7—Digital portfolio rubric

Digital Portfolio Rubric

CATEGORY	Exemplary	Proficient	Developing	Unsatisfactory	RATING
Selection of Artifacts	All artifacts and work samples are clearly and directly related to the purpose of portfolio.	Most artifacts and work samples are related to the purpose of the digital portfolio.	Some of the artifacts and work samples are related to the purpose of the digital portfolio.	None of the artifacts and work samples is related to the purpose of portfolio.	
Reflections	All reflections clearly describe growth, achievement and accomplishments, and include goals for continued learning (long and short term).	Most reflections describe growth and include goals for continued learning. It is clear student put thought and consideration into writing.	A few of the reflections describe growth and include goals for continued learning. It is not clear student put thought into his/her writing.	None of the reflections describes growth and does not include goals for continued learning. It is clear student put little thought into these writings.	
Use of Multimedia	Photographs, graphics, audio and/or video files enhance understanding of concepts, ideas and relationships, create interest, and are appropriate for chosen purpose.	Most of the graphic elements and multimedia contribute to understanding concepts, ideas and relationships, enhance the written material and create interest.	Some of the graphic elements and multimedia do not contribute to understanding concepts, ideas and relationships.	None of multimedia contribute to understanding concepts, ideas and relationships. The inappropriate use of multimedia detracts from content.	
Documentation & Copyright	All images, media and text follow copyright guidelines with accurate citations. All content throughout portfolio displays appropriate copyright permissions.	Most images, media and text created by others are cited with accurate, properly formatted citations.	Some images, media or text created by others are not cited with accurate, properly formatted citations.	No images, media or text created by others are cited with accurate, properly formatted citations.	
Ease of Navigation	Navigation links are intuitive. The various parts of portfolio are labeled, clearly organized and allow reader to easily locate an artifact.	Navigation links generally function well, but it is not always clear how to locate an artifact or move to related pages or different section.	Navigation links are confusing and it is often unclear how to locate an artifact or move to related pages or section.	Navigation links are confusing, and it is difficult to locate artifacts and move to related pages or a different section.	
Layout and Text Elements	Digital portfolio is easy to read. Fonts and type size vary appropriately for headings, sub-headings and text. Use of font styles (italic, bold, underline) is consistent and improves readability.	Digital portfolio is generally easy to read. Fonts and type size vary appropriately for headings, sub-headings and text. Use of font styles (italic, bold, underline) is generally consistent.	Digital portfolio is often difficult to read due to inappropriate use of fonts and type size for headings, sub-headings and text or inconsistent use of font styles (italic, bold, underline).	Digital portfolio is difficult to read due to inappropriate use of fonts, type size for headings, subheadings and text, and font styles (italic, bold, underline).	
Captions	All artifacts are accompanied by a caption that clearly explains importance of item including title, author, and date.	Most artifacts are accompanied by a caption that clearly explains importance of item including title, author, and date.	Some artifacts are accompanied by caption that explains importance of item including title, author, and date.	No artifacts are accompanied by a caption that explains importance of item.	
Writing Mechanics	There are no errors in grammar, capitalization, punctuation, and spelling.	There are few errors in grammar and spelling. These require minor editing and revision.	There are four or more errors in grammar and spelling requiring editing and revision.	There are more than six errors in grammar and spelling requiring major editing and revision.	

Askatechteacher©

EMAIL ETIQUETTE

1. Use proper formatting, spelling, grammar
2. CC anyone you mention
3. Subject line is what your email discusses
4. Answer swiftly
5. Re-read email before sending
6. Don't use capitals—THIS IS SHOUTING
7. Don't leave out the subject line
8. Don't attach unnecessary files
9. Don't overuse high priority
10. Don't email confidential information
11. Don't email offensive remarks
12. Don't forward chain letters or spam
13. Don't open attachments from strangers

Article 7—Which Internet Start Page is Best

Which Internet Start Page is Best?

The Internet is unavoidable in education. Students go there to research, access homework, check grades, and a whole lot more. As a teacher, you do your best to make it a friendly, intuitive, and safe place to visit, but it's challenging. Students arrive there by iPads, smartphones, links from classroom teachers, suggestions from friends—the routes are endless. The best way to keep the Internet experience safe is to catch users right at the front door, on that first click.

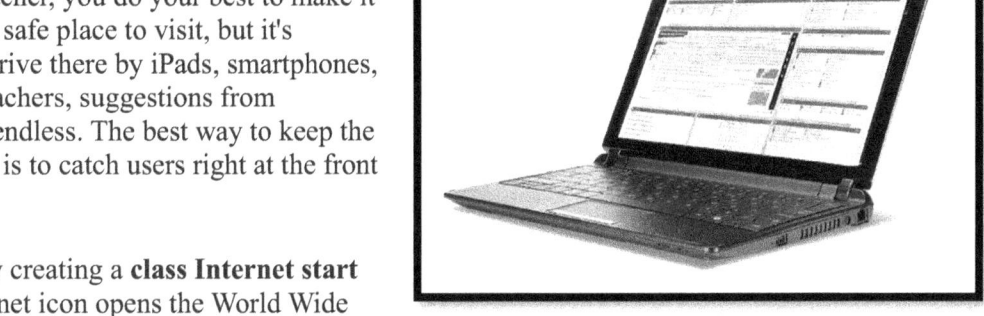

How do you do that? By creating a **class Internet start page**. Clicking the Internet icon opens the World Wide Web to a default page. Never take your device's default because there's no guarantee it's G-rated enough for a typical classroom environment. Through the 'settings' function on your browser, enter the address of a page you've designed as a portal to all school Internet activity, called an 'Internet start page'. Sure, this takes some time to set-up and maintain, but it saves more than that in student frustration, lesson prep time, and the angst parents feel about their children entering the virtual world by themselves. They aren't. You're there, through this page. Parents can save the link to their home computer and let students access any resources on it, with the confidence of knowing you've curated everything.

In searching for the perfect Internet start page, I wanted one that:

- *quickly differentiates for different grades*
- *is intuitive for even the youngest to find their page*
- *is customizable across tabbed pages to satisfy changing needs*
- *presents a visual and playful interface to make students want to go there rather than find work-arounds (a favorite hobby of older students)*
- *includes an immediately visible calendar of events*
- *hosts videos of class events*
- *provides collaborative walls like Padlet*
- *includes other interactive widgets to excite students about technology*

Here are the ones I looked at:

Symbaloo

A logo-based website curation tool with surprising flexibility in how links are collected and displayed. It's hugely popular with educators because collections are highly-visual and easy to access and use. Plus, Symbaloo collections made by one teacher can be shared with the community, making link collections that much easier to curate.

The downside: Links are about all you can collect on Symbaloo.

Ustart

Offers a good collection of useful webtools for students including links, news, calendar, notes, even weather. It provides tabs for arranging themed collections (like classes) and is intuitive to set up and use. It even includes options for embeddable widgets like Padlet. This is the closest to what I needed of all three.

Overall: This is a good alternative to the one I selected.

Protopage

Protopage did everything on my list. It's flexible, customizable, intuitive, and quick to use with a scalable interface that can be adjusted to my needs (2-5 columns, resize boxes, drag widgets between tabs—that sort). I set up a separate tab for each grade (or you can set up tabs for subjects). The amount of tabs is limited only by space on the top toolbar. Resources included on each tab can be curated exactly as you need. Mine includes:

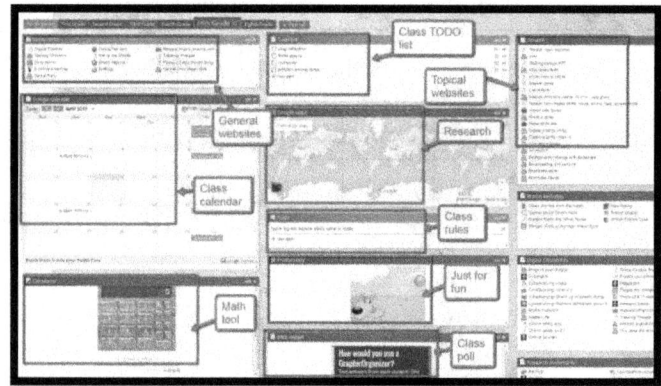

- *oft-used websites*
- *themed collections of websites*
- *a To Do list*
- *an interactive map*
- *a calculator*
- *a calendar of events*
- *edit-in-place sticky notes*
- *pictures of interest*
- *RSS feeds of interest*
- *weather*
- *news*
- *widget for polling the class (Padlet)*

In addition, the Protopage folks are helpful. Whenever I have a problem (which is rare), they fix it quickly.

Article 8—13 Ways Blogs Teach Common Core

13 Ways Blogs Teach Common Core

If you aren't blogging with your students, you're missing one of the most effective tools available for improving student literacy and math. Blogs are easy to use, fun for students, encourage creativity and problem-solving, allow for reflection and feedback, enable publishing and sharing of work, and fulfill many of the Common Core Standards you might be struggling to complete. Aside from math and literacy, Common Core wants students to become accomplished in a variety of intangible skills that promote learning and college and career readiness. Look at these 13 benefits of blogging and how they align with Common Core:

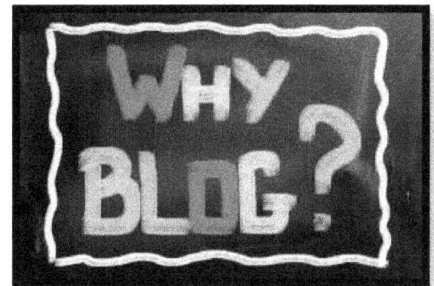

1. **provide and get feedback**—building a community via comments is an integral part of blogging. If you didn't want feedback, you'd publish a white paper or submit work the old fashioned hard copy way. When students publish their ideas in blogs, other students, teachers, parents can provide feedback, join the conversation, and learn from the student.
2. **write-edit-review-rewrite**—teachers don't expect students to get it right the first time. Part of the writing process is revising, editing, rewriting. This is easy with blogs. Students publish a topic, collect comments, incorporate these ideas into their own thinking, and then edit their post.
3. **publish**—the idea that student work is created for a grade then stuffed away in a corner of their closet is disappearing. Current educators want students to publish their work in a way that allows everyone to benefit from the student's knowledge and work. There are many ways to do that—blogs are one of the easiest.
4. **share**—just like publishing, students no longer create for a grade; they share with others. Blogs allow for sharing of not only writing, but artwork, photography, music, multimedia projects, pretty much anything the student can create.
5. **collaborate**—blogs can easily be collaborative. Student groups can publish articles, comment on others, edit and rewrite. They can work together on one blog to cover a wider variety of topics and/or make its design attractive, appealing and enticing to readers.
6. **keyboarding**—blogs are small doses of typing—300-500 words, a few dozen for comments. This is an authentic opportunity to practice the keyboarding skills students will need for Common Core Standards.
7. **demonstrate independence**—blogs are about creativity. No two are alike. They offer lots of options for design and formatting so students can tweak it to their preference. Because they are open 24/7, students can do blog work when it suits them, not in the confines of a 50-minute class.
8. **build strong content knowledge**—blog posts can be drafted as the student collects information, posted when the student is ready. Links can be included to provide evidence of student statements, as well as linkbacks for reference and deeper reading for interested students.
9. **respond to the varying demands of audience, task, purpose, and discipline**—Students can create their work in whatever digital tool fits the audience, task, purpose they are focused on, and then embed it into their blog post. This is possible even in a simplified blogging platform like KidBlog. Most online tools (such as Voki, Wordle, and Tagxedo) provide the html codes that can be easily placed in the blog

post. Then, the student at their option can focus on presenting their ideas as music, art, photos, text, an infographic, a word cloud—whatever works for their purposes.

10. **comprehend as well as critique**—student bloggers are expected to critique the posts of others by thoroughly reading the post and commenting based on evidence. If the reader doesn't understand, they ask questions in the comments. This insures that when they evaluate the post, they have all the information required to reach a conclusion.

11. **value evidence**—blogs make it easy to provide all the necessary evidence to support a point of view. Students can link back to sources to provide credit and link to experts to provide credibility for statements. In fact, in the blogosphere, good bloggers are expected to do this as a means of building credibility for opinions they write

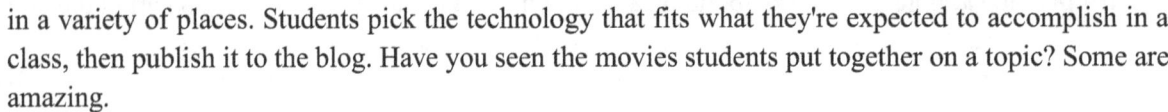

12. **use technology and digital media strategically and capably**—certainly blogs are great for writing, but they're also excellent as digital portfolios to display student work developed in a variety of places. Students pick the technology that fits what they're expected to accomplish in a class, then publish it to the blog. Have you seen the movies students put together on a topic? Some are amazing.

13. **understand other perspectives and cultures**—blogs are published to the Internet. Even private blogs are accessed by many more people than possible with a hand-written paper. Students write knowing that people of all cultures and perspectives will read their material, knowing they can add comments that share their beliefs. This encourages students to develop the habit of thinking about *perspective* as they write.

Don't try all of this at once. Spiral into it. Let student blogging grow with their intellectual skills.

Basics of Posts

Blogs used to be too cutting edge for pedestrian rules like grammar and spelling. That's not true anymore. Before students write their first post, remind them:

- *make content pithy*
- *use correct spelling and grammar*
- *avoid slang*
- *appeal to readers with content and design*
- *interact with readers via questions in the blog and answering comments*
- *avoid mistakes, redundancies, jerky flow by proof reading*

Blogs are everything you want in a school activity—student-centered, independent, supportive of problem solving and creative thinking, transferable to many classes and home activities. If you have questions, add them to the comments. I'll see if I can help.

Article 9—Paper-free Classroom

It's Time to Make Your Classroom Paper-free

Each year, the world produces more than 300 million tons of paper. According to the U.S. Environmental Protection Agency, paper typically found in a school or office environments such as copier paper, computer printouts, and notepads, comprise the largest category. Mitigating the use of paper has long been a goal for schools. Every year, a prodigious number of lesson plans center around dwindling rainforests, the shrinking world forests, and the ever-growing waste associated with paper.

Now, beyond the moral and ethical persuasiveness of a paperless classroom, there is compelling evidence that the time is right to eliminate paper from the classroom:

- **the high cost of printing**: Yale University noted that *"Every 2.5 minutes, a ream of paper was ordered."* No surprise that schools who go paperless experience huge savings in the cost of buying and repairing printers as well as the investment in all the fancy printing papers required for newsletters, class projects, announcements, and more. Who would argue about investing these vast savings in faculty salaries, student services, or reduced tuitions?
- **reduced waste:** Most of those tons of paper end up in the trash. We want them to be recycled but studies show that despite best efforts, about half of used paper isn't. Schools who replace paper with a digital distribution of newsletters, announcements, homework, and anything else possible may not increase recycling but do dramatically reduce the amount of paper they use. The results? Among schools who push digital over paper, most report that only about 5% of their usual amount of paper ends up in the trash. Who wouldn't love that number?
- **saves time:** Every teacher knows how much time they spend copying, stapling, sorting, and then searching for lost documents. An increasingly-popular alternative is to upload a document to the computer, server, or cloud and push it out electronically. No copying, stapling, sorting, or losing templates. No last-minute "I forgot to print this". Yes, digital files do get lost but that's a story for another time.
- **increased organization:** All those permission slips, AUPs, and exams can be curated into a digital file folder that is backed up automatically and never lost ("never" being a fungible sort of word). Teachers no longer find themselves frantically searching for misfiled records or the approvals required before a field trip. Instead, they access the digital file folder. If it's not there, most of the time, a universal search on the school server will find the document. Anecdotal experiences (no studies yet on this topic) indicate that teachers who file digitally rather than in paper file folders lose fewer documents.
- **security**: Digital files aren't lost to floods or fires. Even if the server crashes or corrupts, every school I know has backups. No data is lost; just the equipment.

Here are four approaches to removing paper from your classroom:

Digital whiteboard

A **digital whiteboard** is when you project an online whiteboard to your class screen and then use it as you would the one that hangs on the wall in your room. Some teachers wonder why they would do that. It isn't available when the computer is off; it requires set-up; and what if you want to write a formula? In truth, today's digital whiteboards are much like your traditional board. You have a variety of pens, colors, and shapes. You can easily insert images to support the lesson. You can project a website that ties in with your teaching. Probably the best reason to use the digital version of a whiteboard is that everything you write on it can be saved and pushed out to student 1:1 devices, LMSs, or digital portfolios.

Popular choices range from *free to fee* and *may or may not require a log-in*. Many LMSs (like Canvas) have built-in versions available alongside other classroom management tools.

Ebooks

Assigning a book to your class that everyone must then purchase is not only expensive, it's inequitable. For some, those costs challenge a family budget. If you have a book you want students to read, check to see if it's available on one of the many online free libraries and let students know they can use it there. Ebooks have no concern about the "latest edition" because they're automatically updated. Ereaders are often free from the ebook provider (like Kindle) and PDFs can be read on almost every platform.

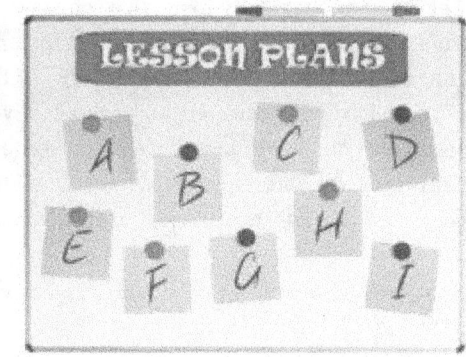

LMS

Most LMSs (Learning Management Systems) make it easy to trade paper for digital. The good news: Most schools now use LMSs be they Google Classroom, Canvas, or another. Through your LMS, you'll find it easy to:

- digitally create and push out assignments
- digitally submit homework
- post announcements, newsletters, and class newspapers
- hold classroom discussions where students share ideas and research

If you're new to an LMS, start with these four activities. Check back next year and I'll have more ideas for you.

Online exams

Exams used to be pages of black-and-white paper. There was limited space to write an answer. The test might be two-sided and good grief — don't forget that second side! If you make a mistake and your eraser wasn't up-to-snuff, the teacher might not realize you knew the answer. The final indignity: If your lead broke — or the entire pencil — it could ruin everything.

Now, exams are increasingly online. That means you access them from the Internet (or a dedicated server). Space for an answer isn't limited to a little square with lines on it, and erasures are a simple backspace. If the computer stops working (akin to a broken pencil), the teacher fixes that for you. With a minimal amount of set-up time, almost any quiz can be offered digitally. If you haven't tried this before, look into Google Forms. You'll be surprised and happy.

Online exams require no print and no day-ahead preparation. Because there is so much variety in these, they can be formative or summative and pretty much everything in between.

Lesson #3—Digital Citizenship

Vocabulary	Problem solving	Skills
• Cyberbullying • Cyberstalking • Digital citizen • Flaming • GPS • Netiquette	• Can't find answer (did you try all options?) • Internet toolbar disappeared (click 'full screen mode') • Online's anonymous! Why do I have to follow so many rules? (do the right thing when no one's watching)	Social media Speaking/listening Problem solving Keyboarding Digital citizenship
Academic Applications research, digcit	**Materials Required** Digital citizenship sites/videos, student workbooks (if using)	**Standards** CCSS: CCRA.L.6 NETS: 2a-d

Essential Question

How should I act in the virtual neighborhood? What are the differences from my physical neighborhood?

Big Idea

Just as in the physical world, the digital world bestows rights and requires responsibilities.

Teacher Preparation

- Know which tasks weren't completed last class and whether they are necessary to move forward.
- Talk with the grade-level team to tie into conversations about using the internet.
- Collect words students don't understand for Speak Like a Geek presentations (if doing this Lesson).
- Something happen you weren't prepared for? Show students how you fix it without a meltdown and with a positive attitude.
- Ask what tech problems students had difficulty with.
- Integrate domain-specific tech vocabulary into lesson.
- Know whether you need extra time to complete lesson.

Assessment Strategies

- Worked independently
- Used good keyboarding habits
- Completed warm-up, exit ticket
- Joined classroom conversations
- [tried to] solve own problems
- Decisions followed class rules
- Left room as s/he found it
- Higher order thinking: analysis, evaluation, synthesis
- Habits of mind observed

Steps

Time required: 90 minutes or more, spread throughout the school year
Class warm-up: Keyboarding on the class typing program, paying attention to posture

_____Required skill level: Basic understanding of digital rights and responsibilities
_____Before beginning, open backchannel on class screen to track student comments. Show students how to access it on their devices.
_____Discuss what it means to be a good digital citizen? Why is this important if no one knows who you are? Must you be honest if you're anonymous? Who does it hurt?
_____What does the quote in *Figure 26* mean—by John Wooden, legendary football coach?

Figure 26—Personal responsibility quote

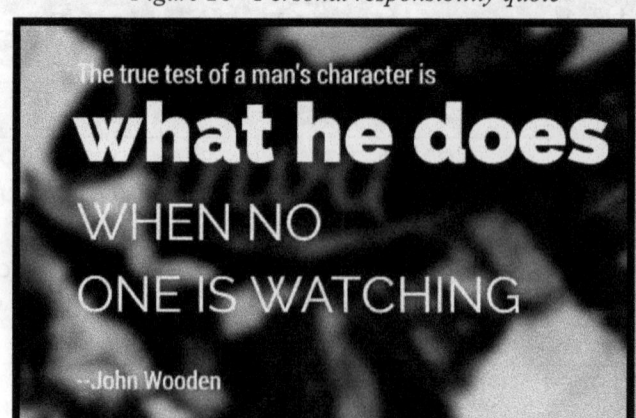

_____Throughout the school year when relevant, discuss the topics listed below. If you haven't covered a topic before, spend more time on it. Where possible, let students lead the discussion, set the pace, and ask questions. Be prepared to spend extra time and adapt to students as needed.

_____Preview the topics to be sure they're appropriate for your unique student group.

Cyberbullying

_____Expand last year's discussion with videos. If you don't have your own favorites, try Ask a Tech Teacher's resource pages for *Digital Citizenship>Cyberbullying*. Review statistics in Think Time: How Does Cyberbullying Affect You (available on YouTube).

_____Watch and discuss You Can't Take it Back (available on YouTube). What precautions can students take to insure they are kind and supportive online?

_____If students have blogs, with this discussion fresh, have them comment on classmate blogs. Include a compliment, suggestion, or question. Keep conversation on topic and relevant.

Digital Communications

_____This includes email, blog comments, texting, cell phones, and discussion forums. Many of these topics are discussed in other sections.

_____Discuss **texting** (see article at end of lesson). Watch and discuss one of these:

_____Is it rude to **text** around other people? Watch and discuss one of these videos:

- *It Can Wait Driving Simulation (7.4 million viewers)*-- video showing driver distracted by texting (search YouTube for video or Ask a Tech Teacher Driver Ed resource page)
- *Texting etc.–Chicken Road YouTube* (search YouTube for video or Ask a Tech Teacher Digital Citizenship resource pages)
- *Texting* (search NYT "Gauging Your Distraction") –a game that gauges your distraction while driving and texting
- *Texting While Walking* (search YouTube—1.9 million viewers)
- *The Last Text* (search AT&T Texting and Driving Documentary—7.8 million viewers)
- *Wait for it* (search YouTube) —sad video about texting and driving

_____Is it rude to text around other people?

_____Does your school allow cell phones? What are the reasons to have one?

- *stay in touch with parents*
- *for emergencies*
- *so parents know where students are (via GPS)*
- *to collaborate and share*

_____What are reasons students shouldn't?
_____How many student parents try to control cell phone use by:
- *limiting their time on it*
- *limiting plan*
- *having them share in cost*
- *set up text-free zones, like dinner*
- *???*

_____Does this work? What else might? Discuss student responsibilities with cell phones, including:

- *don't overuse them; don't over-text*
- *don't let them interfere with classwork*
- *don't use them for academic dishonesty*
- *don't use them for cyberbullying; don't share inappropriate information*

_____Watch and discuss *Digital Passport Communication Video* (available on SchoolTube). Kids who walk with heads down as they text, talk, or play games aren't paying attention to their surroundings.

Digital footprint

_____What is a 'digital footprint'? Have students Google their names to discover their digital footprint.
_____Watch and discuss these videos:

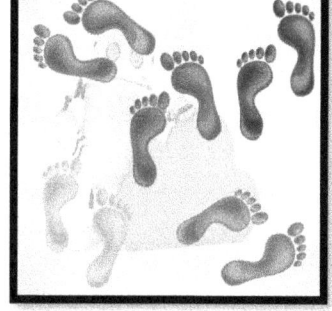

- *What's a Digital Dossier (search YouTube)*
- *Digital Footprint (search YouTube or Ask a Tech Teacher Digital Citizenship resource pages)*
- *Digital Life 101 (search YouTube or Ask a Tech Teacher Digital Citizenship resource pages)*

Digital Law and Plagiarism

_____Some people want to share their work and collaborate with others to create bigger and better things. Watch and discuss this video about Creative Commons licensing *Wanna Work Together* (from Creative Commons.org).
_____What does **'plagiarism'** mean? Why give credit to original authors/artists? What can/can't be 'borrowed' from online sites? Discuss image copyrights, fair use, and public domain. What are repercussions of 'plagiarism'?

_____ Watch this Plagiarism video (from Common Craft or search Ask a Tech Teacher's resource pages for Digital Citizenship).

_____ Discuss **copyright law**. Review summation in *Figure 27 (zoom in if needed)*. What are consequences of infringing copyrights?

Figure 27—Digital law—rephrased

> The law states that works of art created in the U.S. after January 1, 1978, are automatically protected by copyright once they are fixed in a tangible medium (like the internet) BUT a single copy may be used for scholarly research (even if that's a 2nd grade life cycle report) or in teaching or preparation to teach a class.
>
> Askatechteacher©

_____ Discuss how to cite a website. Visit EasyBib or Citation Machine (Google for addresses).

Digital privacy

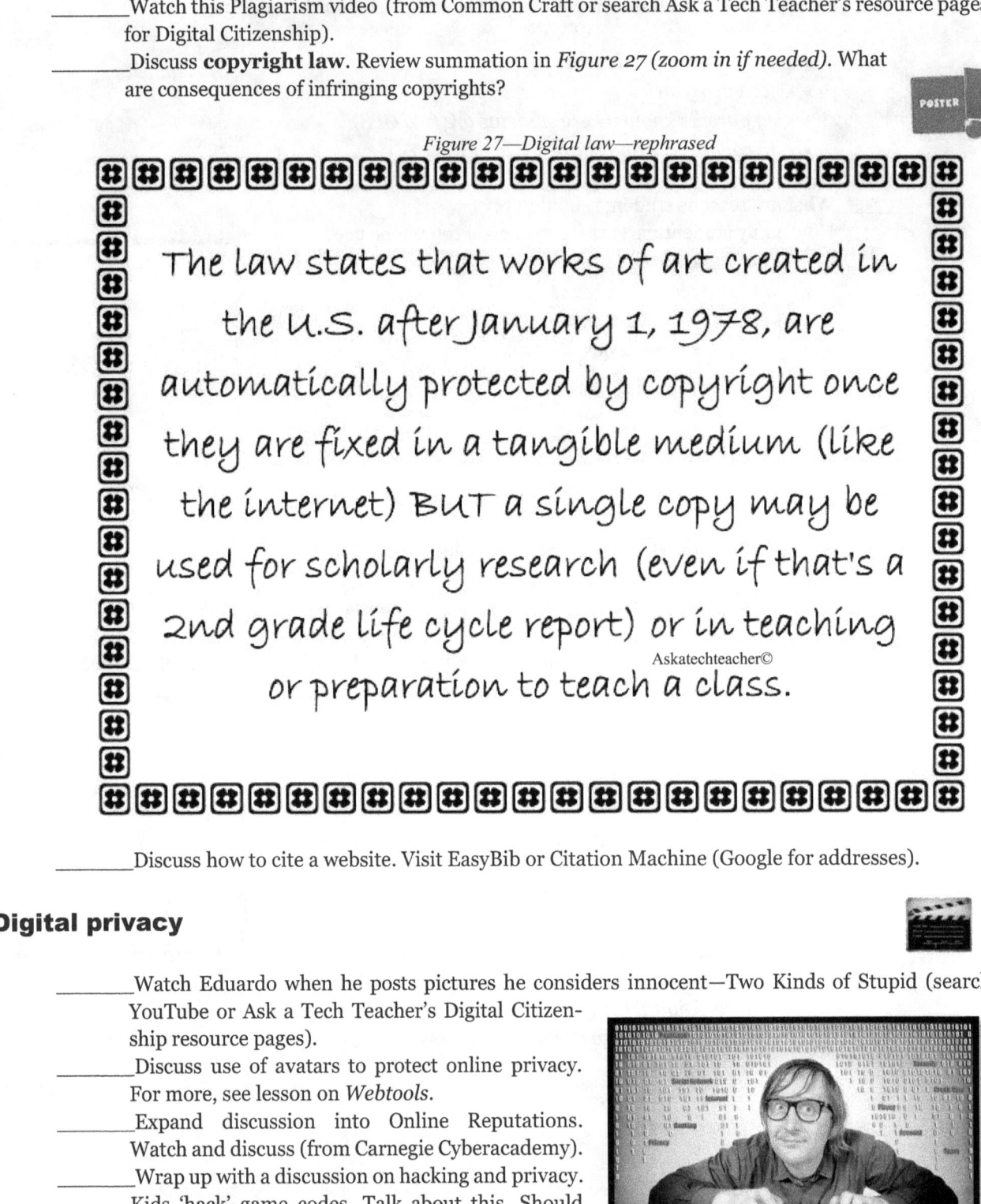

_____ Watch Eduardo when he posts pictures he considers innocent—Two Kinds of Stupid (search YouTube or Ask a Tech Teacher's Digital Citizenship resource pages).

_____ Discuss use of avatars to protect online privacy. For more, see lesson on *Webtools*.

_____ Expand discussion into Online Reputations. Watch and discuss (from Carnegie Cyberacademy).

_____ Wrap up with a discussion on hacking and privacy. Kids 'hack' game codes. Talk about this. Should they do it? Is it a victimless crime? What other issues should they consider? What is the difference between 'hacking' and 'cracking'? Black Hat and White Hat?

Digital rights and responsibilities

_____What are 'digital rights and responsibilities'? Most students come up with 'rights'—access to internet, use of information, creation of documents to be published and shared, freedom of expression—but what are 'responsibilities' of a digital citizen? Help students come up with:

- *Don't share personal information. Don't ask others for theirs.*
- *Be aware of your cyberspace surroundings. Act accordingly.*
- *As in your community, be kind to others. Anonymity doesn't protect you.*
- *If someone is 'flaming' another, help stop it within your abilities.*

_____Review rights and responsibilities inherent to using resources from virtual world.

Digital search and research

_____*Discussed in lesson on Internet Search and Research.*

Fair use, Public domain, Image Copyright

_____*Discussed in lesson on Images.*

Internet safety

_____Discuss password guidelines and rules. Remind students they never share passwords.
_____Watch and discuss Broken Friendship (available on YouTube).
_____Ask students how they protect passwords and online safety on the Internet.
_____What's the difference between 'http' and 'https'? How important is this security?

Netiquette

_____What is '**netiquette**'? Discuss the list of criteria in *Figure 28*. Zoom in if necessary.

Figure 28--Netiquette Rules

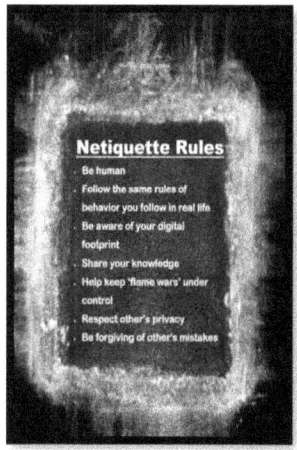

Social Media

_____ Discuss **X/Twitter** (see article at end of lesson)—watch *MSFT Online Safety* (available on YouTube).

_____ Break into groups and discuss **FB, YouTube, Pinterest,** and other social media. What are the challenges of so much openness? Then share group conclusions with the class and share individual thoughts via a blog post or class Twitter feed. Thoughts should be objective, on-point, with domain-specific language appropriate to the task, audience, and purpose.

Class exit ticket: ***Tweet on class Twitter account (or add a comment to class blog) about how the student stays safe online.***

Differentiation

- Assign a student to enter classwork and homework due date into class calendar.
- Full digital citizenship curriculum for K-8 available from StructuredLearning.net.

Article 10—11 Ways X/Twitter improves education

11 Ways X/Twitter Improves Education

A teacher must communicate with students in a way they will hear.
Twitter might be perfect for your class.

Twitter can easily be dismissed as a waste of time in the elementary school classroom. Students get distracted. They might see inappropriate tweets. How does a teacher manage a room full of Tweeple?

But you've read a lot about Twitters usefulness in writing skills and sharing information so you—of the Open Minded Attitude—want to try it. Here's ammunition for what often turns into a pitched, take-sides verbal brawl as well-intended educators try to reach a compromise on using Twitter (in fact, many Webtools—blogs, wikis, discussion forums, and websites that require registrations and log-ins—can be added to the list) that works for all stakeholders:

You learn to be concise
Twitter gives you limited characters to get the entire message across. *Letters, numbers, symbols, punctuation and spaces all count as characters on Twitter.* Wordiness doesn't work. Twitter counts every keystroke and won't publish anything with a minus in front of the word count.

At first blush, that seems impossible. It's not. It challenges students to know the right word for every situation. People with a big vocabulary are at an advantage because they don't use collections of little words to say what they mean. All those hints from English teachers about picture nouns and action verbs and getting rid of adverbs and adjectives take on new importance to the Twitter aficionado.

Twitter isn't intimidating
A blank white page holds hundreds of words, demanding you fill in each line margin to margin is intimidating. limited characters aren't. Students learn to whittle back, leave out emotional words, adjectives and adverbs, pick better nouns and verbs because they need the room. Instead of worrying what to say on all those empty lines, they feel successful.

Students learn manners
Social networks are all about netiquette. People thank others for their assistance, ask politely for help, and encourage contributions from others. Use this framework to teach students how to engage in a community—be it physical or virtual. It's all about manners.

Students learn to focus
With only limited characters, you can't get off topic or cover tangential ideas. You must save those for a different tweet. Tweeple like that trait in writers. They like to hear the writer's thoughts on the main topic, not meanderings. When forced to write this way, students will find it doesn't take a paragraph to make a point. Use the right words, people get it. Consider that the average reader gives a story seven seconds before moving on.

Students learn to share
Start a tweet stream where students share research on a topic. Maybe it's Ancient Greece. Have each student share their favorite website (using a #hashtag — maybe #ancientgreece) and you've created a resource others can use. Expand on that wonderful skill learned in kindergarten about sharing personal toys. Encourage students to RT (retweet) posts they found particularly relevant or helpful.

Writing short messages perfects the art of "headlining"
Writers call this the title. Bloggers and journalists call it the headline. Whatever the label, it must be cogent and pithy enough to pull the audience in and make them read the article. That's a tweet.

Tweets need to be written knowing that tweeple can @reply
This is a world of social networks where people comment on what you say. That's a good thing. It's feedback and builds an online community, be it for socializing or school. Students learn to construct their arguments expecting others to respond, question, and comment. Not only does this develop the skill of persuasive writing, students learn to have a thick skin, take comments with a grain of salt and two grains of aspirin.

#Hashtags develop a community
Create #hashtags that will help students organize their tweets—#help if they have a question, #homework for homework help. Establish class hashtags to deal with subjects you want students to address.

Students learn tolerance for all opinions
Why? Because Tweeple aren't afraid to voice their thoughts. Because the Twitter stream is a public forum (in a classroom, the stream can be private, visible to only class members), students understand what they say is out there forever. That's daunting. Take the opportunity to teach students about their public profile. Represent themselves well with good grammar, good spelling, and well-chosen tolerant ideas. Don't be emotional or spiteful because it can't be taken back. Rather than shying away from exposing students to the world, use Twitter to teach students how to live in it.

Twitter, the Classroom Notepad
I tried this out after I read about it through my PLN. Springboarding off student engagement, Twitter can act as your classroom notepad. Have students enter their thoughts, note, and reactions while you talk. By the time class is done, the entire class has an overview of the conversation with extensions and connections that help everyone get more out of the inquiry.

Twitter is always open
Inspiration doesn't always strike in that 50-minute class period. Sometimes it's after class, after school, after dinner, even 11 at night. Twitter doesn't care. Whatever schedule is best for students to discover the answer, Twitter is there. If you post a tweet question and ask students to join the conversation, they will respond in the time frame that works best for them. That's a new set of rules for classroom participation, and these are student-centered, uninhibited by a subjective time period. Twitter doesn't even care if a student missed class. S/he can catch up via tweets and then join in.

Article 11—Will texting destroy writing skills?

Will Texting Destroy Writing Skills?

Across the education landscape, student text messaging is a bone of contention among teachers. It's not an issue in the lower grades because most K-5 schools successfully ban cell phones during school hours. Where it's a problem are grades 6-12, when teachers realize it's a losing battle to separate students from their phones for eight hours.

The overarching discussion among educators is texting's utility in providing authentic experiences that transfer learning from the class to real life. Today, I'll focus on a piece of that: Does text messaging contribute to 1) shortening student attention span, or 2) destroying their nascent writing ability

Let's start with attention span. TV, music, over-busy daily schedules, and frenetic family life are likely causes of a student's short attention span. To fault text messaging is like blaming the weather for sinking the Titanic. Texting has less to do with the inability to spit out a full sentence than a student's 1) need for quickness of communication, 2) love for secrecy, and 3) joy of knowing a language adults don't.

What about writing? In the thirty years I've been teaching everyone from kindergarteners to college, I can tell you with my hand on a Bible that children are flexible, masters at adjusting actions to circumstances (like the clothes they wear for varying events and the conversations they have with varying groups of people). There is no evidence to support that these elastic, malleable creatures are suddenly rigid in their writing style, unable to toggle between casual texting shorthand with friends and a professional writing structure in class.

In general, I'm a fan of anything that encourages student writing, and there are real benefits to giving students the gift of textual brevity rather than the stomach-churning fear of a five-paragraph structured essay. I've done quite a few articles on the benefits of Twitter's limited-character approach to writing and my teacher's gut says the same applies to text messaging. Truth, studies are inconclusive. Some suggest that because young students do not yet have a full grasp of basic writing skills, they have difficulty shifting between texting's abbreviated spelling-doesn't-matter language and Standard English. But a British study suggested students classify 'texting' as 'word play', separate from the serious writing done for class so it results in no deterioration of writing skills. Yet another study found that perception of danger from texting is greater than reality: 70% of the professionals at one college believed texting had harmful effects on student writing skills. However, when analyzed, the opposite was true: Texting was actually beneficial.

It's interesting to note that texting can be a boon to children who struggle with face-to-face situations. These 'special needs' students flourish in an environment where they can write rather than speak, think through an answer before communicating it, and provide pithy conversational gambits in lieu of extended intercourse. In the texting world, socially-challenged children are like every other child, hidden by the anonymity of a faceless piece of metal and circuits.

To blame texting for student academic failures is a cop-out by the parents and teachers entrusted with a child's education. Treated as an authentic scaffold to academic goals, teachers will quickly incorporate it into their best-practices pedagogy of essential tools for learning.

Article 12—Digital Rights and Responsibilities

Teaching Digital Rights and Responsibilities

Teaching used to be based on textbooks used by millions nation- or worldwide. They took an entire school year to finish leaving little time for curiosity or creativity. Some subjects still do fine with that approach because their pedagogy varies little year-to-year.

In my classes, though, that's changing. I no longer limit myself to the contents of a textbook written years, sometimes a decade, ago. Now, I'm likely to cobble together lesson plans from a variety of time-sensitive and differentiated material. Plus, I commonly expect students to dig deeper into class conversations, think critically about current event connections, and gain perspective by comparing lesson materials to world cultures. That, of course, usually ends up not in a library but on the Internet.

Before I set them loose in the virtual world, though, I teach them the "rules of the Internet road" because make no mistake: There are rules. The Internet's Wild West days are fast disappearing, replaced with the security offered by abiding to a discrete set of what's commonly referred to as "**digital rights and responsibilities**". It boils down to a simple maxim:

With the right to discover knowledge comes the responsibility to behave well while doing so.

The privileges and freedoms extended to digital users who type a URL into a browser or click a link in a PDF or scan a QR Code require that they bear the responsibility to keep the virtual library a safe and healthy environment for everyone.

Digital Rights

Most people if asked could easily name the benefits of the Internet:

- *Everyone can speak their mind knowing they'll find like-minded individuals.*
- *Privacy is ensured by its vastness. Think about living in the desert — who could ever find you there? It's that sort of vastness.*
- *As a creator, you can expose a world of people to your creations to purchase or just spread the word.*
- *You can find any information you want just by typing in search terms and slogging through the multitude of hits.*
- *You can create an online persona that doesn't include your faults, lousy personality, or mistakes.*

These rights are so pervasive to our daily activities that many consider them to be inalienable, not unlike those laid out in the UN's Universal Declaration of Human Rights. To these folks, disconnecting people from the Internet is a violation of international law and tramples all over an individual's human rights.

Digital Responsibilities

But there are two faces to this digital coin: Inalienable or not, they require great responsibilities. Some think the Internet's lawlessness (because no world authority holds legal authority over the world wide web) precludes cultural norms like kindness, morality, and ethics. After all, if you purchase porn from a third-world nation where it's legal to sell, who's going to enforce what law?

That's where I teach my students that **with rights come responsibilities**. Think of the Internet as having comparable expectations to a neighborhood:

- *Act the same online as you'd act in your neighborhood.*
- *Don't share personal information. Don't ask others for theirs. Respect their need for privacy.*
- *Be aware of your surroundings. Know where you are in cyberspace. Act accordingly.*
- *Just as in your community, if you are kind to others, they will be kind to you.*
- *Don't think anonymity protects you—it doesn't. You are easily found with an IP address. Discuss what that is.*
- *Share your knowledge. Collaborate and help others online.*

Information Security Education and Awareness posits these **Ten Commandments for computer use**:

- One shall not use a computer to harm other people.
- One shall not interfere with other's computer work.
- One shall not snoop around in another's computer files [and will keep one's own data safe from hackers].
- One shall not use a computer to steal [or plagiarize].
- One shall not use a computer to bear false witness [or to falsify one's own identity].
- One shall not copy or use any materials for which one has not paid.
- One shall not use other's computer resources without authorization or proper compensation.
- One shall not appropriate other's intellectual output [and will legally download all material like music and videos].
- One shall think about social consequences of the program written or of the system designed.
- One shall always use a computer in ways that respect one's fellow humans [and report bullying, harassing, and identify theft when possible].

For the rest of this article, visit Ask a Tech Teacher

Lesson #4—Keyboarding

Vocabulary	Problem solving	Skills
• Cumulative • F row • Hunt-and-peck • Keyboard shortcuts • Mulligan • QWERTY • Shortkey • Tilde • Touch typing • Wpm	• I can't remember key placement (trust yourself muscle memory) • Can't remember some keys on quiz (skip them) • I can't type with hands covered (Keep practicing) • Can't type faster (slow down, relax) • I keep losing home row (find bump on F and J with pointers) • I do fine with 2-4 fingers (but not fast)	Keyboarding Touch typing Posture at digital device Problem solving Speaking-listening
Academic Applications Writing, research, any topic requiring keyboarding	**Materials Required** Keyboarding tool, keyboard websites, student workbooks (if using)	**Standards** CCSS: W.9-10.6,7 NETS: 1d, 6a

Essential Question

How is it possible to type three-six pages in a single sitting?

Big Idea

Work on essential elements of keyboarding—technique, speed, and accuracy—with goal of typing 3-6 pages in a sitting.

Teacher Preparation

- Know which tasks weren't completed last class.
- Something happen you weren't prepared for? Show students how you calmly fix it.
- Collect words students don't understand for Speak Like a Geek Board (if completing this activity).
- Integrate domain-specific vocabulary into lesson.
- Ensure all required links are on student devices.
- Review article at end of lesson, *"How to Prepare Students for Year-end Tests"*.
- See the article at the end of this lesson, *"5 Ways to Make Keyboarding Fun"*.

Assessment Strategies

- Annotated workbook (if using)
- Used good keyboarding habits
- Completed warm-up
- Joined classroom conversations
- [tried to] solve own problems
- Decisions followed class rules
- Left room as s/he found it
- Higher order thinking: analysis, evaluation, synthesis
- Habits of mind observed

Steps

Time required: Spread throughout the school year with time set aside for quizzes
Class warm-up: Keyboarding on the class typing program, paying attention to posture

This lesson is spread throughout the year.

_____Required skill level: keyboard basics.
_____Using *Figure 29*, discuss why students should care about keyboarding:

Figure 29—Why learn to keyboard

_____This lesson's activities include:

- *review keyboarding*
- *in-class keyboarding*
- *authentic keyboard practice*
- *shortkeys*
- *formative assessments*
- *speed/accuracy quizzes*
- *blank keyboard quizzes*
- *Important Keys quizzes*
- *keyboarding challenge*

Review keyboarding

_____Review posture and computer positioning (*Figures 30a-b*). Have students check their neighbor. If correct posture isn't a habit, encourage students to sit this way when they use a digital devices at home, in school, at the library, and everywhere:

Figure 30a-b—Keyboarding posture

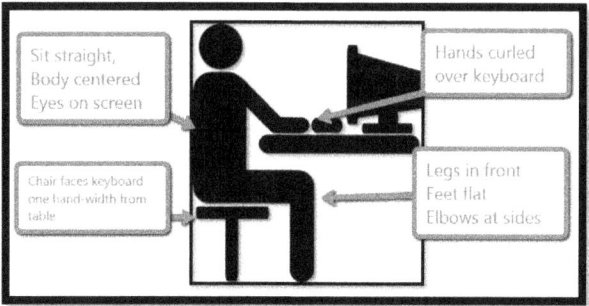 

_____Keyboarding is cumulative. What can be learned depends heavily upon what was learned earlier. If hunt 'n peck or keying with thumbs becomes ingrained, it's difficult to develop competence later.

_____Review keyboarding best practices that you will observe as students work (see *Figure 31* for hand position):

- Keep hands curved over home row.
- Use correct posture:
  - Sit straight, shoulders back, head up, body centered one hand's width from the table, feet flat on the ground.
  - Keep elbows close to sides.
  - Reach for keys—don't move hands (only fingers).
- Touch type with a steady, even pace.
- Keep copy to side of keyboard, eyes on copy or screen—NOT keyboard.
- Effectively use software and internet-based sites for keyboarding.
- Use keyboard shortcuts (i.e., Ctrl+B, Shift+Alt+D).

Figure 31—Keyboarding hand position

_____High school keyboarding is a combination of:

- touch typing
- practice with a program
- covered hands during typing
- reinforcement of shortkeys
- anecdotal observation by teacher
- quizzes
- keyboard challenge (at end of lesson)

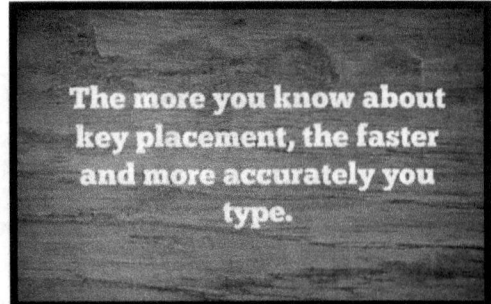

The more you know about key placement, the faster and more accurately you type.

_____Add each student's keyboarding milestone to class calendar. Proudly recognize this!

_____This year's speed and accuracy goal: Type three pages in a sitting. Do the math:

- There are about 300 words per page (show how you got this).
- Student who types 35 wpm will take 8.5 minutes per page.
- Three pages will take about twenty-five minutes without a break.

_____By end of this year, students:
- touch type 35-45 wpm
- easily compose at keyboard
- keep eyes on copy
- know twenty shortkeys (i.e., Alt+F4, Esc, Ctrl+P, Ctrl+S, Ctrl+C, Ctrl+V, Ctrl+Alt+Del, Ctrl+B/I/U, double-click to enlarge window, Alt+Tab, Win key, Shift+tab, right mouse button key, Ctrl+, Ctrl-, ???)
- reach fingers to keys so when viewed, hands are still with fingers moving
- present thoughts quickly with good formatting, minimal errors
- understand keyboard parts and functions

> **Keep Keyboarding Fun**
> 1. In-class keyboarding
> 2. Varied quizzes
> 3. Authentic practice
> 4. Shortkeys
> 5. Keyboard Challenge

_____If your students have just started to practice keyboarding, pick only a few of these criteria to assess. As they practice, they'll develop a greater facility and you can expect more.

_____Any time possible, invoke the Mulligan Rule giving students a do-over on quizzes. **What's the Mulligan Rule?** Students can retake any assessment covered by the Mulligan Rule without losing credit. It's for those times students weren't ready, didn't know about a quiz, were sick, or shouldn't be graded because [fill in the blank]. Few take advantage of this opportunity. It requires little from you, yet you seem like the world's fairest teacher.

Occasional in-class keyboarding

_____Occasionally, take class time to observe student typing. As they type, anecdotally observe posture, hand position, and eye placement based on *Assessment* at the end of lesson.

_____With endemic problems, make suggestions to class.

Monthly homework

_____Monthly homework is keyboarding. Here's a schedule for the **first three months**:

- *Month 1: home row on Popcorn Typer*
- *Month 2: QWERTY row using KidzType*
- *Month 3: lower row using Peter's Online Typing*

If you don't have these apps, visit Ask a Tech Teacher's *Keyboarding* resource pages.

_____Students type first with hands uncovered. By mid-month, repeat lessons with hands covered.

_____At month end, review next month's homework. Questions? Problems?

> **SHORTKEYS**
>
> CTRL+S
> CTRL+P
> CTRL+Z
> CTRL+C
> CTRL+V
> CTRL+X
> CTRL+B
> CTRL+U
> CTRL+I
> CTRL+
> CTRL-

Authentic keyboarding using inquiry-based projects

_____Typing is best learned through inquiry. As soon as possible, begin project-based typing.
_____These can be short reports, magazines, trifolds, a story—one that works for your school. *Figures 33a-d* are some projects that reinforce keyboarding authentically:

Figure 33a-d—Project-based learning and keyboarding

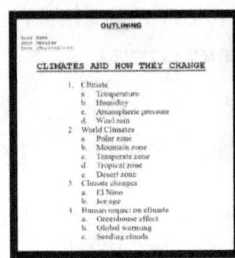

Shortkeys

_____If using student workbooks, students take a screenshot of *Figure 32*, print, and tape to their digital device or notebook.
_____See *Figures 34a-d* for platform-specific shortkeys (full-size posters at end of lesson):

Figure 34a-d—Shortkeys for iPads, Chromebooks, PCs, and Internet

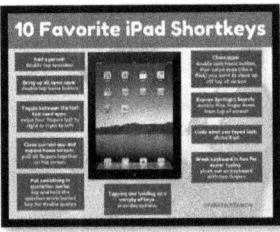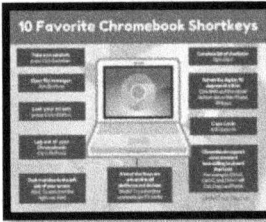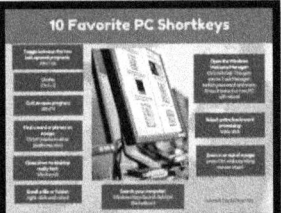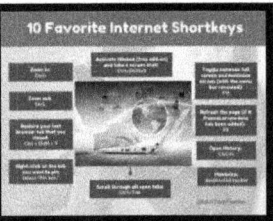

_____**Consistently throughout the year:** Reinforce keyboard shortcuts. Students love to show off their techie-ness with these.

Formative assessments

_____Once a month, practice on a site like TypingTest.com to see how fast/accurately students are typing. More than five errors? Slow down. Less than five—speed up.

Summative speed/accuracy quizzes

_____**Each grading period:** Students test speed and accuracy to track improvement.
_____The first quiz is a benchmark—to evaluate skills. The rest are graded based on improvement. If students do homework (if you assign keyboarding homework) and use good habits when typing, they'll do fine.

- 20% improvement   10/10
- 10-20% improvement   9/10

- *1-10% improvement   8/10*
- *No improvement   7/10*
- *Slowed down   6/10*

_____Grade level standard: 45-75 WPM by the end of High School.

_____The speed quiz can be delivered in several ways:

- *Place a page from a book being read on the class screen. Students copy it. This method forces their heads up rather than on their hands.*
- *Print a page from a book being read in class. Students place it to the side of their keyboard and type from it.*
- *Use an online typing test like TypingTest.com.*

_____Students type for three-five minutes, then save/share/print.

_____Load a digital copy of the *Assessment* at end of this lesson onto your iPad or laptop and fill it in for each student as you walk around observing. Use an annotation tool like Notability or Adobe Reader.

Blank keyboard quiz

_____**Each grading period**, students take a blank keyboard quiz (*Figures 35a-b* are two different keyboards—adapt as needed for your digital device. See end of Lesson for *Assessments*) to test knowledge of key placement. They can work in pairs and must retake until they pass. Success here translates to speed and accuracy.

_____Pass out blank keyboard to student or group. They get 10 minutes to complete.

_____The first iteration of this quiz is a baseline. Next, grade quiz like the keyboard speed quiz.

_____Discuss why it's important that students memorize keys

_____Common mistakes are forgetting *Esc* at the left side of the F row, forgetting the tilde at the left side of the number row, and getting the QWERTY row wrong.

Figure 35a-b—Blank keyboard quiz for PC and Chromebook

Important Keys Quiz

_____**Each grading period:** Students take a blank Important Keys quiz (see *Assessment* at the end of the Lesson—adapt it to your digital device) to test key placement. They can work in pairs and must retake until they pass. Success here translates to speed and accuracy.

_____Discuss why it's important that students memorize keys.

_____Pass out blank *Important Keys* quiz to student or a group. They get 10 minutes to complete.

_____If you are going to give this quiz more than once (say, once a grading period), use this first one as a baseline. Next time, students must improve. Score it like the keyboard speed quiz.

Keyboarding Challenge

_____With the *Keyboarding Challenge*, students get to have fun with their keyboarding knowledge. Divide students into teams. Select a captain—this will be the only person who can answer questions. Answers must be quick—to show that the team knows the right key.

_____See *Assessment* at end of this lesson for sample questions.

_____Ask Team #1 a question, i.e., *Which finger types f?* Give the team 3 seconds to answer (answer may be visual). If they can't, go to Team #2, but don't repeat the question. If they don't know the question or can't answer, move to Team #3 and then Team #4. If no one can answer, provide answer.

_____Next question goes to Team #2—even if they were the ones who answered Team #1's question. This is how teams get ahead. Pose the question to Team #2 and repeat the step above.

_____Sound dull? I thought so, too, but students love it. Every time I play it, it's a hit and they want to repeat it.

_____Prizes are optional.

Class exit ticket: None.

Differentiation

- *Assign a student to enter keyboarding assignment dates.*
- *Put Keyboard Challenge into a Jeopardy template.*
- *K-8 Keyboard Curriculum available in K-8 Keyboard Curriculum (available from Structured Learning LLC).*

Assessment 8—Keyboarding quiz

Student _____

Keyboarding Technique Checklist
Duplicate for each student
Rate 1-4

Technique	Date	Date	Date	Date	Date
Feet placed for balance and sits up straight					
Body centered to the middle of keyboard					
Eyes on the screen					
Types with correct fingering					
Types with a steady, even rhythm					
Keeps fingers on home row keys					
Has a good attitude and strives for improvement					
WPM (words per minute)					
Accuracy percent					

High School Technology Curriculum Book 1: Teacher Manual

Assessment 9—Important Keys

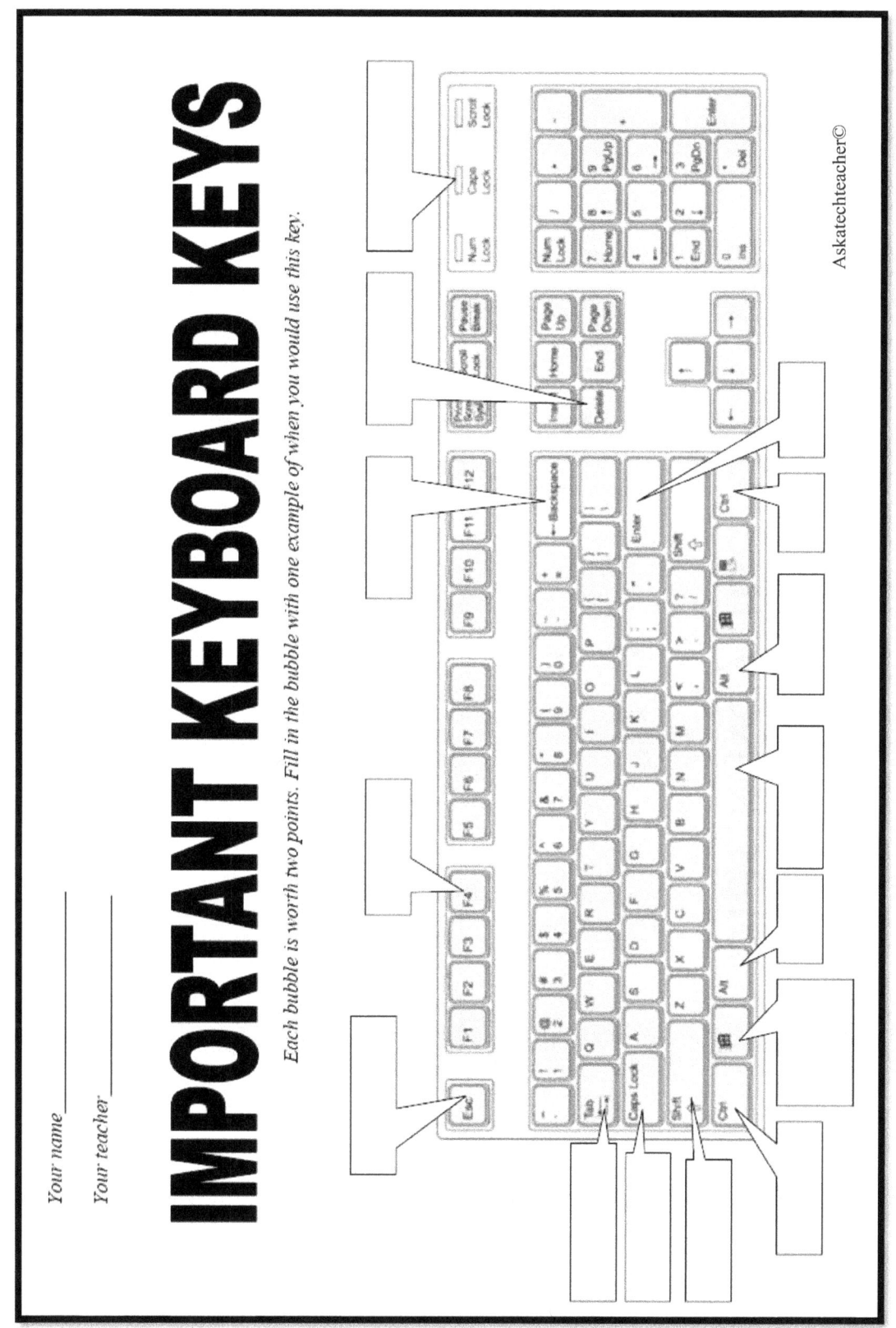

Page 77

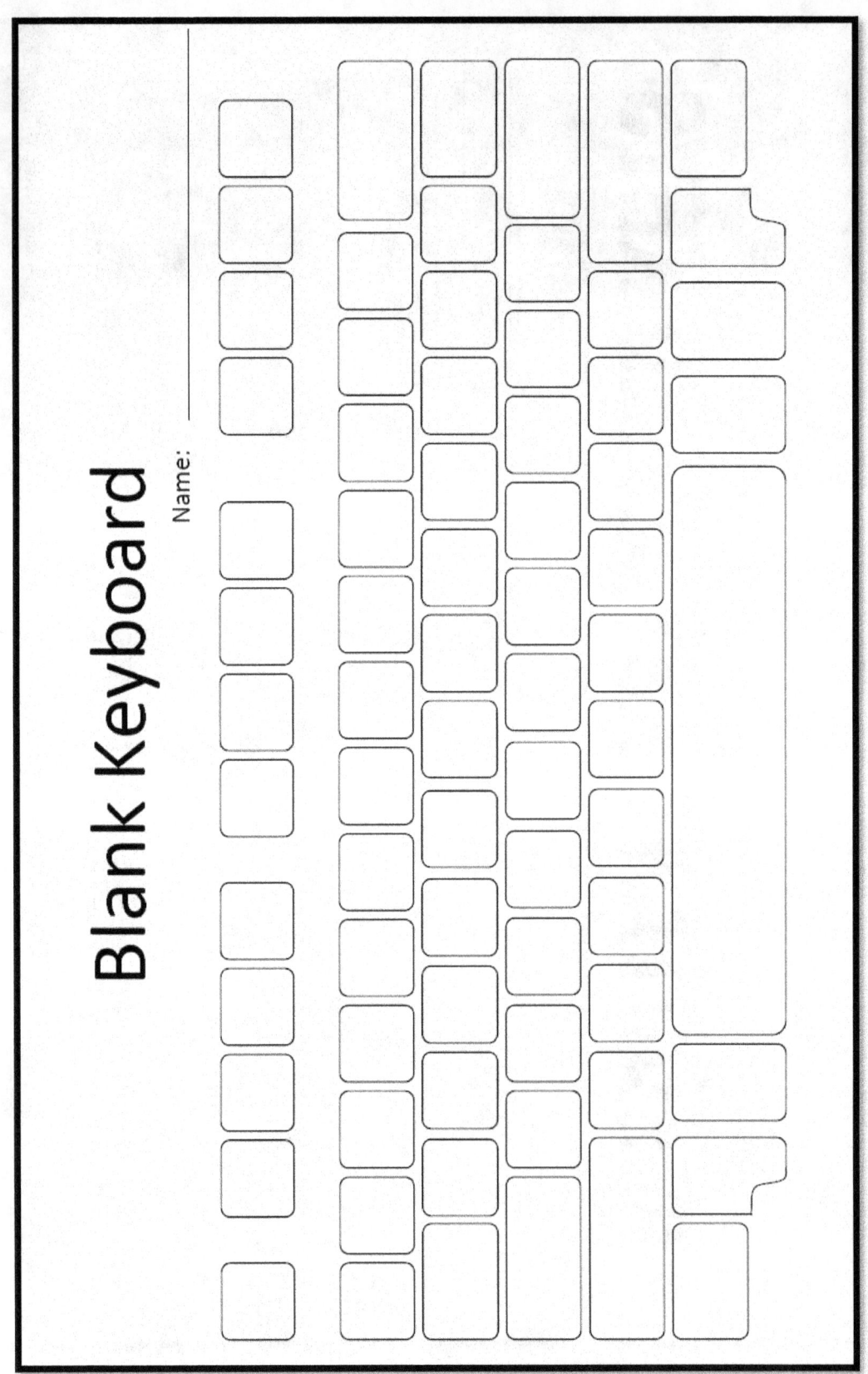

High School Technology Curriculum Book 1: Teacher Manual

Assessment 11—Chromebook blank keyboard quiz

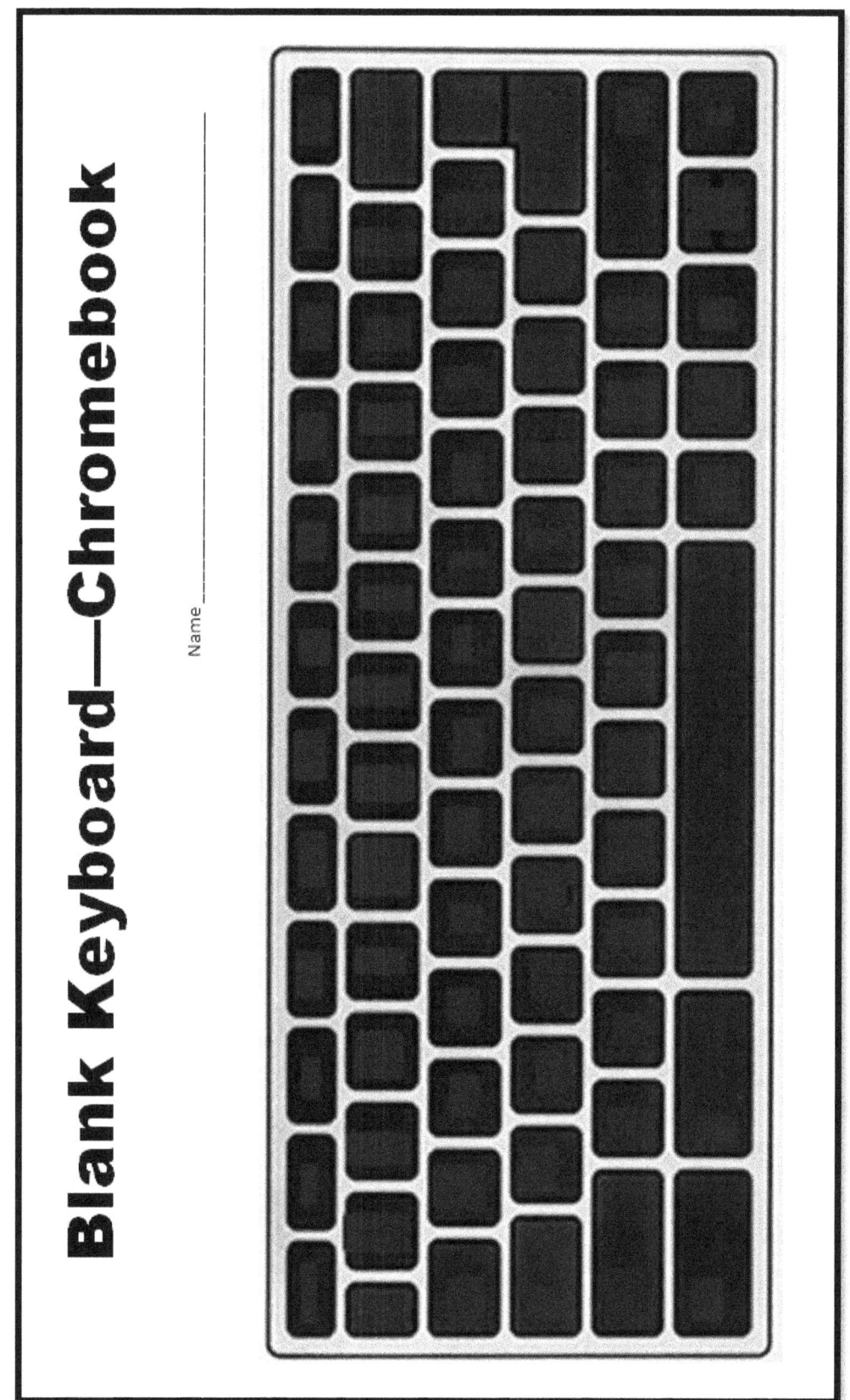

10 Favorite PC Shortkeys

- **Open the Windows Welcome Manager:** Ctrl+Alt+Del. This gets you to Task Manager, switch password and more. Press it twice in a row, PC will reboot
- **Select entire line in word processing:** triple click
- **Zoom in or out of a page:** press Ctrl while scrolling mouse wheel.
- **Search your computer:** Windows Key+Search field (at the bottom)
- **Toggle between the two last-opened programs:** Alt+Tab
- **Undo:** Ctrl+Z
- **Quit an open program:** Alt+F4
- **Find a word or phrase on a page:** Ctrl+F (works in other platforms, too)
- **Close down to desktop really fast:** Win Key+D
- **Email a file or folder:** right-click and select

©AskATechTeacher

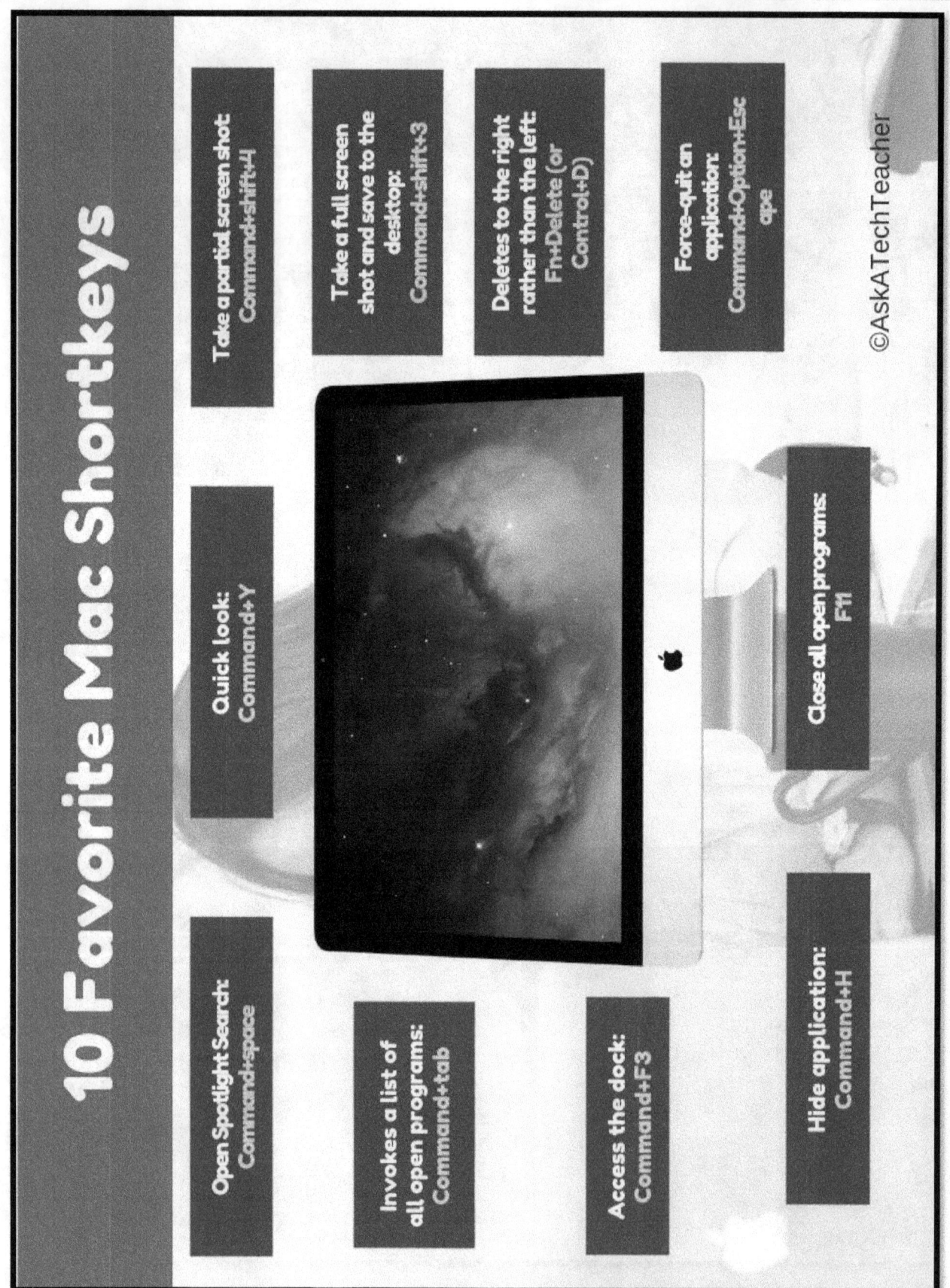

10 Favorite Chromebook Shortkeys

- **Take a screenshot:** press Ctrl+Switcher.
- **Open file manager:** Alt+Shift+m
- **Lock your screen:** press Ctrl+Shift+L
- **Log out of your Chromebook:** Ctrl+Shift+Q
- **Dock a window to the left side of your screen:** Alt+[. To dock it on the right, use Alt+]
- **Complete list of shortkeys:** Ctrl+Alt+?
- **Rotate the display 90 degrees at a time:** Ctrl+Shift and the reload button above the #3 and #4 keys
- Chromebooks support all standard web browser keyboard shortcuts
- Chromebooks support most standard text-editing keyboard shortcuts. For example, Ctrl+X, Ctrl+C, and Ctrl+V will Cut, Copy and Paste.
- A lot of shortkeys are universal to all platforms and devices. Stuck? Try a shortkey you know; see if it works

©AskATechTeacher

10 Favorite iPad Shortkeys

Close apps: double click home button, then swipe apps (like a flick) you want to close up off top of screen

Expose Spotlight Search: quickly flick finger down from top of screen

Undo what you typed last: shake iPad

Break keyboard in two for easier typing: pinch out on keyboard with two fingers

Tapping and holding on a variety of keys provides options.

Add a period: double tap spacebar

Bring up all open apps: double tap home button

Toggle between the last two used apps: swipe four fingers left to right or right to left

Close current app and expose home screen: pull all fingers together on the screen

Put something in quotation marks: tap and hold the question mark/period key for double quotes

©AskATechTeacher

Assessment 12—Keyboarding Challenge

KEYBOARDING TEAM CHALLENGE

Review the following concepts. These are similar to questions that will be asked during the upcoming Team Challenge to find the year's most tech-savvy student!

1. What's the computer log in
2. What's the computer password
3. What's your password for ***
4. What row do your fingers start on before you even type a letter
5. What's the row above home row
6. What's the row below home row
7. How do you find the f and j key without looking
8. Name three keys you use your pinkie to push
9. Name three keys you use your ring finger to push
10. Name three keys you use your middle finger to push
11. Name three keys you use your pointer to push
12. Name one key you use your right thumb to push
13. Which finger do you use for the backspace key
14. Which finger do you use for the shift key
15. Which finger do you use for the escape key
16. What are three rules of how you sit at the keyboard
17. Do you have cat's paws or dog paws at the computer
18. Why (do you use cat's paws or dog paws)
19. What part of the chair do you sit on when keyboarding
20. Where are your elbows when keyboarding
21. Where does your right thumb rest when keyboarding
22. What is typing without looking at the keys called
23. Which finger pushes the a key
24. Which finger pushes the b key
25. Which finger pushes the ac key
26. Which finger pushes the d key
27. Which finger pushes the e key
28. Which finger pushes the f key
29. Which finger pushes the g key
30. Which finger pushes the h key
31. Which finger pushes the i key
32. Which finger pushes the j key
33. Which finger pushes the k key
34. What finger pushes enter
35. What's the keyboard shortcut to exit a program
36. What's the shortkey for Find
37. What's the shortkey for moving between windows (or sites)
38. As a general rule, which finger pushes a key
39. How do you capitalize a letter
40. As a general rule, do your fingers move or your hands in finding the keys
41. What is one keyboard shortcut
42. What is a desktop
43. What's the ~ (tilde) for
44. Name one function of an F key

Article 13—5 Ways to make classroom keyboarding fun

5 Ways to Make Classroom Keyboarding Fun

When you teach typing, the goal isn't **speed and accuracy**. The goal is that students type well enough that it doesn't disrupt their thinking.

Let me say that again:

The goal of keyboarding is students type well enough that it doesn't disrupt their thinking.

Much like breathing takes no thought and playing a piano is automatic, students want to be able to think while they type, fingers automatically moving to the keys that record their thoughts. Searching for key placement shouldn't interfere with how they develop a sentence. Sure, it does when students are just starting, but by third grade students should be comfortable enough with key placement to be working on speed.

To type as fast at the speed of thought isn't as difficult as it sounds. When referring to students in school, 'speed of thought' refers to how fast they develop ideas that will be recorded. 30 wpm is the low end. 45 wpm is good.

Students used to learn typing in high school, as a skill. Now, it's a tool for learning. So much of what we ask students to do on the way to authentic learning requires typing. Consider the academic need to:

- *write reports*
- *comment on Discussion Boards and blogs*
- *journal in blogs and online tools like Penzu*
- *research online (type addresses into a search bar)*
- *take digital notes (using Evernote, OneNote and similar)*
- *collaborate on Google Apps like Docs, Sheets, Presentations*
- *take online quizzes (like PARCC, SB)*
- *use online tools for core classes (Wordle, Animoto, Story Creators)*

The myth is that students will teach themselves when they need it. That's half right. They will teach themselves, but it won't necessarily be in time for their needs. If you're in a tech-infused school, it's your obligation to teach them the right way to type so they can organically develop the tools to support learning.

Most teachers roll out typing with a graduated program like Type to Learn. In September of the new school year, students start Lesson 1. Sometime around May, they are through all the lessons and considered trained. Everything is on auto-pilot with little intervention from the teacher. That works for about ten percent of students. Those are the ones who are intrinsically motivated to learn and nothing gets in their way.

The other 90% need a little more help. Here are six ideas to make your typing lessons fun and effective:

Drill

Drill is part of every granular typing program. Students must learn key placement, finger usage, posture, and all those other details.

There are a lot of options for this—both free like Typing Web and fee-based like QwertyTown. Students usually start enthusiastically, which wanes within a few months as it becomes more of the same rote practice.

Games

When your organic typing program shows signs of wearing on students, throw in a sprinkling of games that teach key placement, speed and accuracy. NitroTyping is great for high school students. Offer games sporadically, not on a schedule. Make it a reward for keyboarding benchmarks.

Team Challenge

Students work in teams to answer keyboard-related questions in a game show format. You can use a Jeopardy template that includes not only keyboard questions, but shortkeys that students use often.

Integrate into Class Inquiry

Within a month of starting a keyboarding program, have students use their growing skills authentically in class projects. This can be book reports, research, a brochure for history class, or a collaborative document through Google Apps. The keyboarding is a tool to communicate knowledge in a subject, much like a pencil, an artist brush or a violin. The better their keyboarding skills, the easier it is to complete the meat of the project, like a blog response, trading cards on characters in a book, or a family tree.

Remind students to use the keyboarding skills they've learned to make this real-life experience easier—hands on their own side of the keyboard, use all fingers, good posture, elbows at their sides. Let their team of grade level teachers know what traits to look for as students research in class or the library. Get parents to reinforce it at home.

ASCII Art

ASCII Art uses keyboarding skills to create artistic representations of class learning. This is a fun way to use keyboarding in other classes. All students do is find a picture that represents the class inquiry topic being addressed, put it as a watermark into the word processing program, type over the washed out image with a variety of keys, then delete the watermark. This takes about thirty minutes usually and always excites students with the uniqueness of their work.

Article 14—How to Prepare Students for PARCC/SBA Tests

How to Prepare Students for Year-end Tests

As part of my online tech teacher persona, I get lots of questions from readers about how to make technology work in an educational environment. This one from Terry is probably on the minds of thousands of teachers:

> *Any help for identifying and re-enforcing tech skills needed to take the online PARCC tests (coming in 2014-15)? Even a list of computer terms would help; copy, cut, paste, highlight, select; use of keys like tab, delete, insert; alt, ctrl and shift. There does not seem to be any guidelines as to prepping students on the "how to's" of taking an online test and reading and understanding the directions. It would be great to take advantage of the time we have before the PARCC's become a reality. Thanks!*

Every spring, more than 4 million students in 36 states and the District of Columbia will take near-final versions of the PARCC and Smarter Balanced efforts to test Common Core State Standards learning in the areas of mathematics and English/language arts. Tests will be administered via digital devices (though there are options for paper-and-pencil). The tests won't produce detailed scores of student performance (that starts next year), but this field-testing is crucial to finding out what works and doesn't in this comprehensive assessment tool, including the human factors like technophobia and sweaty palms (from both students and teachers).

After I got Terry's email, I polled my PLN to find specific tech areas students needed help with in preparing for the Assessments. It boils down to five tech areas:

Keyboarding

Students need to have enough familiarity with the keyboard that they know where keys are, where the number pad is, where the F row is, how keys are laid out. They don't need to be touch typists or even facilely use all fingers. Just have them comfortable enough they have a good understanding of where all the pieces are. Starting next school year, have them type fifteen minutes a week in a class setting and 45 minutes a week using keyboarding for class activities (homework, projects—that sort). That'll do it.

Basic computer skills

These skills—drag-and-drop, keyboarding with speed and accuracy, highlighting, playing videos—are not easy for a student if they haven't had an instructive course in using computers. It won't surprise any adult when I say using and iPad isn't the same as using a computer. The former has a bunch more buttons and tools and the latter more intuitive. And typing on an iPad virtual keyboard is not the same as the reassuring clackity-clack of a traditional set-up. Will students get used to that? Yes, but not this month.

Make sure students are technologically proficient in their use of a variety of digital devices, including computers and iPads. This means students have an understanding of what defines a digital device, how it operates, what type of programs are used on various types (for example, apps are for iPads and software for laptops) and how do they operate, and what's the best way to scaffold them for learning? Being comfortable with technology takes time and practice. Make digital devices and tech solutions available at every opportunity—for notetaking, backchannel communications, quick assessments, online collaboration, even timing an activity. Make it part of a student's educational landscape.

One area Terry asks about is vocabulary. The words she mentioned—*copy, paste, cut, highlight*—these are domain-specific. Use the correct terminology as you are teaching but observe students. If they don't understand what you're saying, help them decode it with context, affixes, or an online dictionary for geek words. Keep a list of those words. Soon, you'll have a vocabulary list for technology that's authentic and specific to your needs.

Stamina

Expect students to type for extended periods without complaint. Common Core requires this. The Assessments expect students have that sort of stamina. They're long tests with lots of keyboarding and other tech skills. Make sure your students have practiced working at computers for extended periods.

A good idea is to have students take some online assessments prior to this summative one. These can be created by the teacher using any number of online tools like Google Forms or use already-created tests like those on BrainPop videos.

Problem Solving

Make sure students know what to do when a tech problem arises. They should be able to handle simple problems like 'headphones don't work' or 'caps lock won't turn on' or 'my document froze'. This is easily accomplished by having students take responsibility for solving tech problems, with the teacher acting as a resource. They will soon be able to differentiate between what they can handle and what requires assistance.

A great starting point when teaching problem solving are Common Core Standards for Mathematical Practice. These are aligned with the Math Standards but apply to all facets of learning.

Teacher Training

Make sure teachers administering the online tests are familiar with them and comfortable in that world. They should know how to solve basic tech issues that arise without calling for outside help. This is effectively accomplished by having teachers use technology in their classroom on a regular basis for class activities, as a useful tool in their educational goals. Helps teachers make this happen.

Lesson #5—Problem Solving

Vocabulary	Problem solving	Skills
• Backchannel • Cerebral • Context • Delineate • Mulligan • Sequence • Shortkeys • Strategic	• I can't solve problem (what strategies have you tried?) • I don't like the reflection method I picked. (why?) • Sign-up website doesn't work (use your problem-solving strategies) • Did poorly on assessment (Mulligan Rule)	Speaking and listening Problem solving Keyboarding Digital citizenship
Academic Applications math, other academic topics	**Materials Required** Backchannel device, class calendar (updated)	**Standards** CCSS: Stds for Math.Practice NETS: 4a, 5c

Essential Question

How does tech help problem solving and logical thinking?

Big Idea

Problem solving is challenging and cerebrally-stimulating.

Teacher Preparation

- Integrate domain-specific vocabulary into lesson.
- Ensure required links are on student digital devices.
- Ask what tech problems students had difficulty with.
- Have Problem-solving Board sign-up available.
- Something happen you weren't prepared for? Show how you solve it.
- Know which tasks not completed last class are necessary to move forward.
- Review *"How to Teach Students to Problem Solve"* and *"How to Teach Critical Thinking"* at the end of the lesson.

Assessment Strategies

- Annotated workbook (if using)
- Signed up for Board
- Worked independently
- Completed warm-up, exit ticket
- Joined classroom conversations
- [tried to] solve own problems
- Left room as s/he found it
- Higher order thinking: analysis, evaluation, synthesis
- Habits of mind observed

Steps

Time required: 90-270 minutes, spread throughout the class grading period
Class warm-up: Keyboard on class typing program, paying attention to posture

This lesson is integrated into many lessons—not a stand-alone. Students learn to consider themselves 'problem solvers'.

_____Required skill level: Enthusiasm for thinking and problem solving.
_____Discuss Problem Solving. This life skill transcends a subject.
_____Discuss what it means to be a 'problem solver'. Who do students go to when they need a problem solved? Parents? Do students believe that person gets it right more often than others? Would they believe most people are wrong half the time?

_____ Problem solving is closely aligned with logical thinking, critical thinking, reasoning, and thought habits. Discuss why students should become problem solvers (hint: refer to prior point—most people students go to for assistance are wrong half the time). Discuss characteristics of a 'problem solver' (from Common Core):

- value evidence
- attend to precision
- comprehend as well as critique
- understand other perspectives
- demonstrate independence
- make sense of problems and persevere in solving them
- use appropriate tools strategically

_____ Discuss 'Big Idea': Is problem solving 'cerebrally-stimulating? Is it fun? Why or why not? Discuss great quotes in *Figure 36* (zoom in if necessary).

Figure 36—Problem-solving quotes

Great Quotes About Problem Solving

"In times like these it is good to remember that there have always been times like these."
— Paul Harvey *Broadcaster*

"Never try to solve all the problems at once — make them line up for you one-by-one."
— Richard Sloma

"Some problems are so complex that you have to be highly intelligent and well-informed just to be undecided about them."
— Laurence J. Peter

"Life is a crisis - so what!"
— Malcolm Bradbury

"You don't drown by falling in the water; you drown by staying there."
— Edwin Louis Cole

"The significant problems we face cannot be solved at the same level of thinking we were at when we created them."
— Albert Einstein

"It is not stress that kills us. It is effective adaptation to stress that allows us to live."
— George Vaillant

"The most serious mistakes are not being made as a result of wrong answers. The truly dangerous thing is asking the wrong questions."
— Peter Drucker *Men, Ideas & Politics*

"The problem is not that there are problems. The problem is expecting otherwise and thinking that having problems is a problem."
— Theodore Rubin

It's not that I'm so smart, it's just that I stay with problems longer.
—Albert Einstein

No problem can stand the assault of sustained thinking.
—Voltaire

The problem is not that there are problems. The problem is expecting otherwise and thinking that having problems is a problem.
—Theodore Rubin

Problems are only opportunities with thorns on them.
—Hugh Miller

_____ Discuss shortkeys. How are they problem solving? Demonstrate this by asking students to tell you how to perform a skill. Is it easier to share the shortkey?

_____ Discuss problem-solving strategies:

- Act out a problem
- Be aware of surroundings
- Break a problem into parts
- Distinguish between relevant and irrelevant information
- Draw a diagram
- Guess and check
- Never say 'can't'
- Notice the forest and the trees
- Observe and collect data
- See patterns
- Think logically
- Try to solve before asking for help
- Try, fail, try again
- Use Help files
- Use tools available
- Use what has worked in past
- Work backwards

_____See *Figure 37* for list of problem-solving strategies (zoom in if necessary):

Figure 37—How to solve a problem

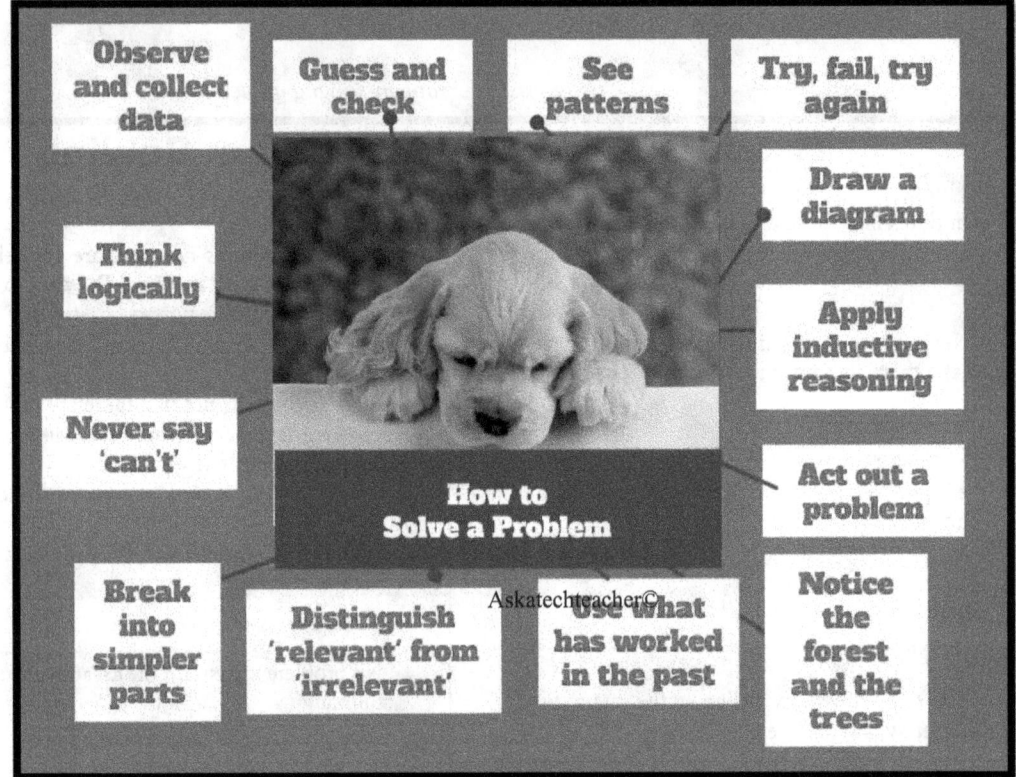

_____When students face a problem, use problem solving strategies before asking for assistance.
_____Here are two projects to reinforce problem solving in everyday life:

- *Problem-solving Board*
- *Analysis of authentic problem-solving skills*

Problem-solving Board

_____Students sign up to teach classmates common problems faced when using technology. Ideally, you have collected these throughout the year from students, other teachers, and parents—the types of problems that stopped students as they tried to use tech. This list might include:

Figure 38—Common tech problems

Problem	
My browser doesn't work	I can't find a tool
Browser toolbar missing	My screen is frozen
The website doesn't work	I'm worried about security
The document is read-only	Can't find Bold, Italic
Double click doesn't work	Can't find the program
I can't find XXX on page	Internet toolbar's gone
Program disappeared	My computer doesn't work
Erased my document	My programs are gone

_____Students sign up via a Padlet wall embedded into the class start page, SignUp Genius, a shared spreadsheet or another method that works for you.

Figure 39a-b—Problem-solving Board sign-ups

_____Review digital rights and responsibilities before using the internet search functions.

_____Here's how the Problem-solving Board works. Students:

- *Select presentation date.*
- *Select problem to teach classmates.*
- *Get solution from tech tools, online resources, family, friends, teacher as a last resort.*
- *Teach classmates how to solve problem.*
- *Take questions. Audience is responsible for making sure speaker makes sense.*

_____Students can get answers through:

- *Help files*
- *Google Searches*
- *family and friends*
- *online resources like age-appropriate videos*
- *other resources*

_____Students must come prepared, having researched material. They may use visual displays to clarify information, such as screenshots, screencasts, and other graphics.

_____Entire presentation takes about three minutes. *Figure 40 (Assessment at end of lesson)* is a sample rubric you can fill out from your iPad.

Figure 40—Problem-solving Board rubric

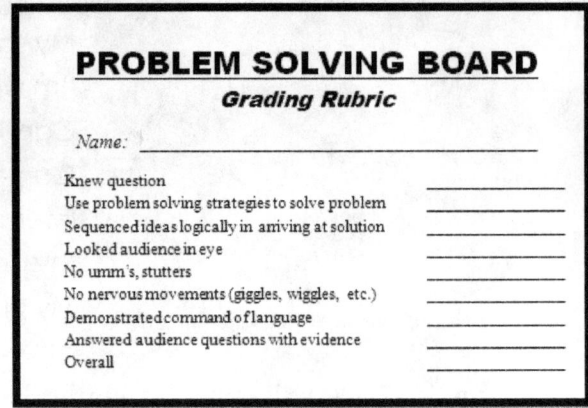

_____Students should own these tech problems by end of class.

Analysis of authentic problem-solving skills

_____During the grading period, student must identify five problems they faced in any part of their life—home, school, or personal—and what problem-solving strategy they used to solve it.
_____Here's how this works:

- *Student records 5 problems faced during the grading period in a Google Spreadsheet created by you and shared with students.*
- *Student answers a Google Forms poll (like* Assessment 14*) that you created and share. It tracks common solutions they used. They must have 5 of these during grading period:*

Assessment 13—Problem solving authentic data

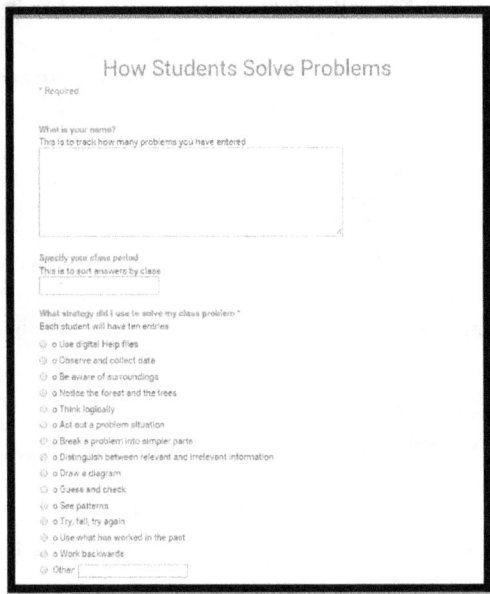

_____At the end of the class, share collected data with students.
_____Throughout class, check for understanding.

Class exit ticket: *Enter one problem already encountered into Google Form.*

Differentiation

- *Have one student create the Problem Solving Google Form to track class results.*
- *Add 'other' to the poll and let students share their own unique strategy with classmates.*
- *Add homework or classwork due date to class online calendar for each month.*

Assessment 14—Problem-solving Board

PROBLEM SOLVING BOARD Rubric

Name: _____

Knew question _____

Use problem-solving strategies to solve problem _____

Sequenced ideas logically in arriving at solution _____

Looked audience in eye _____

No umm's, stutters _____

No nervous movements (giggles, wiggles, etc.) _____

Demonstrated command of language _____

Used visual props to aid communication _____

Answered audience questions with evidence _____

Overall _____

Assessment 15—Problem-solving Presentation Assessment

Problem Solving Presentation Assessment

Project: Problem Solving   Student/Team:

Pts	Investigate	Design	Plan	Create	Evaluate	Group
0	Team does not complete investigation to standard discussed in class	Team does not complete design to standard discussed in class	Team does not complete plan to standard discussed in class	Team does not complete work to standard discussed in class	Team does not complete evaluation to standard discussed in class	Team does not work together to standard discussed in class
1-2	Team states problem but not clearly, vaguely, understanding skills required. Students have difficulty verbalizing steps required to complete	Team addresses some detail about how project will be presented with selected tool, but leaves critical elements out	Team project plan contains some goals for completing project; timeline is not sustainable	Team creates at least part of storyboard, timeline, product/solution	Team evaluates product/solution as they work, but does not adapt plan or project to problems that arise	Team occasionally works well as a group, but has difficulty allocating work and arriving at consensus
3-4	Team states problem clearly with a strong understanding of skills required. Team shows evidence of researching and describes solution in detail	Team addresses all specifics required to create a how-to and present to class	Team produces a plan that contains a clear and achievable goal for using time wisely during class	Team uses appropriate techniques and equipment, storyboard is effective. Team follows plan, and modifies when required, resulting in good quality project	Team evaluates how-to project and their performance; suggests ways to improve, and tests solution before presenting to class	Team frequently incorporates group member input into project, showing respect for the value of all members
Subtotal						
Total					Askatechteacher©	/20

Article 15—How to Teach Students to Solve Problems

How to Teach Students to Solve Problems

Of all the skills students learn in school, **problem solving** arguably is the most valuable and the hardest to learn. It's fraught with uncertainty—what if the student looks stupid as he tries? What if everyone's watching and he can't do it—isn't it better not to try? What if it works, but not the way Everyone wants it to? When you're a student, it's understandable when they decide to let someone tell them what to do.

But this isn't the type of learner we want to build. We want risk-takers, those willing to be the load-bearing pillar of the class. And truthfully, by a certain age, kids want to make up their own mind. Our job as teachers is to provide the skills necessary for them to make wise, effective decisions.

It's not a stand-alone subject. It starts with a habit of inquiry in all classes—math, LA, history, science, any of them. I constantly ask students questions, get them to think and evaluate, provide evidence that supports process as well as product. Whether they're writing, reading, or creating an art project, I want them thinking what they're doing and why.

Common Core puts problem solving front and center. It comes up in ELA ("*Students will be challenged and asked questions that push them to refer back to what they've read. This stresses critical-thinking, problem-solving, and analytical skills that are required for success in college, career, and life.*"), but is inescapable in Math. In fact, students cannot fully meet the Math Standards without understanding how to effectively approach the unknown. Consider the Standards for Mathematical Practice that overlay all grade levels K-12:

- *Make sense of problems and persevere in solving them*
- *Reason abstractly and quantitatively*
- *Construct viable arguments and critique the reasoning of others*
- *Model*
- *Use appropriate tools strategically*
- *Attend to precision*
- *Look for and make use of structure*
- *Look for and express regularity in repeated reasoning*

Do these sound like great strategies for more than math? How about deciding what classes to take? Or whether to make a soccer or basketball game on the weekend? Or which college to attend? Using these eight tools strategically, with precision, and tenaciously is a great first step.

The question becomes: How do students **learn to use them**? Certainly, as they accomplish their grade-level math curriculum, you as teacher remind them they aren't doing a multiplication problem (or an Algebra one); rather they're reasoning abstractly or using appropriate tools strategically, or expressing regularity in repeated reasoning. But for deep learning, hands-on authentic experience is required. Let's say, for example, the class is investigating the purchase of an MP3 player. Should they purchase an iPod, a smartphone, a dedicated use MP3 player, or a different option? How do students arrive at a decision—solve that problem? Ask students to work through the steps below as they address a decision. Ask them to note where they accomplish one or more of the Standards for Mathematical Practice above:

1. What do you want in an MP3 player? Should it play music, show videos, pictures, communicate with others, be a phone also? Make that list so you know how to evaluate information as you collect it (**compare/contrast**).
2. What do you know about the topic (**evidence**)? Have you seen some you liked or didn't like? What have you heard about those on your list? You are a good resource to yourself. Don't discount that. You'll be surprised how much you know on a variety of topics. This step is important to college and career. Future employers and schools want you to think, to use your intelligence and your knowledge to evaluate and solve problems.

3. What advice do knowledgeable friends have (**perspective taking, collaboration**)? You want the input of MP3 users. Your friends will think whatever they own is the best, because they're vested in that choice, but listen to their evidence and the conclusions they draw based on that. This is important to a team-oriented environment. Listen to all sides, even if you don't agree.
4. **Dig deeper (close reading).** Check other resources (**uncover knowledge**). This includes:
   o *people who don't like the product*
   o *online sources. Yep, you might as well get used to online research if you aren't yet. Statistics show more people get their news from blogs than traditional media (newspapers, TV) and you know where blogs are.*
   o *your parents who will bring up topics friends didn't, like cost, longevity, reliability*
5. **Evaluate your resources (integration of knowledge).** How much money do you have? Eliminate the choices that don't fit your constraints (money, time, use, etc.) If there are several choices that seem to work, this will help you make the decision. You might have to save money or get a job so you can afford the one you've chosen. Or, you might decide to settle for a cheaper version. Just make sure you are aware of how you made the choice and are satisfied with it.
6. What are the **risks involved** in making the decision (**reflection**)? Maybe buying an MP3 player means you can't do something else you wanted. Are you comfortable with that choice?
7. **Make a decision (transfer learning).** That's right. Make a decision and live with it knowing you've considered all available information and evaluated it logically and objectively.

Optionally, you might have students evaluate problem solving in their favorite game, say, Minecraft. All it requires is that as they play, think about what they're doing:

- *What is the goal of Minecraft? How is it best achieved*
- *What does the student know about playing the game that can be used in achieving the goal?*
- *Does working with friends and gaining feedback make life easier in Minecraft?*
- *How does experience in the game affect progress?*
- *And so on...*

This is how students become the problem solvers required of their Future. When the day comes that how they solve a problem affects the direction their life takes (college, career, marriage, children, a tattoo), they'll be happy to have strategies that make it easier.

Article 16—Teach Critical Thinking

How to Teach Critical Thinking

There's a reason why the brain uses 25% of the calories you eat: Thinking is hard work. Subjects like math and science — the ones only "smart" kids do well in — demand that you find patterns, unravel clues, connect one dot to another, and scaffold knowledge learned in prior lessons. Worse, you're either right or wrong with no gray areas.

Wait. Where have we heard those characteristics before? In games! Do these descriptions sound familiar (or ask your game-playing students)?

Take the helm of your own country and work together with others to solve international problems!

Manage your city so it's energy efficient and sustainable.

Solve a mysterious outbreak in a distant tropical jungle and save the scientists.

All torn straight from the taglines of popular games. Kids love playing games, leveling up, and finding the keys required to win. They choose the deep concentration and trial-and-error of gameplay over many other activities because **figuring out how to win is exciting**. So why the disconnect among teachers and parents when applying gameplay to learning?

Surprisingly, all you need is one simple mindshift to do this: **Create a classroom environment where thinking isn't considered work**. Don't say science and math are hard. Don't jump in to solve problems. Let students thrill with the excitement of finding their own solutions. The great thinkers of our time understand that **everyone can find solutions**:

"Failure isn't falling down; it's not getting up." — Mary Pickford

"No problem can withstand the assault of sustained thinking." — Voltaire

"Life is a crisis. So what?" — Malcom Bradbury

I've discussed problem-solving before (see *How to Teach Students to Solve Problems*). Today, I want to share five favorite websites that turn the deep-thinking required for solving problems into fun:

60-second Adventures in Thought

by Open University

Can a cat be both alive and dead (Schrödinger's Cat)? How does a tortoise beat Achilles in a race? What do the secrets of GPS have to do with relativity? **60-second Adventures in Thought** are six sixty-second videos on "thought experiments" that have changed the world. Thought experiments, made famous by both the ancient Greeks and Albert Einstein, are carried out only in the imagination. They start with "what if" and proceed to prove/disprove a hypothesis without raising a pencil. The six you'll find on this website are the most famous, covering subjects like time travel, infinity, quantum mechanics and artificial intelligence *humorously and mind-blowingly. Voiced by comedian David Mitchell, they will not fail to enthrall students.*

The Crossing

by Ramon Vullings and Igor Bytterbier

The Crossing *is a video showing how a society of nearlings tries, fails, and tries again to cross a chasm. It's easy-to-follow, less than two minutes, and humorous. The moral is the nearlings' tenacity; They just won't give up. BTW, a* **nearling** *is a positive word for something that was done with the right intentions but has yet to lead to the right results. Think "nearly" and you've got it.*

How to Critically Think

George Polya presented by the Mathematical Association of America

George Polya *is the most brilliant unknown mathematician to ever live. When he became frustrated with the process of memorizing and regurgitating, he published a book called* How to Solve it *(1945) to share his four-step process to solve problems. This one-hour [quite old] wildly-famous video shares his discussion of that method. It validates what many teachers already teach, the problem-solving steps included in Common Core, as well as how most of us intuitively set out to solve a problem. I'll give you a hint: Where many of us go wrong is we give up too soon.*

Inference Riddles

by Phil Tortuga

Phil Tortuga's inference riddles *are designed to provide students with a fun and engaging activity to practice* **inference and prediction** *at a variety of skill levels. In this online game, players make guesses based on clues provided by the website. When players think they know the answer, they type it in a dialogue box provided on the website and check to see if they're right.*

Quandary

by MIT

Quandary *is MIT's free, award-winning space-themed online game that requires decision-making, critical-thinking, perspective-taking, and ethical evaluation to make decisions that can save a dying planet. To do so requires you solve the problems that threaten to end this world. The trick is to separate fact from fiction, assess varied viewpoints, and make ethical decisions that are best for all world citizens. Once you've made a decision, you can see how it plays out in this virtual world.*

***

To me, problem-solving is one of life's great highs. I love the feeling of getting it right, especially after failure. If you struggle with students who give up too quickly, these five online sites are perfect.

Lesson #6—Screenshots, Screencasts, Videos

Vocabulary	Problem solving	Skills
<ul><li>Embed</li><li>PDF</li><li>Screencast</li><li>Screenshot</li><li>Storyboard</li><li>Voice-over</li></ul>	<ul><li>I can't find the screencast tool (use search)</li><li>Can't figure it out (breathe deeply, check screen, you can do it)</li><li>How do I edit a video (either start over or use native video editing tools)</li><li>My partner isn't helping</li></ul>	Screencasting Digital citizenship Keyboarding Screenshots Speaking/listening
Academic Applications Writing, research, history	**Materials Required** keyboard program, Evidence Board badges, student workbooks (if using)	**Standards** CCSS: SL.9-10.4 NETS: 3d, 4c, 6b

Essential Question

What is the best way that I can help a classmate solve a problem?

Big Idea

A visual is much easier to understand for many people than words

Teacher Preparation

- Ask what tech problems students had difficulty with.
- Integrate domain-specific vocabulary into lesson.
- Ensure required links are on student digital devices.
- Know whether you need extra time to complete lesson.
- Collect words for Speak Like a Geek Board.
- Know which tasks weren't completed last class and whether they are necessary to move forward.
- Have screencast and screenshot tools available as software, webtools, or add-ons.

Assessment Strategies

- Completed project
- Worked well in a group
- Worked independently
- Used good keyboarding habits
- Completed warm-up, exit ticket
- Joined classroom conversations
- [tried to] solve own problems
- Decisions followed class rules
- Left room as s/he found it
- Higher order thinking: analysis, evaluation, synthesis
- Habits of mind observed

Steps

Time required: 90 minutes
Class warm-up: Keyboarding on the class typing program, paying attention to posture

This lesson should follow *Problem Solving* as it expects familiarity with that.

_____Screenshots and screencasts are digital recordings of what appears on your screen, with or without audio, video, and notes.

_____This project discusses three options:

- screenshots
- screencasts
- video recording

Screenshot

A screenshot is a still photo of your screen, likely annotated. Students use this process to fill in quizzes and rubrics in their student workbooks (if you use the companion PDFs). *Figures 41a-b* are examples:

Figure 41a-b—Samples of screenshots

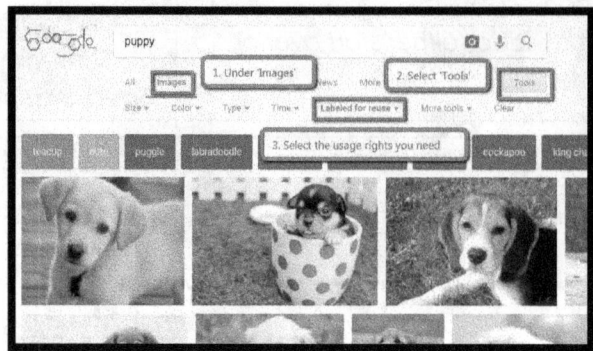 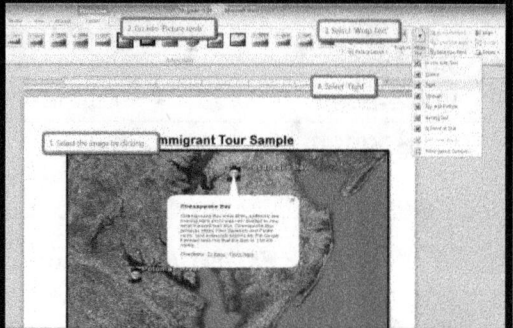

Most digital devices come with a built-in screenshot tool:

- ***Windows***: *Snipping Tool (Figure 42b)*
- ***Chromebook***: *hold down the control key and press the window switcher key*
- ***Mac***: *Command Shift for a full screenshot and Command Shift 4 for a partial*
- ***Surface tablet***: *hold down volume and Windows button at the same time*
- ***iPad***: *hold Home button and power button at same time*

Other options (search Google for addresses):

- *Nimbus — Chromebook add-on, screencasts too*
- *Screen Capture*

Depending upon the tool, it may include a range of annotation functions. These may include:

Figure 42a-b—Annotation Tools

 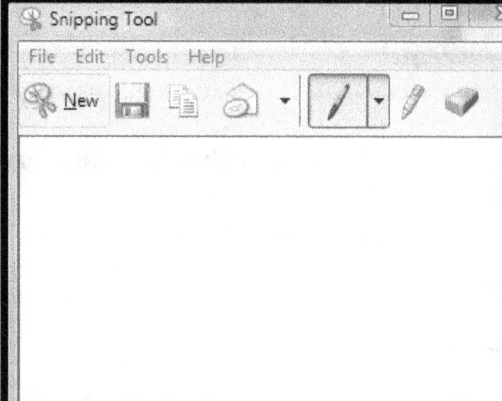

- *arrows*
- *blur tool*
- *boxes*
- *freehand drawing*
- *highlighting*
- *shapes*
- *stickies*
- *text*

_____Screenshot tips:

- *pick a clear image*
- *make annotations easy to read*
- *check grammar and spelling*

_____*Figure 43* use a screenshot to sequence activities, in this case, how to run an iPad slideshow (zoom in if necessary):

Figure 43—Sequencing in a screenshot

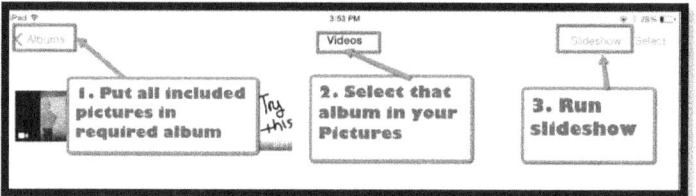

Screencast

_____A screencast is a video of what's happening on your screen. For example, *Figure 44* illustrates a screenshot of what is actually a 16-minute video on creating a classroom backchannel.

Figure 44—Sample screencast

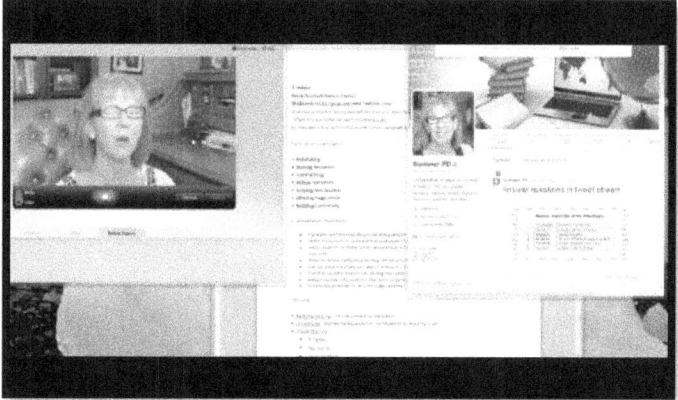

_____ It can be simple or sophisticated. Tools available to convey your message may include:

- *a spotlight for the mouse*
- *the presenter picture*
- *ability to edit*
- *ability to upload to YouTube, the Cloud, or another file sharing location*

_____Popular screencasting tools include ScreenPal (check Ask a Tech Teacher resource pages for more options).
_____For iPads, try:

- *Educreations*
- *Explain Everything*
- *Show Me*

Screencast tools

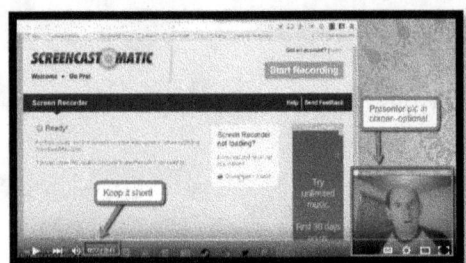

_____Screencasting tips:

- *keep screencasts short—a couple of minutes*
- *speak conversationally but avoid slang, umm, and giggles*
- *don't worry about mistakes—you can re-record*
- *pause the video, find a resource, and start again*
- *keep on topic; don't get distracted*
- *use a simple background that doesn't distract*

Video

_____A video can use the native recorder in the digital device. It may be a video of the student talking and holding up items that they want the audience to see. At your option, it may also be a student using a traditional camcorder as they talk into the camera.
_____Options for iPads: iMovie for iPad
_____Other options:

- *Animoto*
- *YouTube—tape directly using camera on laptop, iPad, desktop, Chromebook*

Activity

_____A good way to start using screenshots, screencasts, and videos is to task students with showing how to solve a problem in the Problem Solving lesson. Expect them to:

- *sequencing ideas logically*
- *be clear about the process, not simply the goal*
- *understand and present all steps required to complete a task*

_____Students can work in small groups. Select one (or more) of the problems solved during the problem-solving lesson.

_____Write a storyboard to make sure all topics are covered—or simply use notes.

_____Students should expect to practice several times before recording.

_____When done, share the screencast, screenshot, or video by publishing or embedding it to the class common areas (blog or website).

_____By the end of this Lesson, students will have a library of how-to videos for tech problems.

Class exit ticket: ***Watch a neighbor's screencast, screenshot, or video.***

Differentiation

- *Make audio how-tos instead. Here are programs that work well for this purpose:*
  - *QuickVoice Recorder*
  - *VoiceThread (both apps)*
  - *Sonic Pics–voice-over slideshow of pictures*
- *Add homework or classwork due dates to class online calendar.*

High School Technology Curriculum Book 1: Teacher Manual

Lesson #7—Word Processing Summative

Vocabulary	Problem solving	Skills
• Alignment • Format • Hyperlinks • Right click • Toolbar • Word processing • Word wrap	• I want to indent outline (tab) • I want to exdent (Shift+tab) • I want a new page (Ctrl+Enter) • I want a hyperlink (Ctrl+K) • I got out of the outline (backspace to last point. Push enter) • Why do I use word processing?	Word processing Outlining Problem solving Keyboarding Digital citizenship
Academic Applications Writing, research, notetaking	**Materials Required** Backchannel device, Homework info, student workbooks (if using)	**Standards** CCSS: CCRA.L.6 NETS: 1d, 3d

Essential Question

How can I use technology to help me organize and prioritize my ideas?

Big Idea

There are many ways word processing can organize your ideas

Teacher Preparation

- Have a book or chapter for students to outline.
- Collect words for Speak Like a Geek Board.
- Have word processing summative available.
- Ask what tech problems students had difficulty with.
- Integrate domain-specific tech vocabulary into lesson.
- Ensure all required links are on student digital devices.
- Know whether you need extra time to complete this lesson with your student group.

Assessment Strategies

- Completed outline
- Worked independently
- Used good keyboarding habits
- Completed warm-up, exit ticket
- Joined classroom conversations
- [tried to] solve own problems
- Decisions followed class rules
- Left room as s/he found it
- Higher order thinking: analysis,

Steps

Time required: 45-90 minutes for each activity
Class warm-up: Keyboarding on the class typing program, paying attention to posture

_____ Required skill level: word processing basics.

_____ Before beginning, put backchannel device onto class screen (Padlet, class Twitter account, or another) to track student comments. Show students how to access it on their devices. During class, pay attention to student concerns.

_____ Discuss word processing with students. What is it? How have students used it (see *Figures 45a-d* for examples)? What are examples of word processing programs students have used? Which do they like and why?

- *Blogs*
- *Digital storytelling*
- *Discussion Boards*
- *Evernote*
- *Google Docs/Word*
- *Twitter*

Figure 45a-d—Word processing examples from elementary and middle school

   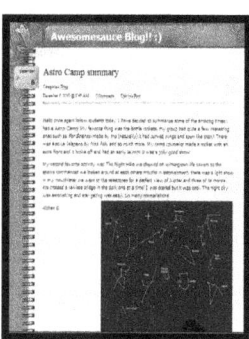

_____If students don't think of 'Evernote' or 'Twitter' as word processing, discuss.

_____Compare word processing to other communication methods students use (*Figure 46*—zoom in if necessary):

Figure 46—Compare-contrast: Productivity tools

Element	Presentation	Word processing	Spreadsheets	DTP
Purpose	Share a presentation	Share words	Turn numbers into information	Share information using a variety of media
Basics	Graphics-based. Design is important to content. Layout communicates. Few words, lots of images	Text-based. Design is secondary to content. Layout may detract from words. Primarily words communicate	Number-based. Focus on tables, graphs. Little text; lots of statistics and date. Almost no words	Mix of media—equal emphasis on text, images, layout, color
Sentences	Bulleted, phrases	Full sentences with proper conventions	None	Full sentences, bullets,
Content	Slides cover basics, to remind presenter what to say	Thorough discussion of a topic. Meant to be complete document	Statistics, data, charts, graphs	To draw an audience in;
Use	As a back-up to presentation	As complete resource	To support other presentation methods	Good way to group information for easy consumption
Presentation	Speaker presents with their back to the slideshow	Speaker reads from document	Speakers uses it in a presentation or 1:1	Speaker passes out as a handout or take-way
What else				

_____If you're using student workbooks, ask students to complete the table in it, alone or with a partner. Assessment 17 is an example of what they'll see. Alternatively, you can display Assessment 17 on the class screen and fill it out together:

Assessment 16—Compare-contrast productivity tools

Element	Slide-show	Word processing	Spread-sheets	DTP
Purpose	Share a presentation	Share words		
Basics		Text is essential to design; layout may detract		
Sentences		Full sentences with proper conventions		
Content	Slides cover basics, remind presenter what to say			
Use		As complete resource		
Presentation		Speaker reads from document		
What else				

_____Open a document in the class word processing program. Go to 'save as' and click drop down box with 'save as type'. What's available? What do those 'types' mean? What's 'plain text'? RTF? Open Source? Why would student save in a different format than what they created the document in?

_____Have a knowledgeable student review the **program menu bar, ribbons, toolbars** (*Figure 47*):

Figure 47—Toolbar, menu bar

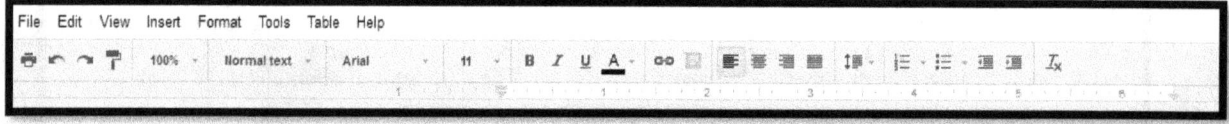

- *Alignment*
- *Bullets*
- *Icons*
- *Drop down menus*
- *Font options*
- *Indent*
- *Ruler*

_____Discuss **tools**. Remind students how similar they are to other software like Excel, PowerPoint, Publisher, Google Sheets, or Numbers (*Figure 48*):

Figure 48—Tools on toolbars

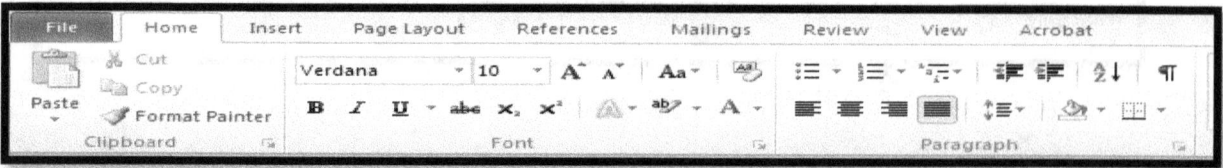

_____Discuss right click menu options—what are those? What do they bring up?

_____Pick one or both of this lesson's projects to complete with students:

- outlining
- word process summative

Outlining

_____As a class, **review outlining** (bullets or numbers). What is its purpose? What do students remember about outlining from earlier grades?

_____Today, they will independently create an outline using a textbook they brought from a different class (see outline sample *Figure 49a in MS Word, 49b* in Google Docs, and *49c* in Workflowy).

Figure 49a-c—Examples of outlines in word processing programs

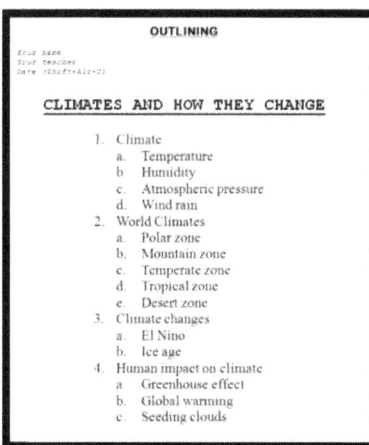 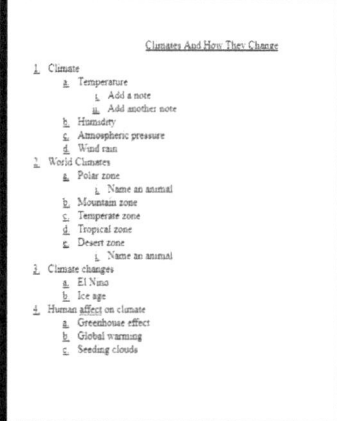 

_____If you don't use MS Word or Google Docs on your digital device, try these independent outlining tools:

- *OneNote—software, a web app, or an iPad app*
- *Workflowy*

_____If you're an iPad school and don't have access to Google Docs, Mac, or Microsoft Word apps, try one of these:

- *The Google Docs or MS Word app*
- *Quicklyst*
- *OmniOutliner*

_____Any time students go online, remind them how to do so safely. If you haven't covered the lesson on digital citizenship, spend as much time on this as needed, until you are comfortable students understand this concept.

_____When students have completed outlining the assigned chapter, ask them to add information not included in the chapter, that they learned during class, through independent research, and/or in discussions with classmates or the teacher by adding points and subpoints. Let them see how easy it is to edit an outline.

Word processing summative

_____Give students a word processing skills assessment (at the end of the lesson). *Figure 50a* is the completed assessment in Word and *Figure 50b* is in Google Docs. Adapt as needed for iPads:

Figure 50a—MS Word; 50b—Google Docs

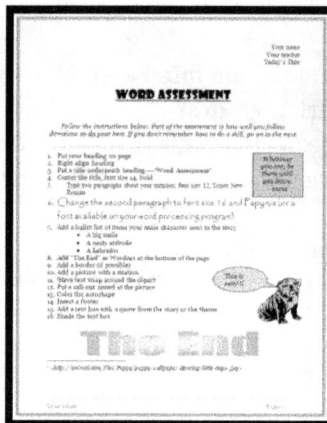 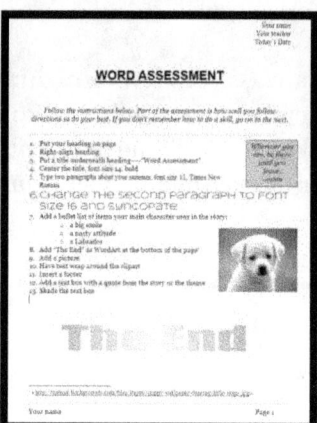

_____Adjust the assessment to include only skills students have learned by this year, such as:

- *heading is right-aligned at the top of the page*
- *title centered underneath in Comic Sans, 14 font size, bold*
- *story written in 12 font size, Times New Roman*
- *2nd paragraph written in 16 font size, Papyrus*
- *bulleted list (maybe items your main character took with them)*
- *'The End' in Word Art or another title font and appearance*
- *footer includes student name*

_____If students are using workbooks, they can access assessment there.
_____Allow 30-45 minutes to complete—enough to share what students know. You're assessing knowledge, not experimentation. Save and share.
_____Evaluate assessments before the next class to determine holes in word processing knowledge.
_____Spend the next class reviewing identified holes. If most students remembered most skills, add new tools such as how to adjust margins, add hyperlinks (Ctrl+K), move text within a document, force a new page, insert images, create/use embedded links, and find synonyms.
_____Remind students: Every time they use a digital device, practice good keyboarding.

Class exit ticket: ***Have neighbor review work for completeness.***

Differentiation

- *Complete word processing skills with a journal rather than a document.*
- *After submitting Assessment, student highlights words that indicate effective technique, descriptive details, and clear event sequences.*
- *Provide opportunity for students to get Word certification through Certiport—or get yourself licensed to administer test at your school. This will take longer than allocated time.*

Assessment 17—Word processing summative

Your name
Today's Date

WORD PROCESSING ASSESSMENT

Follow the instructions below. Part of the assessment is how well you read and complete directions. Do your best. If you don't remember how to do a skill, go on to the next.

- Put your heading on page
- Right-align heading
- Put a title underneath heading——"Word Processing Assessment"
- Center the title, font Comic Sans, font size 14, bold
  - Type two paragraphs about yourself, font size 12, Times New Roman
- Change the second paragraph to font size 16 and Papyrus
- Add bullets with
  1. Your daily activities
  2. What you like to read
  3. Who you play with
- Add "The End" as WordArt at the bottom of the page
- Add a border

> *Wherever you are, be there until you leave.*
> —*Anonymous*

- Add a picture
- Have text wrap around the clipart
- Put a call-out aimed at the picture
- Add an autoshape
- Color the autoshape pink or red
- Insert a footer

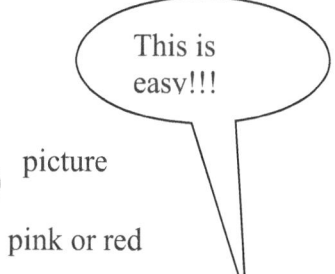

"This is easy!!!" said the most this summer three times during the day each time of day

- Add a text box with what your mom
- Shade the text box
- Add a table with seven columns and
- Add information for each day and
- Add footer with student name and class

Sunday	Monday	Tuesday	Wednesday	Thursday	Friday	Saturday
Ate breakfast						
Ate lunch						
Ate dinner						

Lesson #8—Writing with Comics, Twitter, More

Vocabulary	Problem solving	Skills
• Avatar • Installments • Panel • Serialized novel • Twitter novel • Vignette	• Can I string tweets together to cover a topic? • I don't read comics (try creating one—they are a different style of writing) • Comics communicate with pictures. How about Twitter (add images there, too)	Writing with comics/cartoons, a Twitter novel or a serialized novel Word processing tools
Academic Applications Writing, research, publishing	**Materials Required** Comic creator, Twitter, sample of a serialized and Twitter novel, student workbooks (if using)	**Standards** CCSS: W.9-10.6 NETS: 6a, 6d

Essential Question

How do I communicate my message with less text and more other media?

Big Idea

Students learn writing skills without focusing on writing or word processing

Teacher Preparation

- Have examples of Twitter novels and comics.
- Know which tasks weren't completed last class and whether they are necessary to move forward.
- Talk with the grade-level team so you tie into inquiry.
- Ask what tech problems students had difficulty with.
- Ensure required links are on student digital devices.
- Collect words for Speak Like a Geek Board.
- Integrate domain-specific tech vocabulary into lesson.
- Know whether you need extra time to complete lesson.
- Something happen you weren't prepared for? Show students how you solved it without a meltdown.

Assessment Strategies

- Annotated workbook (if using)
- Worked independently
- Completed project
- Used good keyboarding habits
- Completed exit ticket
- Joined classroom conversations
- [tried to] solve own problems
- Decisions followed class rules
- Left room as s/he found it
- Higher order thinking: analysis, evaluation, synthesis
- Habits of mind observed

Steps

Time required: 90+ minutes—varies by activity; may be spread over one class or several
Class warm-up: None

_____Students use unconventional word processing tools to write fiction or non-fiction (whatever works best for your unique group). The goal is to learn important writing skills without all the text and typing normally required. These include:

- *Comics/Cartoons*
- *Twitter novel*
- *Serialized novel*

Comics/Cartoons

_____Students have used comics to explore a topic, develop a story, and/or share perspective. Writing with comics is appropriate for both fiction and nonfiction. *Figures 51a-c* are examples of comics students created:

Figure 51a-c—Comic samples

_____Discuss how comics relay a story differently from other storytelling methods. Why focus on drawings? Do they make a serious theme light-hearted? What do students like about comics?
_____Writing with comics includes the same elements students include in a story:

- *Each panel includes detail to support the plot, characters, and setting.*
- *Each panel flows into the next, just as story paragraphs and scenes flow.*
- *Images, text, bubbles, and captions communicate ideas, story, and empathy.*

_____Comics include these parts (zoom in on *Figure 52* if necessary):

- *more than four panels (#6 in Figure 52)*
- *dialogue—delivered via speech bubbles (#1 in Figure 52)*
- *thoughts—delivered via thought bubbles (#2 in Figure 52)*
- *captions—to summarize action (#4 in Figure 52)*
- *sound effects—delivered via bubbles like 'Blam!' or 'And then' (#3 in Figure 52)*
- *student avatar—a character that represents the student. Fold this into a discussion of digital citizenship (#5 in Figure 52)*

Figure 52—Decoding a comic strip

_____Before starting, chat with students about how the topic they'll cover in their comic strip fits into class discussions.

_____Have students open an online comic creator like:

- *Powtoons -- Figure 52*
- *Storyboard That -- Figure 51c*

_____If you're an iPad school, try:

- *Pixton – Figure 51a*
- *Google Draw*

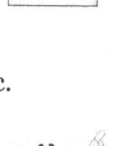

_____Note: When using the internet, remind students how to do that safely.

_____Students can work in pairs, small groups, or as a large group to write narratives that recount a sequenced event. Include opening, plot, details, temporal words to signal event order, and a sense of closure.

_____If you have workbooks, students can use included panels to sketch out their comic.

_____Done preparing? Open the comic tool and select the desired number of panels. Use available tools to select any or all of:

- *background*
- *captions*
- *characters*
- *props*

- *sound effects*
- *speech bubbles*
- *text*
- *thought bubbles*

_____Follow class writing conventions. An exception may be in speech bubbles. Explain why. *Hint: Think about task-audience-purpose as it relates to writing and comics.*

_____When done, students read their comic with a partner before publishing. Revise and edit as needed, then save as a PDF and print/publish/share as is the custom in your class. Students may find it easier to save as a screenshot using the appropriate tool in their digital device.

Twitter Novel

There's a lot Twitter brings to education:

- anyone can write limited characters
- it forces concise and pithy writing
- wasted, fluff words aren't an option
- students want to try 'forbidden fruit'

In this activity, students write a novel in Twitter. Just to be clear: We're talking about squeezing all those novel parts required for a manuscript—

- *plot/pacing*
- *character development*
- *theme*
- *story arc*
- *scene*

...into limited characters. *Figure 53* is David Mitchell's Twitter novel in 288+ tweets (available on Twitter).

Here's a sampling of Twitter novels you can find on the internet:

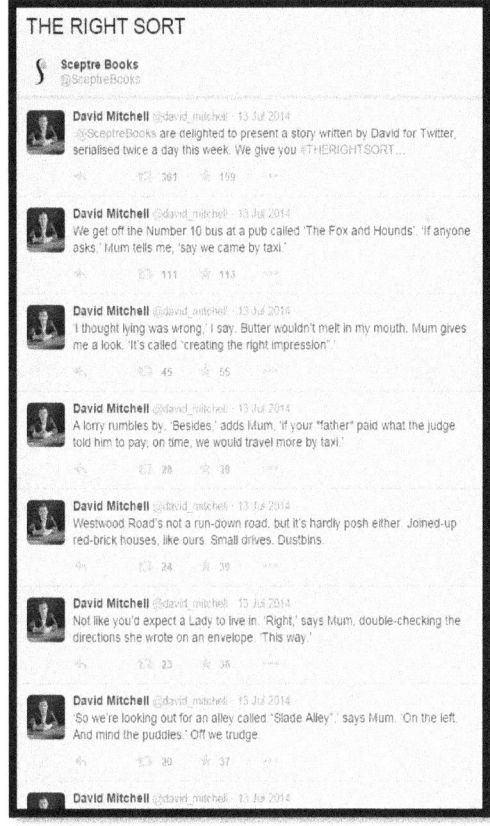

Figure 5—Twitter novel sample

'He said he was leaving her. "But I love you," she said. "I know," he said. "Thanks. It's what gave me the strength to love somebody else." **James Meek**

I opened the door to our flat and you were standing there, cleaver raised. Somehow you'd found out about the photos. My jaw hit the floor. **Ian Rankin**

Rose went to Eve's house but she wasn't there. But Eve's father was. Alone. One thing led to another. He got 10 years.
Rachel Johnson

Clyde stole a lychee and ate it in the shower. Then his brother took a bottle of pills believing character is just a luxury. God. The twins. **Andrew O'Hagan**

"It's a miracle he survived," said the doctor. "It was God's will," said Mrs. Schicklgruber. "What will you call him?" "Adolf," she replied. **Jeffrey Archer**

Here are tips on how to create exciting, satisfying Twitter novels:

- **Think token action,** dialogue and description.

<u>Not this</u>:
He sat and looked at the computer for a full ten minutes before he grasped it and experienced the icy weight of his first laptop.

<u>Rather:</u>
Laptop in hand, he wrote.

- **Think installments.** Releasing the novel over time increases suspense. Douglas Sovern released 1600 tweets at the rate of about 5 to 12 a day.
- **Think multimedia** and add links to images, video, articles or anything else that will add excitement to the story. A Twitter novel allows you to combine text with other media.
- **Think movement.** Every tweet should advance the plot. You don't want your readers ignoring tweets out of boredom.

Serialized novel—one author

_____Discuss the meaning of a serialized novel—a normal length novel published by chapter—smaller bites for people to read. Many early writers were published this way including Leo Tolstoy, Joseph Conrad, and Charles Dickens.

_____Show examples of serialized novels from authors students are reading (say, Charles Dickens).

_____Why are serialized novels making a resurgence? Consider these statistics:

Figure 6—Serialized novel by Conrad

- *The average person's attention span is 8.8 seconds.*
- *The average goldfish's attention span is 9 seconds.*

_____A serialized novel can be a stand-alone activity or an optional approach to the lesson, *Writing and Publishing an Ebook.*

_____Here's how this will work:

- *Write an outline of the planned story.*
- *Write a character study of each character.*
- *Develop a plot line of what happens when.*
- *Research settings characters will visit.*
- *Every class, students write one installment of their serialized novel and publish it to their blog. They can use a word processing tool, a comic creator, or even an audio tool, but it must be embeddable into their blog. Let them select the best tool for their communication style.*

_____When done, students will visit and comment on three of the stories written by classmates.

Serialized novel or vignettes—multiple authors

_____Discuss the meaning of 'vignettes'. Help students understand it is a verbal sketch, a brief **essay**, or a carefully crafted short work of fiction or **nonfiction**. Authors include:

- *Dickens' Sketches by Boz*
- *Cisneros' The House on Mango Street*

_____In this option, students work in groups to write vignettes around a cast of characters and a central atmosphere. Discuss what *atmosphere* means. Why is this important to a vignette—so important that it sets it apart from other forms of writing?

_____Here are basic rules to follow when writing vignettes:

- *Each vignette abides by the collection's atmosphere.*
- *Each vignette is approximately 800 words. They can be shorter, but not usually longer.*
- *The vignette must evoke emotion.*
- *The vignette shares a moment (including its power and emotion) rather than a plot point.*

_____There are lots more rules, but they vary depending upon your writing curriculum. Share what is necessary to fit your unique student group.

_____Here's how this works:

- *Students work in groups organized by the format they wish to use in writing their vignettes. For example, those who wish to use a comic creator join the same group.*
- *As a group, write a character study of each character.*
- *As a group, decide on setting and atmosphere.*
- *Develop a schedule of who will publish their vignette when. Alternatively, students have three-five weeks to write their vignette, and then use the balance of the time to meld all the pieces into one.*
- *These will be published in a collaborative student blog or another location you have selected to curate these stories.*

_____When done, students visit and comment on three of the stories written by classmates.

Class exit ticket: ***Tweet a comic or a link to a blog of a novel the student created.***

Differentiation

- Add homework and classwork due dates to class online calendar for each month.
- Use Twitter novels as a less-intimidating approach to dialogue and stories.

Lesson #9—Desktop Publishing I

Vocabulary	Problem solving	Skills
• Banner heading • Design elements • Dialogue box • DTP • Graphic design • Placeholder • Place saver • Pull-out • Sidebar • Template • Text box • Works cited	• My text disappeared (Ctrl+Z) • I can't find my file • I typed, but it doesn't show (is there an A… at cell bottom? Enlarge box) • How do I undo? (Ctrl+Z) • Screen froze (clear dialogue box) • It's difficult to toggle between two programs (Alt+Tab) • Article doesn't fill white space (enlarge picture) • Why do I have to learn DTP? Why not put work in a slideshow? WP?	Curation of resources DTP Problem solving Keyboarding Digital citizenship Newsletter Flier Magazine Calendar
Academic Applications Writing, research, history, journalism	**Materials Required** DTP tools, Inquiry that DTP projects support, DTP samples, workbooks (if using)	**Standards** CCSS: CCRA.L.6 NETS: 1d, 3a-d, 6a, 6c

Essential Question

How can color, images, and layout aid communication with a variety of audiences, for a variety of tasks?

Big Idea

Formatting and page layout contribute significantly to communication of ideas

Teacher Preparation

- Ensure required links are on student devices.
- Talk with the grade-level team to tie into inquiry.
- Integrate domain-specific vocabulary into lesson.
- Ask what tech problems students had difficulty with.
- Collect words students don't understand for Speak Like a Geek Board presentations.
- Know which tasks weren't completed last class and whether they are necessary to move forward.
- Know whether you need extra time to complete this lesson with your student group.

Assessment Strategies

- Annotated workbook (if using)
- Completed DTP project
- Worked independently
- Used good keyboarding habits
- Completed warm-up, exit ticket
- Joined classroom conversations
- [tried to] solve own problems
- Decisions followed class rules
- Left room as s/he found it
- Higher order thinking: analysis, evaluation, synthesis
- Habits of mind observed

Steps

Time required: 15 minutes introduction; 90-180 minutes per project
Class warm-up: Keyboarding on the class typing program, paying attention to posture

_____Required skill level: DTP and webtool basics, keyboarding basics.

_____Students create a variety of projects using desktop publishing and understand how this communication alternative is different from word processing, presentations, and spreadsheets.
_____Before beginning, put backchannel device onto the class screen.
_____If students have been using the SL curriculum since elementary school, they have created a wide variety of projects using desktop publishing including cards, a magazine, stories, trifolds, and newsletters:

Figure 55a-e—DTP project samples

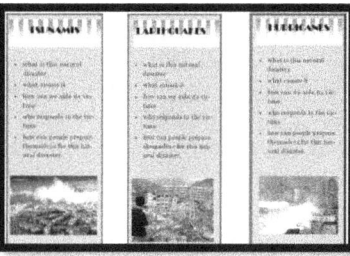

_____What is 'desktop publishing' (DTP)? In short, DTP is a good choice when a balance of communication elements is required—text, images, color, and layout.
_____Compare/contrast this to word processing, presentation tools, and spreadsheets. What are the pros and cons of each approach? *Figure 56* is a table you can display on the class screen with a few traits filled in:

Figure 56—Compare-contrast digital tools—incomplete

Element	Slide-show	Word processing	Spread-sheets	DTP
Purpose	Share a presentation	Share words		
Basics		Text is essential to design; layout may detract		
Sentences		Full sentences with proper conventions		
Content	Slides cover basics, remind presenter what to say			
Use		As complete resource		
Presentation		Speaker reads from document		
What else				

_____If using student workbooks, students take five minutes to fill in blank cells (using the annotation tool) with their best guess. *Figure 57* shows it filled in:

Figure 57—Compare-contrast digital tools—complete

Element	Presentation	Word processing	Spread-- sheets	DTP
Purpose	Share a presentation	Share words	Turn numbers into information	Share information using a variety of media
Basics	Graphics-based Design is important to content Layout communicates Few words, lots of images	Text-based Design is secondary to content Layout may detract from words Primarily words communicate	Number-based Focus on tables, graphs Little text; lots of statistics and date Almost no words	Mix of media—equal emphasis on text, images, layout, color
Sentences	Bulleted, phrases	Full sentences with proper conventions	None	Full sentences, bullets,
Content	Slides cover basics, to remind presenter what to say	Thorough discussion of a topic. Meant to be complete document	Statistics, data, charts, graphs	To draw an audience in;
Use	As a back-up to presentation	As complete resource	To support other presentation methods	Good way to group information for easy consumption
Presentation	Speaker presents with their back to the slideshow	Speaker reads from document	Speakers uses it in a presentation or 1:1	Speaker passes out as a handout or take-way
What else				

_____Over the next two lessons, students will work in groups to complete up to four projects that cover desktop publishing's most popular uses:

- *calendar*
- *flier*
- *magazine*
- *newsletter*

Newsletter

_____A newsletter is *informative/explanatory text that examines a topic and conveys ideas via formatting (e.g., headings), illustrations, design, and multimedia.*
_____Show samples of newsletters, maybe your school's or your class's. Do students see the following critical elements?

- *bold name*
- *short stories with relevant information and concise, pithy titles*
- *attractive, colorful layout*
- *pull-out with info audience will want to read*

_____Students bring two stories in digital format to class about an assigned topic such as:

- *arguments in support of claims*
- *informative/explanatory texts to examine a topic and convey ideas*
- *narratives using effective technique, descriptive details, and event sequences*

_____Students will work in groups to create a newsletter on a theme that supports class inquiry. Open the digital stories or articles each student prepared for today's lesson.

_____Now open the desktop publishing tool you use in your school. Two you may have are MS Publisher (*Figure 58a*) and Google Docs (*Figure 58b*):

Figure 58a—Newsletter in Publisher; 58b—in Google Docs; 58c—online tool

_____If you don't have a desktop publishing tool, try a PowerPoint template *(Figure 59a* or a Word template from Microsoft's website (*Figure 59b*):

Figure 59a-c—Newsletter

  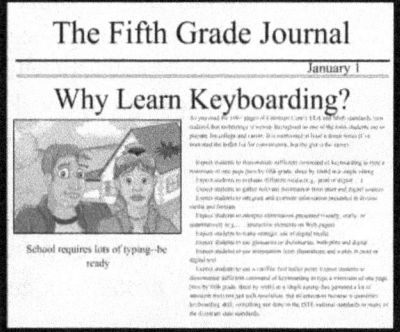

_____If you have iPads, you can use free Microsoft or Mac apps but know these will have differences from the fully-functioning software/online tools. Other iPad apps you might like include:

- *Quark Design —Figure 60a*
- *Pages*
- *My Newspaper*
- *Canva — Figure 60b*
- *Lucid Press — Figure 60c*

_____Several of these also work with laptops, PCs, Macs, and Chromebooks.

Figure 60a-c—DTP examples

 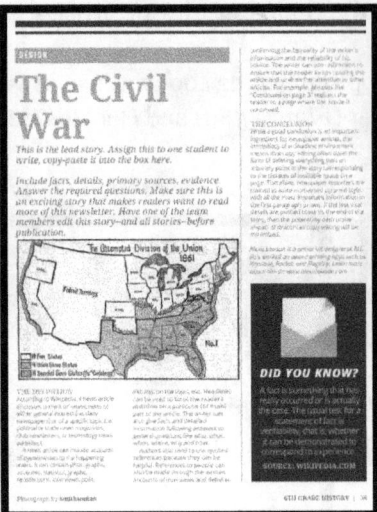 

_____Adapt lesson instructions to your digital device and platform.

_____Open the class DTP and demonstrate on the class screen while students follow on their digital devices. This newsletter will be one page, but you can make it longer if desired.

_____Discuss a newsletter layout. This will include supporting information (volume number, tagline, etc.), layout of the articles, size of the titles, the table of contents, pictures, multiple pages, advertising, images and their captions, titles and fonts, and pull-out information. Fill in as many as possible.

_____Students work together to select a newsletter title. If you haven't discussed the importance of titles before, do so now. It should be short, meaningful, summative, and pithy. Students also collaborate on story titles, and then copy-paste stories from the digital copy into columns. Review stories to be sure they explore the topic and share information clearly. Use a drop cap to start each article (if desired).

_____Student groups will review, revise, edit, and rewrite articles, with a goal of developing and strengthening the newsletter writing. Where relevant:

- *demonstrate command of English grammar and usage*
- *analyze central ideas of a primary or secondary source*
- *provide an accurate summary distinct from prior knowledge or opinions*
- *organize key steps in the description of a process*
- *summarize in words and visually (i.e., flowchart, diagram, model, graph, table)*

_____Writing should be appropriate to task, purpose, and audience.

_____Include one chart, graph, photo, or map per article.

_____Insert footer with names of team members.

_____Save (Ctrl+S) to digital portfolio; save-as to a back-up location; share/print/publish as is the custom in your class.

_____If using the grading rubric at the end of the Lesson, students can fill it out as a paper copy or on their digital workbooks (if you have those). If using the digital option, students take a screenshot of the completed rubric and email it to you.

_____If using the grading rubric, make it available to students early.

_____If time is an issue, create a newspaper clipping from Fodey *(Figure 59c)*.

Magazine

_____Magazines will (where relevant):

- *demonstrate command of English grammar and usage*
- *analyze central ideas of a primary or secondary source*
- *provide accurate summary of information distinct from prior knowledge or opinions*
- *organize key steps in description of a process*
- *summarize information textually and visually (i.e., a flowchart, diagram, model, graph, or table)*

_____If you have iPads or Chromebooks, you can use the free Microsoft and Mac apps but be familiar with these. Each platform is different as is the app when offered as software, online tools, or iPad apps. Check the Ask a Tech Teacher resource pages for ideas.
_____Students work in groups or individually (either way) to create a magazine themed to the class inquiry topics.
_____Open class desktop publishing tool. Show students how to find magazine templates.
_____Students bring to class multiple stories in digital format about the assigned topic. These include:

- *arguments in support of claims*
- *informative/explanatory texts to examine a topic and convey ideas*
- *narratives using effective technique, descriptive details, and event sequences*

_____**Add a cover** (*Figures 61a-d*). Decide on the layout—should the title be at top or in the middle? How many articles should be spotlighted? Then, adjust the color/font schemes to fit the theme and the student vision of the magazine. Experiment until it suits the taste of all group members.
_____Be sure the cover includes a title, author names, a hint what's included, and a tagline if desired.

Figure 61a-d—Magazine cover examples

_____Through discussion as a class or within the student group, decide how many pages are required for the magazine and add them to the project.
_____Add a footer with student names, page numbers, and other information the student group would like to appear on all pages.
_____**Page 2:** Add a Table of Contents (*Figures 62a-b*). Add topics as required to suit class needs.

Figure 62a-b—Magazine table of contents

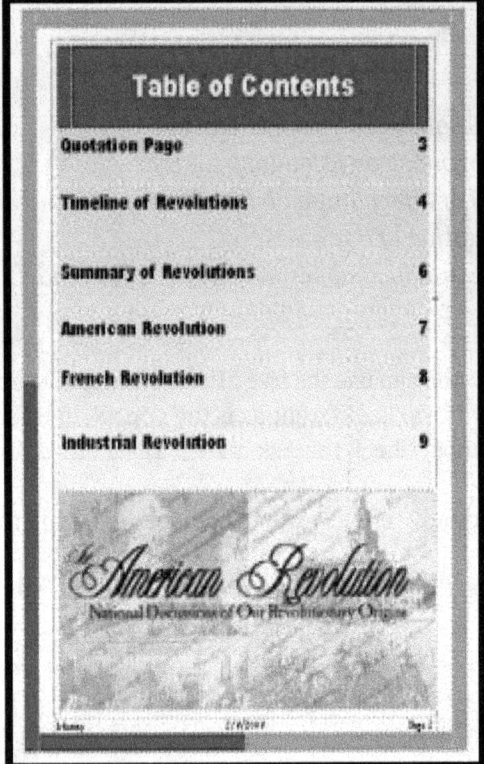

_____**Pages 3-10 (or the balance of pages in the magazine):** Depending upon your tool, add creative page elements such as a border and a banner heading. Layer them behind the title. Once you settle on the page design, add it to each page. This adds continuity to the magazine.

_____**At least one page** should be a Photo Journal (*Figures 63a-b*), Quotations (*Figure 63c*), or another collage of your choice. Caption each picture with source credit. Fill all white space.

Figure 63a-c—Magazine internal pages

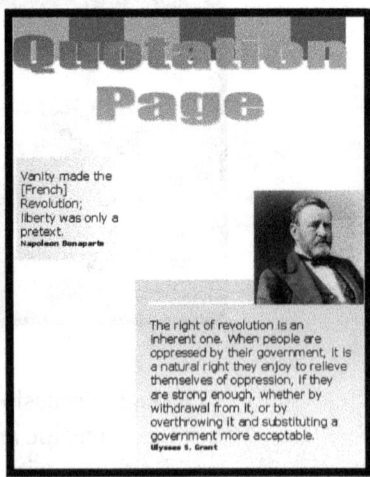

_____Two pages side-by-side will be a timeline. This may be created in a spreadsheet program or an online timeline creator like Tiki-toki and pasted into the magazine.

Figure 64—Magazine timeline

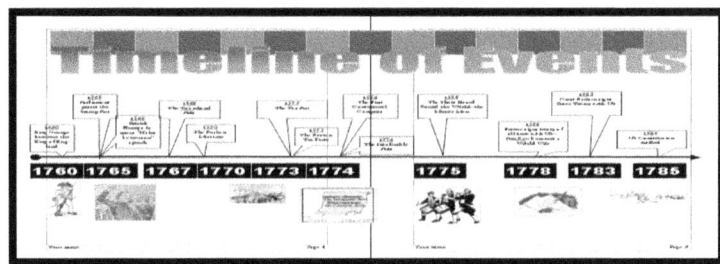

_____**Compare-contrast two ideas**. For example: Discuss the British/American participation in the American Revolution, effects of a revolution, and/or inventions resulting from a revolution. Use text boxes, pictures, and decorative items. Add pull quote to each page if desired.

Figure 65a-d—Magazine compare-contrast

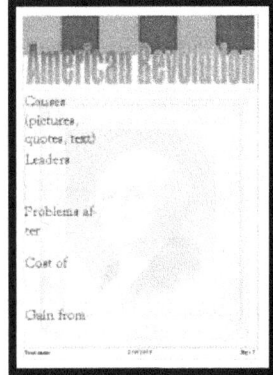 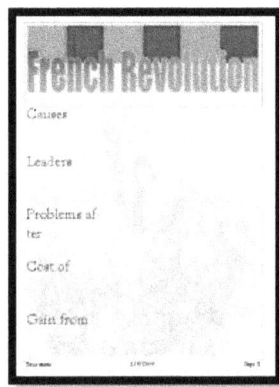 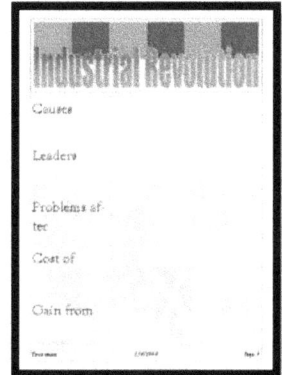 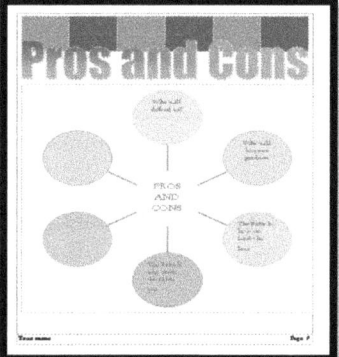

_____At least one page should use **tables**. For example: famous people in a revolution or summary of important events. Format table so titles stand out.

Figure 66a-b—Magazine graphic organizers

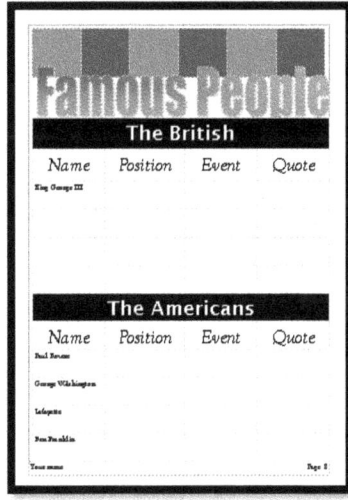 

_____At least one page should include a primary source document. Give credit to the source.

_____Last page: 'The End' (*Figure 67b*).

Figure 67a—Magazine primary source; 67b—The End

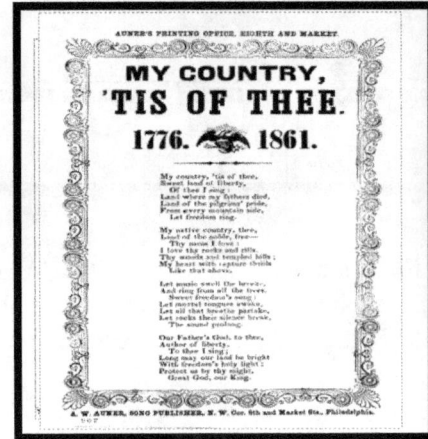 

_____Save (Ctrl+S) to digital portfolio; print (Ctrl+P), share/ publish, as is the custom in your class.
_____If using a grading rubric (*Assessment* is at the end of the lesson), make it available to student groups early.

Curating Online Articles

_____Rather than creating original content, you may want students to curate online resources into a magazine they can share with classmates. This can be done with webtools like:

- *Scoop It! – Figure 689a*
- *Flipboard – Figure 68b*

Figure 68a-b—Curating articles

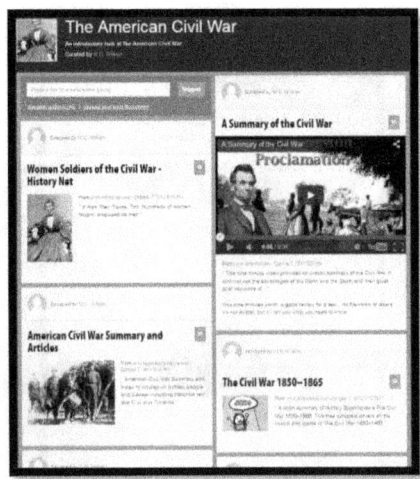 

_____This is more research-based than other activities and may appeal to your specific needs.
_____Whichever activity students complete, have them add it to their digital portfolio. Remind students that digital portfolios are graded.

Class exit ticket: *Share student project with a neighbor. If it allows comments, have students add their thoughts to their classmate's work.*

Differentiation

- *Magazine can be in a debate format, tied in with The Debate lesson.*
- *Create a literary magazine, published once per grading period, where students share their thoughts on literature read during the school year.*
- *Add homework and classwork due dates to class online calendar for each month.*
- *Early finishers: visit class internet start page for websites that tie into classwork.*

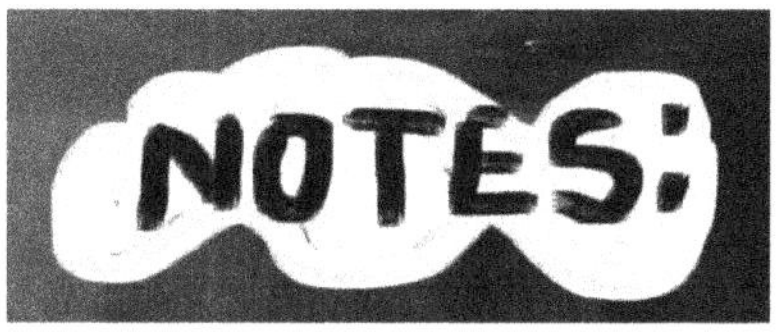

NOTES:

Assessment 18—Newsletter rubric

Newsletter
Grading Rubric

Your name: _____
Your homeroom teacher: _____

1. Newspaper title — **4 points** _____
   a. Title stands out— large font _____
   b. Spelling _____

2. Lead story — **2 points** _____
   a. Headline is creative _____
   b. Headline summarizes story _____
   c. Picture applies to story _____
   d. Grammar/spell check _____
   e. White space _____

3. Secondary story — **2 points** _____
   a. Headline is creative _____
   b. Headline summarizes story _____
   c. Picture applies to story _____
   d. Grammar/spell check _____
   e. No white space _____

4. Quotation — **2 points** _____
   a. On topic _____
   b. Spell/Grammar check _____

5. Four points of interest — **2 points** _____
   a. All deal with topic _____
   b. All deal with significant information _____
   c. Spell/grammar check _____

6. Additional — **4 points** _____
   a. Date included _____
   b. Volume and issue included _____
   c. Unnecessary template info deleted _____
   d. Only one page _____
   e. Keep info inside blue print border _____

7. Overall Professional Look — **4 points** _____
   a. Fonts/colors consistent _____
   b. Design pleasing _____
   c. Attention to detail _____

Askatechteacher©

Assessment 19—Magazine rubric

Magazine Grading Rubric

Your name(s):_____

1. **Title Page**   _____2 points_
   a. Magazine title in large font
   b. Subtitle in smaller font
   c. Your name in smaller font
   d. Picture related to topic

2. **Table of Contents**   _____3 points_
   a. Correct layout
   b. Topics match pages
   c. Border
   d. Picture matches topic

3. **Each Magazine Page**   _____10 points_
   a. Decorative banner heading
   b. 'Photo Journal'—photos fill page
   c. 'Famous People' with table
   d. 'Pros and Cons' with graphic organizer
   e. Timeline accurate
   f. Timeline with pictures
   g. Timeline with callouts
   h. 'The British' filled with quotes
   i. 'The Americans' filled with quotes
   j. Two pages with original documents
   k. Spell-check
   l. Grammar check
   m. Page filled (text/pictures)

4. **The End Page**   _____1point_
   a. 'The End' in WordArt

5. **Overall Professional Look**   _____2 points_

6. **Teamwork**   _____2 points_

Askatechteacher©

Lesson #10—Desktop Publishing II

Vocabulary	Problem solving	Skills
• Banner heading • Design elements • Dialogue box • Graphic design • Placeholder • Place saver • Sidebar • Text box	• My text disappeared (Ctrl+Z) • I can't find my file (Start-Search) • I typed, but it doesn't show (is there an A... at cell bottom? Enlarge box) • It's difficult to toggle between two programs (Alt+Tab) • Why do I have to learn DTP? Why not put work in slideshow? WP?	DTP Problem solving Keyboarding Digital citizenship Fliers Posters Calendars
Academic Applications Writing, research, reports	**Materials Required** DTP tools, inquiry for DTP projects, links to online tools, student workbooks (if using)	**Standards** CCSS: CCRA.L.6 NETS: 1d, 3a-d, 6a, 6c

Essential Question

How can adding color, images, and layout aid communication with a variety of audiences and tasks?

Big Idea

Formatting and page layout contribute significantly to communication of ideas

Teacher Preparation

- Ensure required links are on digital devices.
- Integrate domain-specific vocabulary into lesson.
- Talk with the grade-level team to tie into inquiry.
- Ask what tech problems students had difficulty with.
- Collect words students don't understand for Speak Like a Geek Board (if doing this).
- Know which tasks weren't completed last class and whether they are necessary to move forward.
- Know whether you need extra time to complete this lesson with your student group.

Assessment Strategies

- Annotated workbook (if using)
- Completed project
- Worked independently
- Used good keyboarding habits
- Completed warm-up, exit ticket
- Joined classroom conversations
- [tried to] solve own problems
- Decisions followed class rules
- Left room as s/he found it
- Higher order thinking: analysis, evaluation, synthesis
- Habits of mind observed

Steps

Time required: 15 minutes for introduction and 15-30 for each activity
Class warm-up: Keyboarding on the class typing program, paying attention to posture

_____ Required skill level: DTP and webtool basics, keyboarding basics.
_____ Students create a variety of projects using desktop publishing, to review this colorful alternative to word processing, presentations, and spreadsheets.
_____ Before beginning, put backchannel device onto class screen.

_____If students have been using the SL curriculum in the past, they have created many DTP projects including cards (*Figure 69a*), a magazine (*Figure 69b*), stories, trifolds, and newsletters (*Figures 69c-e*):

Figure 69a-e—DTP project samples

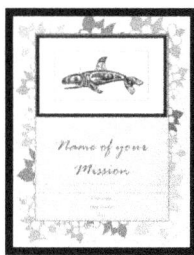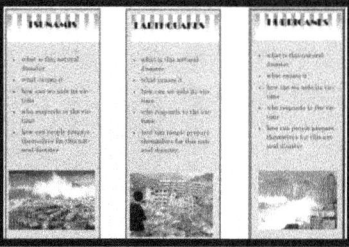

_____What is 'desktop publishing' (DTP)? What is its strength (i.e., a balance of communication elements—text, images, color, layout)?

_____Compare/contrast how it differs from word processing, slideshow tools, and spreadsheets in sharing information. Share the table from the previous lesson and ask students if they can help you fill in the blanks. If you use student workbooks, they can complete the table included in there. *Figure 70* shows a completed table:

Figure 70—Compare-contrast digital tools—complete

Element	Slideshow	Word processing	Spread-sheets	DTP
Purpose	Share a presentation	Share words	Turn numbers into information	Share information using a variety of media
Basics	Graphics-based; design is important to content; layout communicates; few words, lots of images	Text-based; design is secondary to content; layout may detract from words; primarily words communicate	Number-based; focus on tables, graphs; little text; lots of statistics and date; few words	Mix of media—equal emphasis on text, images, layout, color
Sentences	Bulleted, phrases	Full sentences with proper conventions	None	Full sentences, bullets,
Content	Slides cover basics, to remind presenter what to say	Thorough discussion of a topic. Meant to be complete document	Statistics, data, charts, graphs	To draw an audience in;
Use	As a back-up to presentation	As complete resource	To support other presentation methods	Groups information for easy consumption
Presentation	Speaker presents with their back to slideshow	Speaker reads from document	Speakers uses it in a presentation or 1:1	Speaker passes out as a handout or take-way

_____Over two lessons, students complete four projects that cover DTP's popular uses:

- *calendar*
- *flier*
- *magazine*
- *newsletter*

Fliers and Posters

_____Students may have created fliers before in DTP for report covers (*Figure 71a*), project covers (*Figure 71b*), announcements (*Figure 71c*), and cards (*Figure 71d*):

Figure 71a-d—DTP flier examples

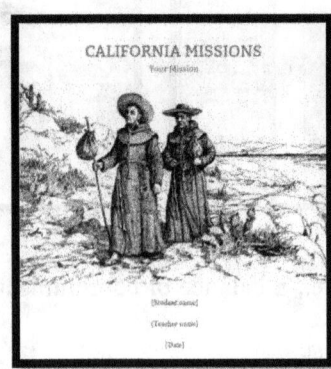

_____Open your class DTP tool, such as:

- *MS Publisher*
- *Canva (webtool or iPad)*

Figure 72a-b—Posters in DTP

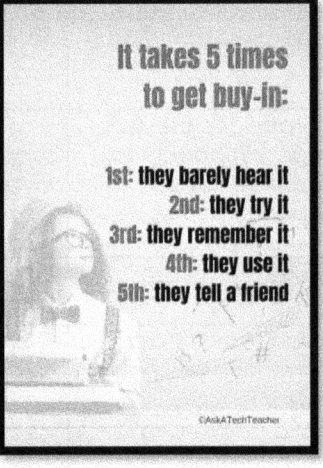

_____Select template; adjust the colors/fonts. Replace place saver pictures and text with what fits the project. Resize fonts and images to fill space.
_____If students are using a new webtool, have them 1) follow directions included with the tool, 2) go to the webtools help files, and/or 3) access how-to videos you make available to them.
_____Save (Ctrl+S) to digital portfolio; print (Ctrl+P), publish/share as is the custom in your school.
_____Rather than save, students may find it easier to take a screenshot and save that. Most digital devices have native programs for that action.
_____If using a rubric (see sample at the end of the lesson), make available to students early.
_____Rather than creating a flier from scratch, you may decide to use one of these quick templates:

- *Big Huge Labs*
- *Eye Chart (from Eye Chart Maker)*
- *Road sign (from Custom Road Sign)*

Figure 73a-d—Online tools to create fliers

   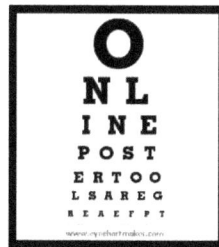

Calendar

_____Select a calendar template with one page for each required month. Change color/font schemes and pictures as desired.

_____If your DTP tool doesn't have calendars, use templates or create a table in Google Docs (*Figure 74b*) or MS Word (*Figure 74c*) and turn it into a calendar:

Figure 74a-c—Calendar samples

_____Go over school events as a class. Have students share what they're doing and add to the calendar. Resize font as needed so text fits in the cell. Add only one event per date. If there's a conflict between a school event and a personal one, have the student choose.

_____Add at least one picture to one date cell. Resize so it fits nicely in cell.

_____Add student name to lower right cell. Print (Ctrl+P); save (Ctrl+S); publish.

_____Share *Assessment* at end of lesson with students to check their work.

Class exit ticket: **Share student calendar with class and have them add holiday events.**

Differentiation

- Create fliers for class dance, meeting, play, or something else that supports the school. Post these around campus.
- Early finishers: visit the class internet start page and use the websites available there that tie into classwork.

Assessment 20—Flier grading rubric

Flier Grading Rubric

Creator: _____

Teacher: _____

Date: _____

1. Cover Page   _____8 points_____

    a. Title in large font   _____

    b. Subtitle in smaller font   _____

    c. Student name in small font   _____

    d. Picture related to topic   _____

    e. Spelling and grammar good   _____

2. Layout   _____8 points_____

    a. Decorative border   _____

    b. Attractive colors   _____

    c. All pieces well-laid out   _____

    d. Spell- and grammar-check   _____

    e. No white space   _____

3. Overall Professional Work   _____4 points_____

    a. Student worked independently   _____

    b. Student solved own problems   _____

    c. Student worked well in group   _____

    d. Student saved, printed, shared   _____

4. Extra Credit   _____

Askatechteacher©

Assessment 21—Calendar grading rubric

Calendar Grading Rubric

Creator: _____

Teacher: _____

Date: _____

1. Layout — 8 points _____
   - *Title in large font* _____
   - *Subtitle in smaller font* _____
   - *Student name in small font* _____
   - *Monthly pics relate to theme* _____
   - *One pic in one date cell/month* _____
   - *Text fits in each date cell* _____
   - *Each month includes all events* _____
   - *One calendar/month* _____

2. Appearance — 8 points _____
   - *Decorative border* _____
   - *Attractive colors* _____
   - *All pieces well-laid out* _____
   - *Spell- and grammar-check* _____
   - *No unusual white space* _____

3. Overall Professional Work — 4 points _____
   - *Student worked independently* _____
   - *Students solved own problems* _____
   - *Student worked well in group* _____
   - *Student saved, printed, shared* _____
   - *Each month matched theme* _____

4. Extra Credit _____

Askatechteacher©

Lesson #11-12—Spreadsheets

Vocabulary	Problem solving	Skills
• Algorithm • Autosum • Axis • F11 • Formula • Model • Spreadsheet • Symbols • Workbook • Worksheet	• Formula doesn't work (put = in front) • Formula still doesn't work (is there extraneous text in cell?) • Graph is empty (is data highlighted) • Can't format plot area (click plot area–not chart) • Chart doesn't look right (highlight ONLY data and headings) • Spreadsheet answer is different from mine (use standard algorithm)	Problem solving Keyboarding Digital citizenship Spreadsheet formulas Graphs and charts
Academic Applications Math, problem solving, compare-contrast	**Materials Required** Spreadsheet tools, backchannel, screenshot program, spreadsheet data, skills assessment	**Standards** CCSS: Math.Practice.MP1-8 NETS: 5a-d, 6a

Essential Question

How do I make data interesting and still allow viewers to draw their own conclusions?

Big Idea

Students turn data into information

Teacher Preparation

- Collect words for Speak Like a Geek Board.
- Ensure required links are on student digital devices.
- Talk with grade-level team so you tie into inquiry.
- Integrate domain-specific vocabulary into lesson.
- Ask what tech problems students had difficulty with.
- Know which tasks weren't completed last class and whether they are necessary to move forward.
- Know whether you need extra time to complete this lesson with your student group.

Assessment Strategies

- Annotated workbook (if using)
- Worked independently
- Completed project
- Completed warm-up, exit ticket
- Joined classroom conversations
- [tried to] solve own problems
- Decisions followed class rules
- Left room as s/he found it
- Higher order thinking: analysis, evaluation, synthesis
- Habits of mind observed

Steps

Time required: **180 minutes**
Class warm-up: **Keyboard on the class typing program, paying attention to posture**

_____ Required skill level: Spreadsheet basics.

_____ In this lesson, students review a variety of spreadsheet formulas they'll use in their academic career.

_____ Before beginning, put backchannel device on class screen (Padlet, class Twitter account, or another) to track student comments.

_____Discuss this Common Core statement—

*Mathematically proficient students consider available tools when solving a mathematical problem. These tools might include pencil and paper, concrete models, ruler, protractor, calculator, **spreadsheet**, computer algebra system, statistical package, or dynamic geometry software.*

_____What does it mean to 'model' a concept? Name models students are aware of. Anyone make model airplanes? Lego models? Discuss how important that modeling is done carefully with precision. Each tool must be exact. Anyone who sees the 'model' gets the message.
_____How does this compare to formulas discussed in class?

Figure 75a-b—Two formulas

_____Formulas are a tool, like a calculator, strategically used to analyze data, and draw conclusions that would be difficult to comprehend without automaticity. But, they do not supplant student responsibility for learning the process.
_____Spreadsheets are a time-proven method for using formulas to model data and solve problems. A familiarity with spreadsheets should start when students begin math. This may be in elementary school with these spreadsheet projects:

Figure 76a-c—Spreadsheet projects

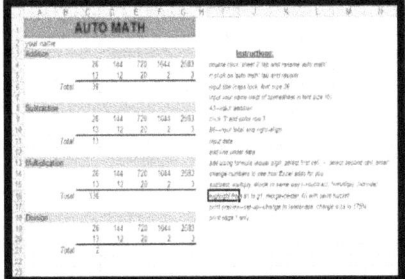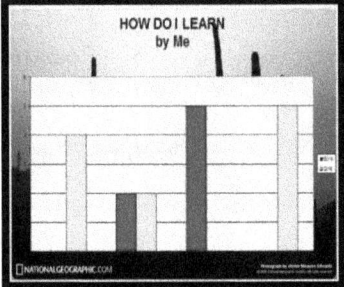

_____For this lesson, you can use Numbers, Excel, or Google Spreadsheets. If you have Chromebooks, use the online versions (Office 365 and Google Drive). If you have iPads, use the app versions but know they differ from the programs. You must adapt the project to accommodate them.
_____If you don't have MS or Google Apps, use an online tool like *Zoho Docs*.

_____Why pick spreadsheets for projects rather than DTP? Have students see if they can fill in the categories under *Spreadsheet* in *Figure 77* (see *Figure 70* in an earlier lesson for completed version). If students use workbooks, have them fill it in there:

Figure 77—Compare spreadsheets to other tools

Element	Presentation	Word processing	Spreadsheets	DTP
Purpose				
Basics				
Sentences				
Content				
Use				
Presentation				
What else				

_____This lesson includes four activities. Students can work individually or in small groups:

- *spreadsheet formulas*
- *automath*
- *charts and graphs*
- *summative spreadsheet skills*

Spreadsheet formulas

_____Build spreadsheet formulas for adding, subtracting, multiplying, and dividing (*Figures 78a-b*).
_____Formulas are composed of:

- = *(introduce formula)*
- **Function** *(add, subtract, multiply, divide)*
- **Location** *(cells function applies to)*
- *( ) (group numbers)*

_____Resulting formula will look like either *Figure 78a* or *78b*:

Figure 78a-b—Formula unpacked

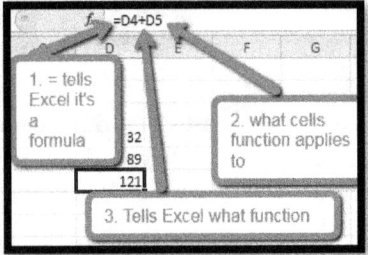 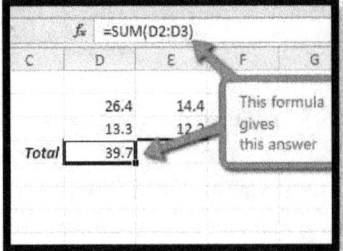

_____Open spreadsheet program. Adapt the directions to the tool you're using (side of *Figure 79*).

Figure 79—Spreadsheet project

	A	B	C	E	F
1	**T2 SPEED QUIZ**				
2		WPM	Grade	**Teach this with each speed quiz:**	
3	1	22	9	rename tab	font size
4	2	21	10	recolor tab	fill
5	3	19	6	enter data	merge cells
6	4	14	8	average column	
7	5	21	8	**Teach this with 3-week training**	
8	6	24	8	add count, min, max, median, mode	
9	7	29	10	add label for WPM and Grade	
10	8	28	10	add labels for formulas	
11	9	19	9	click on cells and see the formula	
12	10	21	10	add separater line under data	
13	11	15	8	B/I rows 21-24	
14	12	17	10	F11 graph	
15	13	16	10	Who's the slowest	
16	14	19	10	Who's the fastest	
17	15	20	10	Who got the highest grade	
18	16	18	10	Who got the lowest grade	
19	17	14	10	Format Graph	
20	18	20	10	rt click--chart options	
21	average	19.83333	9.222222	explore chart options	
22	median	19.5	10	rt-click--chart type	
23	mode	21	10	change colors	
24	count	18	18	change background	
25	max	29	10		
26	min	14	6		

_____Rename worksheet; color tab.

_____**A1**—add title (i.e., *T2 Speed Quiz*). Merge A1 and A2 to span title over two columns.

_____**A2**—add data. Resize column to fit data. 1) Sort data from smallest to largest, 2) Format speed under *35wpm* red, *at 35wpm* black, and *above 35wpm* green.

_____Remind students: Spreadsheet programs can't evaluate letters or symbols—only numbers.

_____Find average. Notice the formula in the cell: **=AVERAGE(H8:H15)**. Copy the formula and replace *AVERAGE* with *median*, or *mode* for those calculations.

_____Calculate 'Count', 'Max', 'Min'. Evaluate formulas. Why do they work?

_____If you're working in groups, discuss first in your group and then as a class: How do equations correspond to given situations? Why is it a good idea to use equations to solve problems? How can this model be replicated for other circumstances? How is precision in building formulas important? Will it always work if the formula is programmed correctly?

Auto Math

_____This project is a review of basic formulas available in most spreadsheet programs.

_____Open workbook and add a tab called 'Auto Math'; change tab color. See *Figure 80*. Zoom in if necessary.

_____**A1**—add title; merge-center A1-G1; color with paint bucket.

_____**A2**—add student or group name.

_____**A3**—type 'Addition'; select entire row; use paint bucket to color.

_____Add 'Total' next to answers; right-align cell.

_____Discuss place value. Show how to format cells for multiple decimal places.

_____Input data (not answers). Add a line beneath bottom row of data.

Figure 80—AutoMath

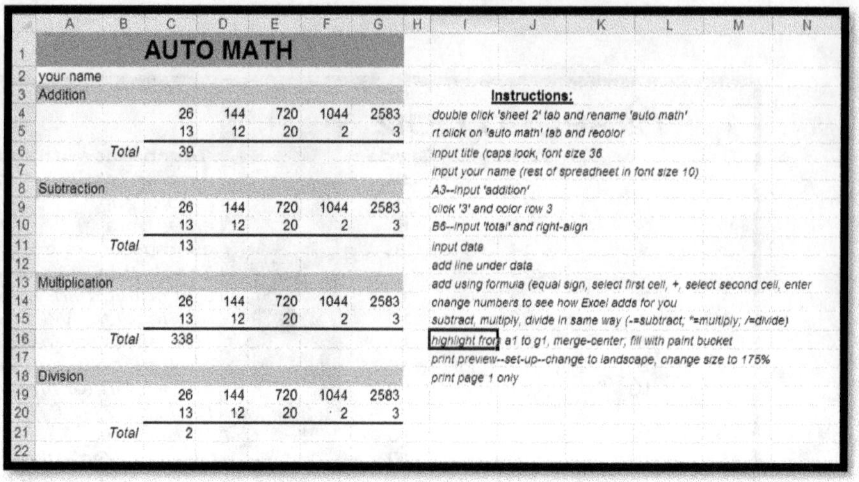

_____The cell beneath the problem (and line) is for a formula. The easy way to create a formula is:

- *start with =*
- *select the first cell with a mouse click*
- *input function—+,- /,**
- *select the second cell*
- *push enter for the answer*

_____When the answer shows up, does it look correct: 1) eyeball answer to determine if logic and experience say it is accurate, 2) use mental math, 3) guess-and-check, 4) use an algorithm.

In short: Students construct a viable argument, and then critique reasoning.

_____Share with students a teacher secret: We roughly know the answer before it comes up. If the spreadsheet is not close to what we expect, we re-evaluate. Did we input the formula correctly? Did we point to the correct cells?

As they work to solve a problem, mathematically proficient students maintain oversight of the process while attending to the details. They continually evaluate the reasonableness of their intermediate results (from Common Core).

_____If the answer is wrong, troubleshoot:

- *Is function correct (+, -, *, /)?*
- *Is formula in the right spot?*
- *Did student type answer rather than formula?*
- *Does formula start with =?*
- *Is column wide enough (or is *** in the answer cell instead of a number)?*
- *Are the cells pointed to by the formula different?*

_____Have students complete problems first with the standard algorithm and then with spreadsheet formulas.

_____In spreadsheet, students identify which are 1) dependent, and 2) independent variables. How does changing one affect the other? Analyze the relationship between these two.

_____Have students look both for general methods and shortcuts. For example, copy formula =b4+b5 and replace addition symbol with * for multiplication. Students understand that will work because they understand the importance of **repeated reasoning**.

_____Save (Ctrl+S). What's the difference between 'save' and 'save-as'? Print (Ctrl+P), share, or publish as is the custom in your class. Embed with code into blog or website if this is available (say, with Google Sheets).

Charts and Graphs

_____What the difference between a table (*Figure 81a*), a chart (can be a table or graph—*Figure 81b*), and a graph *(Figure 81c)*? How does each analyze data? Which tells more? Which is better at 'making sense' of data?

Figure 81a-c—Tables, charts, and graphs

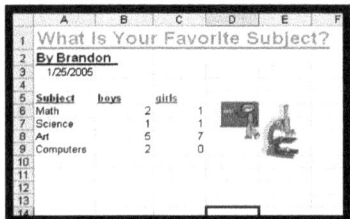 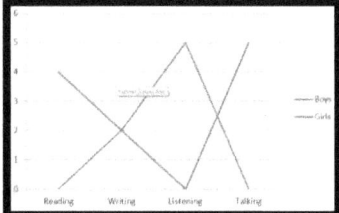 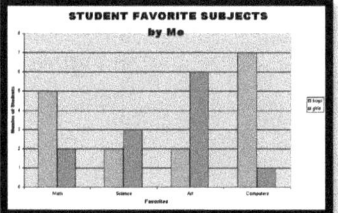

_____Open the spreadsheet program on the class screen while students open it on their digital devices. Today, the class will collect data to create a table and a graph and evaluate which is more useful.

_____Rename 'sheet 1' to subject being analyzed; change tab color. Add table name (i.e., *What is Your Favorite Subject?*), student name, date, column headings (*subject, boys, girls*), and categories (*math, science, art, computers*).

Figure 82—Graph data

_____See 'Instructions' on right side of *Figure 82* (zoom in if necessary)? If this is review, have students complete the steps independently or in groups.

_____When you reach 'Survey Class...' under 'Instructions': Collect data by a show of hands. One vote per student and no one can change their vote (allowing this complicates the process).

_____Demonstrate how to highlight data. In *Figure 82*, that includes a4 to c8 (labels, titles, and data); push *F11* to turn table into a chart similar to *Figure 84b* without the title or formatting.

_____Take a moment to study the graph. Ask students:

- *What does the x axis represent? The y axis? How does legend tie into graph?*
- *What's the ratio of the two types of favorites?*
- *What is the unit rate for the ratio of two favorites?*
- *What is the percent of girls who like reading? How does that compare to boys?*
- *Write a word problem that could be represented by the graph.*
- *If girls 'writing' is distributed equally among other choices, which is the favorite?*
- *Based on the chart, predict whether girls in your class prefer reading or listening?*
- *What is the statistical spread of data? Statistically describe the data collected?*

_____Format chart area, add title, add labels to x and y axes, change background, add student name, and format plot area. Remind students to pay attention to chart clarity. For example, in *Figure 83,* selected background has been made more transparent to make it easier to read the data. And, it has been downsized to not interfere with the x axis and y axis descriptors).

Figure 83—Chart formatted for easier reading

_____In algebraic terms, what is the 1) dependent, and 2) independent variable?

_____Use ratio language to describe a relationship between two quantities in the graph.

_____Ask students to re-form graph as a line graph, a 3D graph, or other options (*Figure 84a* is in MS Word; *Figure 84b* is in Google Sheets).

Figure 84a-b: Graph options in Excel and Google Spreadsheet

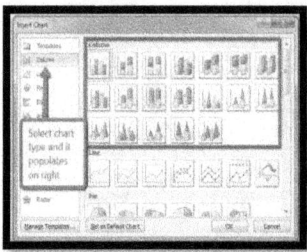 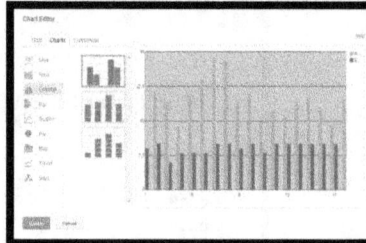

_____Is it clearer or more confusing? Which is best for this data (*Figures 85a* or *85b*)?

Figure 85a-b: Two types of graphs

_____Is there a danger in allowing the chart to interpret data for us—that we won't draw our own conclusions? That we won't critically think about data?

Summative Spreadsheet Skills

_____*Assessment 23* is a sample assessment based on learned skills (zoom in if necessary):

Assessment 22—Spreadsheet summative

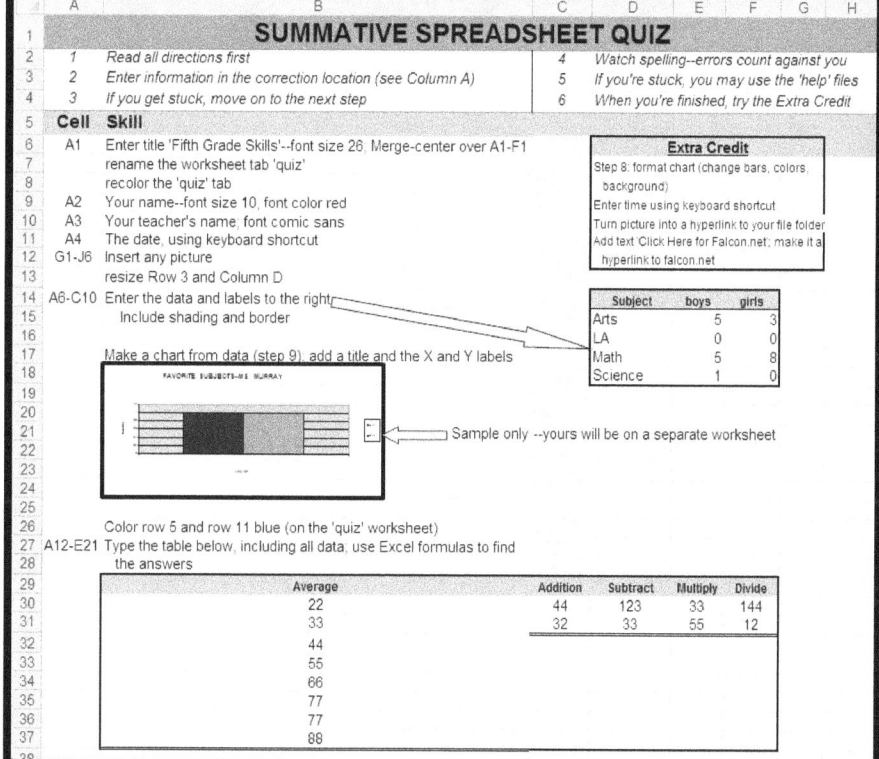

_____Students assess 1) spreadsheet knowledge, and 2) skills likely to be used in High School.
_____Here are some test-taking strategies:

- *Answer questions you know first—go back for others.*
- *Don't know the entire answer? Answer what you know.*
- *Check your work when you're done.*

_____There are two extra credit items. Use these, or add different ones suited to your students.

_____When finished, students upload the quiz to the teacher and save.

_____Give students one class to complete the assessment. Do not answer questions. Adjust assessment as needed to satisfy particular circumstances. You may choose to make this a collaborative exercise or individual.

Class exit ticket: *Tweet or blog about student thoughts on spreadsheets.*

Differentiation

- *Assign a student to enter homework and classwork due dates. Change monthly.*
- *Early finishers: visit class internet start page for websites that tie into classwork.*

_____
_____
_____
_____
_____
_____
_____
_____
_____
_____

Assessment 23—Spreadsheet summative

Spreadsheet Grading Rubric

Name_____ Teacher_____

1. Worksheet title added, font size 26____ in A1 _____

2. Title merge-centered A1-F1 _____

3. Worksheet tab renamed 'quiz' _____ recolored _____

4. Name filled in, font size 10 _____ font color red_____ in A2 _____

5. Teacher's name filled in, font comic sans_____ in A3 _____

6. Date filled in (using keyboard shortcut)_____ in A4 _____

7. Picture added (any picture) _____ in G1-J6 _____

8. Row 3 resized _____ Column D resized _____

9. Data table entered (labels, data) _____ in A6-C10 _____

10. Data table heading row shaded _____ with border _____

11. Chart created from data ____ Titles added (chart name, x/y axis labeled) ____

12. Row 5 colored blue _____ Row 11 colored blue _____

13. Data entered from 2nd table _____

14. Average calculated with formula _____

15. Addition calculated with formula _____

16. Subtraction calculated with formula _____

17. Multiplication calculated with formula _____

18. Division calculated with formula _____

19. No spelling errors _____

20. Overall _____

EXTRA CREDIT

1. *Format chart (change bars, colors, background)* _____

2. *Turn the picture into a hyperlink* _____

3. *Add text 'Click here for Falcon.net'* _____

4. *Enter time using keyboard shortcut* _____

Askatechteacher©

Lesson #13—Financial Literacy

Vocabulary	Problem solving	Skills
- Banking - Budget - Debt - Financial literacy - Stock market - Taxes	- I don't pay my own bills (that will happen soon—be ready) - I'll live at home. Won't I have plenty of money (play one of the games and see) - I already have a bank account that I manage (how's it going?)	Financial literacy Problem solving Digital citizenship
Academic Applications Math, financial literacy, economics	**Materials Required** Links to online programs	**Standards** CCSS: 9-12.A.SSE.1 NETS: 3a, 3d

Essential Question

How can finite money satisfy infinite needs?

Big Idea

Managing money has a lot to do with needs and wants

Teacher Preparation

- Collect words for Speak Like a Geek Board.
- Ensure required links are on student devices.
- Integrate domain-specific vocabulary into lesson.
- Talk with grade-level team to tie into inquiry.
- Know whether you need extra time for this lesson.
- Know which tasks not completed last class are necessary this week.

Assessment Strategies

- Worked independently
- Used good keyboarding habits
- Finished financial literacy program
- Completed warm-up, exit ticket
- Joined classroom conversations
- [tried to] solve own problems
- Left room as s/he found it
- Higher order thinking: analysis, evaluation, synthesis
- Habits of mind observed

Steps

Time required: 90-180 minutes or more, depending upon the tool selected
Class warm-up: Keyboarding on the class typing program, paying attention to posture

_____ Required skill level: Familiar with internet, financial literacy.
_____ Introduce the discussion of 'financial literacy' with a conversation about budgets, bills, and money. What about America's $21 trillion+ debt? Do students understand the consequences of unbalanced budgets? The quandary of infinite wants vs. finite dollars? Or do they think money grows on some fiscal tree that always blooms?
_____ Here are seven activities that can be completed during class:

- *Banzai*
- *Financial Football*
- *Gen-I Revolution*
- *Tools for Financial Literacy*
- *Spent*
- *Rich Kid, Smart Kid*
- *Stock Market Game*

Banzai (search *Teach Banzai*)

   Banzai is a personal finance curriculum to teach students how to prioritize spending decisions through real-life scenarios. Students start the course with a pre-test to determine a baseline for their financial literacy.
   They then engage in 32 life-based interactive scenarios covering everything from balancing a budget to adjusting for unexpected bills like car trouble or health problems. Once they've completed these exercises, they pretend that they have just graduated from high school, have a job, and must save $2,000 to start college while juggling rent, gas, groceries, taxes, car payments, and emergencies. At the end, they take a post-test to measure their improved financial literacy.
   The program is free, takes about eight hours (depending upon the student), and can include printed materials as well as digital.

Rich Kid, Smart Kid

   Rich Kid Smart Kid is a collection of four games where players struggle with real-life scenarios such as running an ice cream stand, raising money for a personal goal, allocating earned money over varied needs, (such as charity, investments, and savings), and the difference between good and bad debt.
   The Rich Kid, Smart Kid program is free, online, and can be completed in four sessions. There are also add-on low-tech options like board games.

Financial Football (from Practical Money Skills)

   Financial Football uses football strategy to teach money management. Teams answer financial questions to score touchdowns. Players pick their NFL team and opponent, the level of difficulty, the age-group, and length of play.
   The Financial Football program is free, online with stunning graphics and authentic NFL music. If you're a fantasy football fan, this is a winner.

Stock Market Game

   Stock Market Game is an online simulation of global capital markets to engage students in economics, investing and personal finance. Students set up market accounts and make decisions about buying and selling based on research and real-life events. It is played by over 600,000 students every year. Once registered, teachers have access to lesson plans and other resources to unpack the game.
   The Stock Market Game is free, suggested for grades 4-12, and delivered via website or mobile app.

Tools for Financial Literacy (at EconEdLink)

_____**EconEdLink** provides hundreds of free online lesson plans on personal finance, economics, and entrepreneurship. This includes interactive tools, videos, and game-like activities.
_____Resources are free and differentiated for learning styles with free professional development.

Gen I Revolution (search for web address or visit Ask a Tech Teacher's Financial Literacy resource page)

_____Developed for high school students, **Gen I Revolution** teaches important personal finance skills through competition with classmates. It includes sixteen Missions in which students help people in financial trouble.
_____The games are free and can be played as part of a class (with a class code) or an individual. Each mission is about thirty minutes.

Spent (from PlaySpent.org)

_____**Spent** postulates that you've lost your job, had your house foreclosed, and are down to your last $1,000. It asks, *Can you make it through the month?*
_____Students select a job and then make decisions. The program tells them the consequences of that choice. The game ends when they run out of money.

Class exit ticket: *Students blog about what they learned from the game they picked.*

Differentiation

- *Early finishers: Try another of the financial literacy websites.*
- *Try an economics link from Ask a Tech Teacher's Economic resource page.*

NOTES:

_____
_____
_____
_____
_____

Lesson #14—Internet Search and Research

Vocabulary	Problem solving	Skills
• Alt+Tab • Copyright • Creative commons • Domain • Extension • Limiters • Refine search • Spoof • Toggle	• Browser too small (double click title bar) • Browser text small (Ctrl+) • How do I switch between windows (Alt+Tab) • How do I know if a website is reliable (evaluate, analyze) • It's on Google—it must be free • Doesn't 'fair use' cover me? • This website looks professional	Problem solving Keyboarding Digital citizenship Internet searches
Academic Applications Research, varied academic subjects	**Materials Required** Backchannel device, notetaking tool, Examples of copyright and plagiarism problems	**Standards** CCSS: WHST.9-10.8 NETS: 2b, 2c, 3a-d

Essential Question

How do I gather information from digital sources, assess credibility, and integrate it while avoiding plagiarism?

Big Idea

Gather information using effective search terms; assess credibility; quote or paraphrase while avoiding plagiarism.

Teacher Preparation

- Ensure required links are on student digital devices.
- Ask what tech problems students had.
- Integrate domain-specific vocabulary into lesson.
- Talk with the grade-level team so you tie into inquiry.
- Collect words students don't understand for Speak Like a Geek Board presentations.
- Know which tasks weren't completed last class and whether they are necessary to move forward.
- Know whether you need extra time to complete this lesson with your student group.

Assessment Strategies

- Annotated workbook (if using)
- Worked independently
- Used good keyboarding habits
- Completed warm-up, exit ticket
- Joined classroom conversations
- [tried to] solve own problems
- Decisions followed class rules
- Left room as s/he found it
- Higher order thinking: analysis, evaluation, synthesis
- Habits of mind observed

Steps

Time required: **90 minutes or 50 minutes per Google class**
Class warm-up: **Keyboarding on the class typing program, paying attention to posture**

_____ Required skill level: internet basics.

_____ Put backchannel device onto class screen (Padlet, class Twitter account, or another).

_____ Today, discuss internet search and research to prepare for two projects heavily-dependent upon research: 1) a slideshow (see the lesson on *Slideshows*), and 2) a debate (see the lesson on *The Debate*). Students will collect notes which require an **understanding of how to safely and**

legally use the internet, as well as how to identify reliable websites.

_____Why research? Encourage students to dig deeper than 'for classwork' or 'to find out something I don't know'. Overarching reasons include to **build and present knowledge**.

_____In this Lesson, students cover three activities:

- *internet safety*
- *internet search and research*
- *identify reliable websites*

Internet Safety

_____Review safe internet use. This is covered in detail in the *Digital Citizenship* Lesson.

Internet Search and Research

_____Discuss internet searches. Then, try Google's 50-minute Power Search classes:

- *how to search*
- *how to interpret results*
- *how to find facts faster*
- *how to check facts*
- *how to put it all together*

_____When students finish these, discuss:

- *keywords to generate qualified hits*
- *pictures, insets, maps for more information*
- *site extensions to categorize results*
- *focusing hits by a general understanding of the topic through discussions, texts, individual interest*
- *sidebars, headings, hyperlinks to locate relevant information*

_____Practice with a topic students are discussing in class (or the topic students will debate in the lesson on *The Debate*). Say, type *Winston Churchill*—no quotes—into the search bar. Lots of hits.

_____Type "Winston Churchill" (with quotes)—less hits.

_____Now type "Winston Churchill" "British Prime Minister"—adding words to refine hits.

_____Type "Winston Churchill" –"World War II"—minus skips sites that include words "world war II".

_____Use notetaking tool to record info, being sure to:

- *rephrase in age-appropriate words*
- *credit source*

_____If you haven't already, discuss how to use online material safely and legally (see the lesson on *Digital Citizenship*). Cover:

- *citations*
- *copyrights*
- *digital rights and responsibilities*
- *plagiarism*

_____Circle back on these concepts during the year.

Identify Reliable Websites

_____Why is website credibility important? Consider:

- *How can you use websites to locate an answer to a question quickly or to solve a problem efficiently if you don't know it is reliable?*
- *How can you quote an author's reasons and evidence if you aren't convinced they're accurate?*
- *How can you integrate information from several texts knowledgeably if you don't know the websites are knowledgeable?*

_____Ask students how they pick a reliable website when they get a long list of hits. Disabuse them of the belief that reliability is related to ranking. Focus on 1) extensions, and 2) the website itself.
_____Discuss the parts of a website address (see *Figure 86*).

Figure 86—What are the parts of a website?

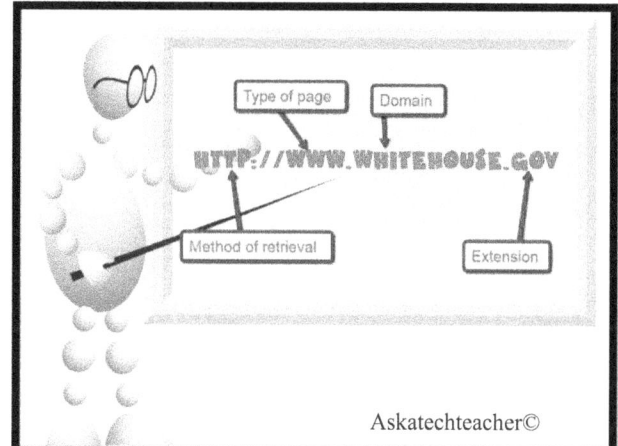

_____Discuss popular extensions. Which are most reliable?

- *.gov—limited to US governmental entities*
- *.edu—limited to educational institutions*
- *.org—used to be non-profit groups.*
- *.net—used to be Internet service providers.*
- *.com—most common extension*

_____Bring a website up on the class screen and demonstrate how you make decisions about the website's credibility based on these questions:

- *Is author(s) knowledgeable on the subject?*
- *Is the website publisher credible?*
- *Is the content accurate based on what you know?*
- *Does the content include depth in the topic?*
- *Is the information up to date?*
- *Is the website unbiased?*
- *Is the website age-appropriate? Can students understand verbiage?*

_____There are a variety of checklists available. Either do an internet search or check Ask a Tech Teacher's resource pages.

_____Have students follow along as you evaluate a website on the class screen.

_____Discuss how some websites are hoaxes and how to identify a fake. Show students a spoof site like Zapatopi. Does it look real? Why? Don't reveal truth until everyone has had their say.

_____During class, check for understanding.

Class exit ticket: ***Tweet (or comment on a class blog) about how to stay safe online.***

Differentiation

- *Practice internet research by filling in the storyboard in the Slideshow lesson and/or preparing for an upcoming debate project.*
- *Try more search skills—definitions, phone numbers, functions, convert currencies, area codes, specific file types, similar sites, time around world, * as general term.*
- *Early finishers: visit class internet start page for websites that tie into classwork.*

Lesson #15—Presentation Boards

Vocabulary	Problem solving	Skills
• Evidence • Geek • Help files • Padlet • Perspective • Virtual wall • Wonders of World	• I forgot my notes. (take a deep breath, smile, and speak!) • I'm not ready for my presentation (can you move to later date?) • My word isn't in the dictionary (what dictionary did you use?) • Definition is wrong (dig deeper)	Speaking and listening Problem solving Digital citizenship Research skills
Academic Applications Presentations, research skills	**Materials Required** Presentation Board materials, backchannel, student workbooks (if using)	**Standards** CCSS: SL.9-10.1-6 NETS: 3b-d, 6a, 6c-d

Essential Question

Why is short, focused research essential to academic success?

Big Idea

A presentation is enhanced by multimedia components

Teacher Preparation

- Sign-ups, grading rubrics for presentation board.
- Ensure required links are on student digital devices.
- Integrate domain-specific vocabulary into lesson.
- Ask what tech problems students had difficulty with.

Assessment Strategies

- Annotated workbook (if using)
- Signed up for Board
- Made presentation
- Used good keyboarding habits
- Completed warm-up, exit ticket
- Joined classroom conversations
- [tried to] solve own problems
- Higher order thinking: analysis, evaluation, synthesis
- Habits of mind observed

Steps

Time required: 10 minutes setup; 3 minutes per student, spread through grading period
Class warm-up: Keyboarding on the class typing program, paying attention to posture

_____Required skill level: Intro to Google Earth, computer basics, several years of tech.
_____Before beginning, put backchannel on class screen (Padlet, Twitter, or another).
_____Presentation Boards require quick research followed by a short class presentation that demonstrates understanding of the subject.
_____A question you'll often get is: **Can I take as long as I want on the presentation?** The answer: **No.** they must say what they need to in a limited amount of time.
_____Consider teaching this with the Twitter novel lesson—they share a goal of short, pithy communication.
_____The entire presentation takes about three minutes. Research may take longer depending upon student ability to focus on solutions and transfer prior knowledge.
_____Overview:

- *Student signs up for a topic and a presentation date.*

- *Student researches via Help files, family, friends, internet, or teacher as last resort.*
- *Student prepared to share knowledge with classmates in a three-five minute presentation.*
- *Student speaks with pertinent descriptions, facts, details, and examples. Student uses appropriate eye contact, adequate volume, and clear pronunciation. Student adapts speech to audience, context and task.*
- *Student avoids nervous movements like stuttering, giggling, playing with hair, words like 'umm' and 'you know' that demonstrate nervousness, slang, and clichés.*
- *Where required, student shares multistep procedure required to solve problem.*
- *When the presentation is completed, student takes questions. They attempt to answer even questions outside of what was researched. You can pitch in when possible.*
- *Grade is based on knowledge, presentation, confidence as well as part student plays as 'audience' in the presentations of classmates.*

_____Demonstrate a presentation.
_____Presentation Board sign-ups can be via:

- *Google Forms*
- *Google Calendar*
- *Sign-up Genius*
- *Padlet — embedded calendar*

Figure 87a-b—Presentation Board sign-ups

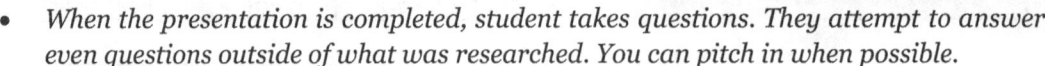
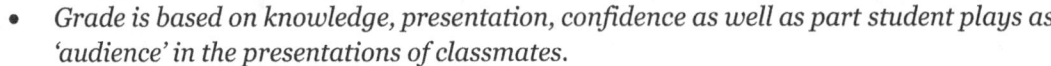

_____Research can blend already-learned material into new.
_____Wherever students acquire the information, they should assess credibility and accuracy, and provide credit where necessary.
_____At the end of this lesson, there is a grading rubric for each of three Boards, also in student workbooks if you use these. Load the rubric into a digital device. Use your annotation tool to grade students as they present and then save a screenshot of the rubric into your grading file for each student. Clear the form for the next student.
_____Each Board can be a summative assessment for a past Lesson (such as the Problem-solving Lesson Plan) or a pre-assessment to determine how much students know before beginning.

High School Technology Curriculum Book 1: Teacher Manual

_____This lesson discusses three examples of Boards but adapt the theme to your inquiry:

1. *Problem-solving Board*
2. *Speak Like a Geek*
3. *Google Earth Board*

Problem-solving Board

_____This activity builds off of the Problem-solving Lesson.
_____Students will choose one common tech problem and teach classmates how to solve it.
_____Samples of problems students may be asked to solve include (*Figure 88*—zoom in if necessary):

Figure 88—Common problems and solutions

	Problem	**Solution**
1	Deleted a file	Open Recycle Bin—right-click—restore
2.	Can't exit a program	Alt+F4
3.	Can't find a program	Type program name into Search bar
4.	Keyboard or mouse doesn't work	Plug cord into back; reboot
5.	Quick zoom in/out of doc	Ctrl+ or Ctrl-
6.	Start button is gone	Push Windows button
7.	No sound	Unmute, turn volume up, plug headphones in, Reboot
8.	Can't find a file	Start button—Search
9.	Double click doesn't work	Push enter
10.	I can't remember how to…	Try right click
11.	Shift key doesn't work	Push caps lock to disengage
12.	I can't find xxxx in document	Ctrl+F
13.	Desktop icons messed up	Right click on screen—arrange icons.
14.	Desktop icons too small	Highlight and Ctrl+ to enlarge (Too large? Ctrl-)
15.	Program frozen	Clear the dialog box; click program on taskbar
16.	I erased my text	Ctrl+Z
17.	Program closed down	Reopen from taskbar (if there)
18.	Website doesn't work	Plug URL into a different browser
19.	Internet toolbar missing	Push F11 key
20.	Internet window too small	Ctrl+ to enlarge; Ctrl- to delarge (or Ctrl+mouse wheel)
21.	Internet doesn't work	Reboot modem
22.	Document is 'read only'	Save-as under a new name
23.	How to quickly hide screen	Alt+Tab (CMD+Tab) moves away from current screen
24.	I worry about security	Cover webcam with a post-it
25.	I still worry about security	Put your mobile device in airplane mode

_____Where can you get a problem list? Try these ideas:

- *Collect student questions one year and use in next year's Board.*
- *Ask teachers what problems students face using class digital devices.*
- *Ask parents about tech problems students face with schoolwork.*
- *Ask students what they are most worried about when they use digital devices.*

_____If students have been learning technology since kindergarten, they have been learning to solve tech problems. If it is a new skill to your students, this may be a challenge. Watch their faces as you share this list. Read their body language. Adapt the difficulty to their expertise.

_____After the student presents, have them add their problem and solution to a Google Form (*Figures 89a-b*) you have designed for that purpose. Then, embed the entire list to the class website or blog to share with everyone.

Figure 89a—Google Form; 89b—answers

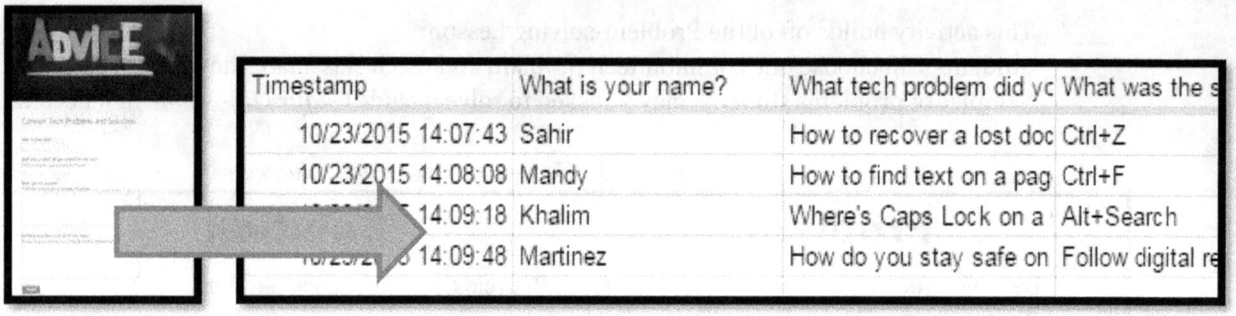

Speak Like a Geek Board

_____Do students understand the domain-specific vocabulary used in *Figure 90*? If they aren't comfortable with tech vocabulary, how will they follow directions for using websites, digital devices, or apps?

Figure 90—Domain-specific vocabulary

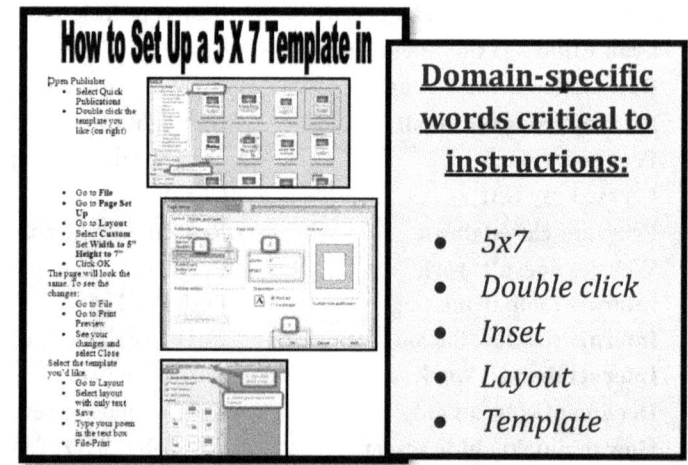

_____Help students come up with more examples of where understanding tech's specific vocabulary will make their educational journey easier. For example:

- to teach themselves to use a new program/widget/online tool
- to troubleshoot a tech problem

_____The Speak Like a Geek Presentation Board explores technology domain-specific words (pick a different topic if you prefer).

_____For six weeks prior to the Board, collect authentic tech words students don't understand onto a virtual wall like Padlet , Linoit, a Google form, or a Twitter stream with #hashtag #vocabulary. You can even use a physical Vocabulary Wall (*Figure 91c*).

Figure 91a-c—Virtual wall options

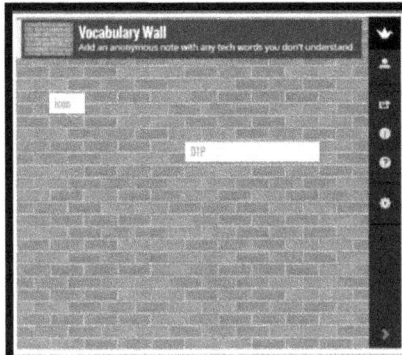 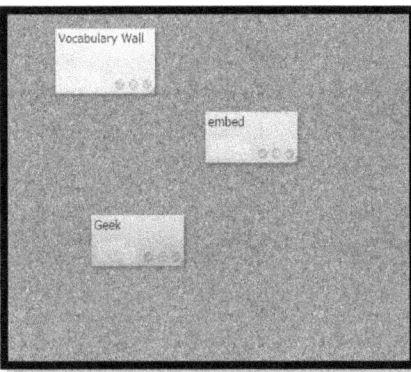 

_____Where else can you get geeky words? Try these ideas:

- *Collect from student questions one year and use them in next year's Board.*
- *Ask teachers what words students don't understand when using technology. These can relate to iPads, Chromebooks, laptops, or desktops.*
- *Ask students what words stop them from understanding technology.*

_____Show students how to find definitions:

- *Google dictionary: type Define:[tech word]. See Figure 92:*

Figure 92—Definitions from Google.com

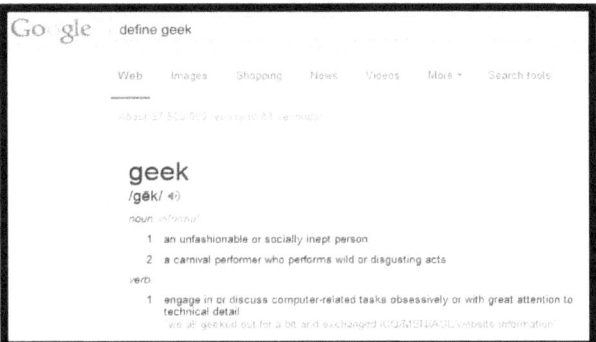

- *internet techtionary like Tech Terms*
- *family, friends, geeky siblings*
- *native grammar tools such as right click for dictionary or thesaurus*

Google Earth Board

_____The Google Earth Presentation Board builds off of the *Google Earth Lit Trip* lesson plan.
_____Student finds a Google Earth location that fits the Board theme.

_____Student researches the location and finds a Fascinating Fact about it to share with the group.
_____Preparation time is limited (see earlier discussion) by design.
_____During presentation, student opens Google Earth on class screen (while classmates open on their digital device), finds location, and placemarks it. In Placemark dialogue box (see *Figure 93*), student adds name of place and Fascinating Fact. Optional: customize placemark.

Figure 93—Google Earth placemark

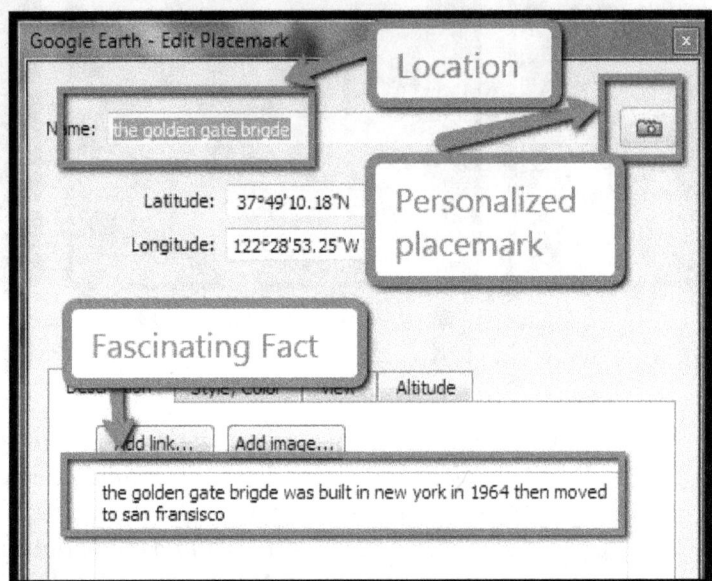

_____Popular Google Earth locations you can use for Board:

- *locations students go during the school year*
- *locations of student homes or their ancestral homeland*
- *locations of the setting in their favorite literary book*
- *student choice*

Class exit ticket: **Blog or Tweet about the Board presentations students watched today.**

Differentiation

- *Add homework and presentation due dates to class online calendar.*
- *Early finishers: visit class internet start page for websites that tie into classwork.*

Assessment 24—Presentation Board assessments

Presentation Grading (General Characteristics)

Name_____ **Teacher**_____

Face audience, eye contact _____

Talk to audience _____

Introduce yourself _____

Introduce topic _____

Speak loudly and clearly _____

Displays good presence _____

No slang or nervous gestures _____

Seemed knowledgeable _____

No 'umms' or stuttering _____

Answer audience questions _____

Audience can help if necessary _____

Overall _____

Speak Like a Geek Grading Extras

Name: _____ *Class:* _____

WORD DEFINED: _____

Knew word _____

Knew definition _____

Used word in sentence _____

Sentence showed student knew definition _____

Askatechteacher©

Lesson #16—Slideshow Summative

Vocabulary	Problem solving	Skills
• Alt+Tab • Animation • Design • GIF • Storyboard • Transition • Wrap	• How do I save with an online tool (or an app on the iPad)? • I forgot some of these skills (think back) • I forgot my storyboard (did you save it to the Cloud?) • It takes time to toggle between the storyboard and slideshow (Alt+Tab)	Add music to slideshow (if using) Problem solving Keyboarding Digital citizenship Slideshows Storyboard
Academic Applications Research, literacy, history	**Materials Required** Slideshow tool, student workbooks (if using)	**Standards** CCSS: WHST.9-10.6 NETS: 1d, 6a-d

Essential Question

How do I share with classmates?

Big Idea

Audio, visual, design layout, images and text all contribute to communicating ideas

Teacher Preparation

- Ensure required links are on student digital devices.
- Integrate domain-specific tech vocab into lesson.
- Talk with grade-level team so you tie into inquiry.
- Know whether you need extra time for this lesson.
- Ask what tech problems students had difficulty with.
- Collect words for Speak Like a Geek Board.
- Know which tasks weren't completed last class and whether they are necessary to move forward.

Assessment Strategies

- Annotated workbook (if using)
- Completed slideshow
- Worked independently
- Used good keyboarding habits
- Completed warm-up, exit ticket
- Joined classroom conversations
- [tried to] solve own problems
- Decisions followed class rules
- Left room as s/he found it
- Higher order thinking: analysis, evaluation, synthesis
- Habits of mind observed

Steps

Time required: 135 minutes
Class warm-up: *storyboard ready to use for slideshow*

_____Required skills: Enough knowledge to prepare a storyboard.
_____Review storyboard (see *Assessment* at end of lesson). What is a storyboard?
_____You can complete the storyboard during class or expect students to bring them to class. If you're using workbooks, students can fill the sample in that's included there.
_____The topic should fit grade-level inquiry—history, science, literacy. This should not require research, rather be completed using information the student already has from class, books, other resources, or personal knowledge.

_____When finished, discuss the difference between writing with a slideshow tool and a word processing program. *Figure 94* provides a few ideas. What else would you add? If using the workbooks, students can fill in the blanks included in their copy.

Figure 94—Presentation tool vs. word processing

Element	Presentation program	Word processing
Purpose	Share a presentation	Share words
Basics	Graphics-based	Text-based
	Design is important to content	Design is secondary to content
	Layout communicates	Layout may detract from words
	Few words, lots of images	Primarily words communicate
Sentences	Bulleted, phrases	Full grammatical sentences
Content	Slides cover basics, to remind presenter what to say	Thorough discussion of a topic. Meant to be complete document
Use	As a back-up to presentation	As complete resource
Presentation	Speaker looks at audience	Speaker reads from document

_____ Remind students of slideshows completed in earlier grades (*Figure 95a-c*) if students did this:

Figure 95a-c Sample slideshows from earlier grades

_____Open slideshow program your school uses and ask volunteers to review basics, layout, screen, tools, ribbons, and place savers.

_____The tool may be PowerPoint or web-based like Google Slides, Office 365, Keynote, Haiku Deck, Kizoa, or another.

_____If you use iPads, you may use the app version of PowerPoint, Keynote, or Google Slides. You may also use Haiku Deck, Adobe Voice, or Adobe Slate:

Figure 96a-c—Slideshows in various digital tools

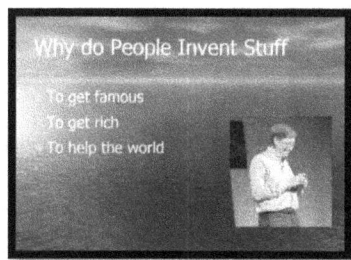  

_____Adapt the instructions in this lesson to the program you use.
_____Show samples of slideshows.

High School Technology Curriculum Book 1: Teacher Manual

_____Now get started by adding nine slides to the blank slideshow (or the number you are using).
_____Students copy information from their storyboard to the slideshow. Remind them to use Alt+Tab to toggle between the two. Demonstrate how much easier it is.
_____**Slide #1**—add title and student name (see *Figures 97a-c*):

Figure 97a-c—Slideshow covers in various slideshow programs

_____**Slide #2**—'Table of Contents'. Bulleted beneath, add topics from storyboard (*Figures 98a-c*):

Figure 98a-c—Table of Contents

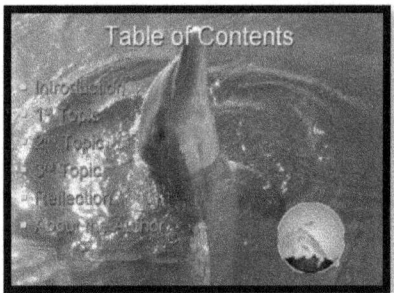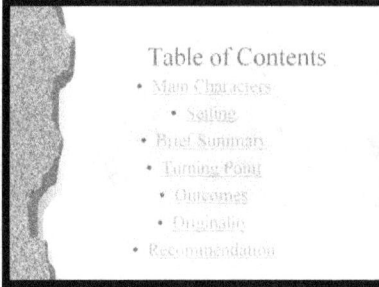

_____Link each Table of Contents topic to its slide (as can be done in PowerPoint and Google Slides) for easy maneuverability.
_____**Slide #3**—'Introduction'—topic and student qualifications for teaching it (*Figures 99a-b*).

Figure 99a-b—Introduction in two digital tools

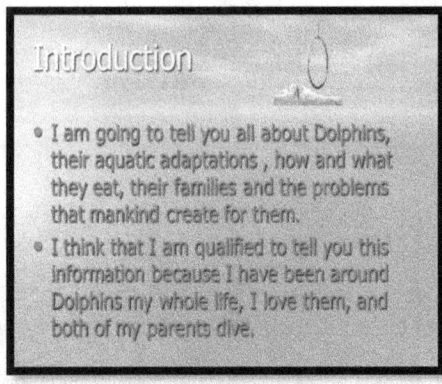

_____**Slide #4-7**—add each Table of Contents topic to a separate slide with bullet points from the storyboard summarizing research (*Figure 100a*) or a graphic organizer (or a table) that visually explains the topic (*Figures 100b-c*).

Figure 100a—Topic and subpoints; 100b-c—graphic organizer

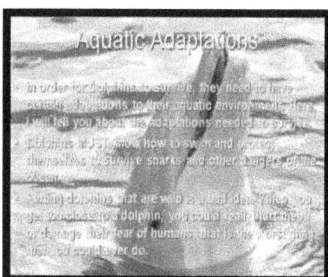 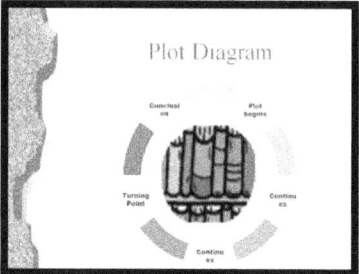 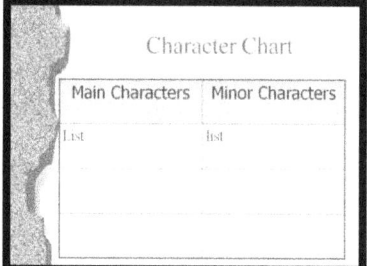

_____**Slide #8**—reflect on how topic affects student life and the world in general. Show an understanding of other perspectives and culture.

_____**Slide #9**—add 'About the author' and three points audience should know (*Figures 101a-b*):

Figure 101a-b—About the author

_____Add additional items listed in the rubric. These won't be taught. Students should know how to complete them and can ask for help if they get stuck. *Figure 102* is a thumbnail; find *a* full-size assessment at end of Lesson:

Figure 102—Slideshow rubric

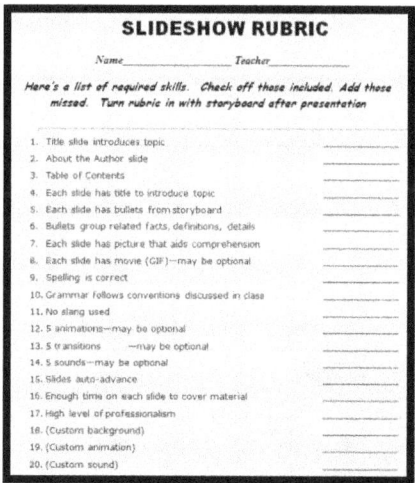

_____Make sure everything is included and that the slideshow runs smoothly from the first slide to the last. Students can work with partners. Does the partner feel the slideshow provides ample evidence to support the topic? Does all media – text, pictures, audio, video – function? Does it all deliver the same message?

Class exit ticket: ***Practice slideshow to be sure each slide provides sufficient time for the material to be shared during the presentation.***

Differentiation

- Add 'Custom Animation' to pictures/words. Select custom path or create one. Warn students not to make paths so complicated they distract from message.
- Add a song that plays from start to finish. Students can use their own song (that fits the slideshow theme) or use one from a collection you provide.
- If using Google Slideshow, embed slideshow into student blog, wiki, website to share with classmates. Have students view these and comment on the work of friends.
- Early finishers: visit class internet start page for websites that tie into classwork.

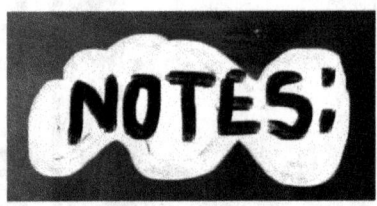

Assessment 25—Slideshow storyboard

Storyboard

Your name: _____ Your teacher: _____

Slide 1:   Cover

Slide 2:   Table of Contents

Slide 3:   Introduction
- _Your name_____
- _Your topic_____
- _Why you're qualified to discuss this topic_

Slide 4:   3 Topics of Discussion
- _____
- _____
- _____

Slide 5:   1st Topic and 3 subpoints
- _____
- _____
- _____

Slide 6:   2nd Topic and 3 subpoints
- _____
- _____
- _____

Slide 7:   3rd Topic and 3 subpoints:
- _____
- _____
- _____

Slide 8:   Reflect on how this topic affects your life
- _____
- _____
- _____

Slide 9:   About Author—three things about you we should know
- _____
- _____
- _____

Assessment 26—Slideshow presentation rubric

SLIDESHOW RUBRIC

Name_____ Teacher_____

Here's a list of required skills. Check off those included. Add those missed. Turn rubric in with storyboard after presentation

1. Title slide _____
2. About the Author slide _____
3. Table of Contents slide _____
4. Each slide has title _____
5. Each slide has bullets from storyboard _____
6. Bullets group related facts, definitions, details _____
7. Each slide has picture _____
8. Spelling is correct _____
9. Grammar follows conventions discussed in class _____
10. No slang _____
11. Slides auto-advance _____
12. Enough time on each slide to cover material _____
13. High level of professionalism _____
14. 5 animations—may be optional _____
15. 5 transitions—may be optional _____
16. 5 sounds—may be optional _____
17. Each slide has movie (GIF)—may be optional _____
18. (Custom background) _____
19. (Custom animation) _____
20. (Custom sound or music) _____
21. **Class presentation** _____
    a. **Face audience** _____
    b. **Talk to audience** _____
    c. **Introduce yourself and topic** _____
    d. **Speak loud enough** _____
    e. **No 'umms' or stuttering** _____

Lesson #17—Slideshows: Presentations

Vocabulary	Problem solving	Skills
• Animation • Auto-advance • Mouse click • Rubric • Slideshow • Transition	• Slide too fast (change transition speed) • Slideshow doesn't advance (spacebar) • I'm not ready for my presentation (can you move to later date?) • Why can't I read my slideshow (that's not this presentation method)	Speaking/listening Presenting with a slideshow
Academic Applications Speaking and listening, many topics	**Materials Required** Class projector, student slideshows	**Standards** CCSS: SL.9-10.4-6 NETS: 6d

Essential Question

How do I change the way I communicate for different audiences, for different purposes?

Big Idea

Technology provides student with tools to adapt to audience, task, and purpose

Teacher Preparation

- Have projector to display student slideshows.
- Integrate domain-specific vocabulary into lesson.
- Know whether you need extra time for lesson.
- Invite parents and grade-level team for presentations.
- Know which tasks weren't completed last class and whether they are necessary to move forward.

Assessment Strategies

- Followed class guidelines for speaking and listening
- Completed presentation
- Completed warm-up, exit ticket
- Joined classroom conversations
- [tried to] solve own problems
- Decisions followed class rules
- Left room as s/he found it
- Higher order thinking: analysis, evaluation, synthesis
- Habits of mind observed

Steps

Time required: **90 minutes**
Class warm-up: **make sure slideshow presentation is ready to go**

_____Required skills: Completion of a slideshow.
_____Explain grading (see *Assessment* at end of lesson:

- *come prepared, having practiced material*
- *keep eyes on the audience, glancing at the screen only when necessary*
- *summarize where necessary; use the bullet item to remember additional information*
- *speak loudly so the whole room can hear*
- *be prepared to respond to specific questions*
- *always sound interested and knowledgeable about the topic*

_____Audience should:

- *pay attention*
- *not fidget*
- *be polite*
- *make comments that contribute to the discussion*
- *link comments to presentation and others' remarks*

_____Presenter grade is based in part on how good s/he is as an audience.

_____When finished, presenter takes three questions. Vary side of the room questions come from, boy/girl, and not the same people called on for the last presentation.

_____Audience must confine questions to what presenter discussed.

If the question comes up as to why the presenter made a mistake, remind audience questions are positive, upbeat—everyone makes mistakes. Focus on what sparked curiosity.

Class exit ticket: ***Thank attendees for joining student in this presentation.***

Differentiation

- *Students can videotape their presentation.*

Assessment 27—Slideshow presentation rubric

SLIDESHOW RUBRIC

Name_____ **Teacher**_____

Face audience _____

Talk to audience _____

Introduce yourself _____

Introduce your topic _____

Speak loudly and clearly _____

No 'umms', slang, stuttering _____

Answer questions _____

Slide show progresses smoothly _____

Lesson #18—Infographics

Vocabulary	Problem solving	Skills
• Font • Infographic • Layout • Multiple intelligence • Piktochart • Visual appeal • Visual organizer	• Browser toolbar disappeared (F11) • Browser text too small (Ctrl+ to zoom in) • I only want part of webpage (highlight, right-click, print) • It's difficult toggling between sources (Alt+Tab) • I forgot information (use what you can)	Infographics Problem solving Keyboarding Digital citizenship Speaking/listening
Academic Applications Any academic topic—history, science, literacy	**Materials Required** Infographic topic, infographic links	**Standards** CCSS: W.9-10.6 NETS: 3d, 4b, 6c-d

Essential Question

How does tech help me communicate as a visual learner?

Big Idea

Use visual communications to clearly share ideas

Teacher Preparation

- Have a list of topics for infographic.
- Ensure links for infographic templates are available.
- Know whether you need extra time for this lesson.
- Integrate domain-specific tech vocabulary into lesson.
- Know which tasks weren't completed last class and whether they are necessary to move forward.

Assessment Strategies

- Displayed creativity and critical thinking in completing project
- Worked independently
- Completed warm-up
- Joined classroom conversations
- [tried to] solve own problems
- Decisions followed class rules
- Left room as s/he found it
- Higher order thinking: analysis, evaluation, synthesis
- Habits of mind observed

Steps

Time required: 270 minutes
Class warm-up: Select a topic from a teacher-provided list for today's infographic

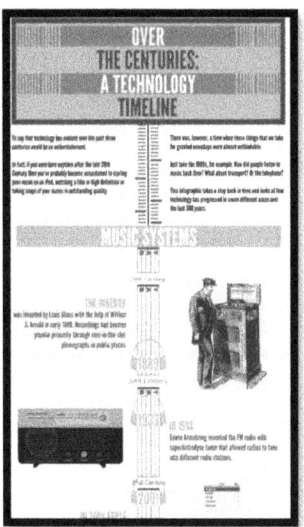

_____Required skills: knowledge of topic; facility with internet searches and internet in general; completion of several graphic organizers. If students have been studying technology for a few years, they are prepared. For new students, adapt expectations.

_____Use a backchannel program to encourage class participation.

_____This lesson uses an infographic to summarize what students learned about a particular topic.

_____Divide class into groups. Give them five minutes to organize thoughts on one topic below:

- Discuss learning styles—logical (mathematical), visual, linguistic, kinesthetic, musical, interpersonal intrapersonal, naturalistic, existential. This can be discussed anecdotally by students. Personal experiences are fine.
- Discuss what it means to organize ideas visually rather than textually? Hint: It's more than pictures. Think of examples completed in the past (Venn Diagrams, org charts, pyramids). What's the difference between sharing via 'text' and 'visually'? Would blending both be more effective?
- How do visual organizers:

- build content knowledge
- use media strategically
- understand perspectives

_____Student groups share their thoughts with classmates, abiding by class speaking and listening skills. If you have time, allow questions.

_____Why are you taking time to discuss student learning style? Why is that important?

_____Ask students to take the following two surveys to determine what their best learning style is (or check Ask a Tech Teacher's resource pages):

- *Edutopia's Multiple Intelligences quiz*
- *North Carolina State University's Learning Styles quiz*

_____Discuss infographics:

- *What are they?*
- *How can organization and style be appropriate to audience, task purpose?*
- *How can they encourage students to interact and collaborate?*

_____They are NOT graphic organizers (see *Figures 103a-c*). Graphic organizers are:

Figure 103a-c—Graphic organizers examples

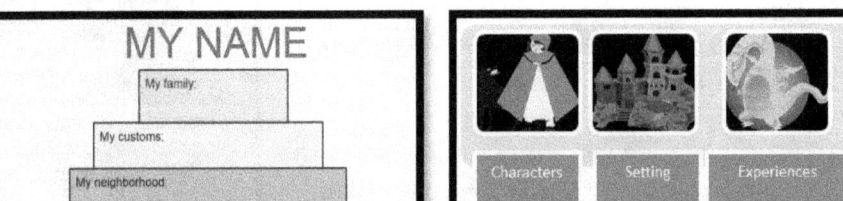

- *much simpler*
- *much quicker*
- *much less information*

_____Before continuing, review legalities of using internet images (in-depth discussion in *Online Image Legalities* lesson).

_____Infographics are popular because they sum up a great volume of information that would take reader hours to process. Layout and visual appeal are as important as information.

_____In *Figures 104a-c*, how does the layout make you want to look closer?

Figure 104a-c—Sample infographics

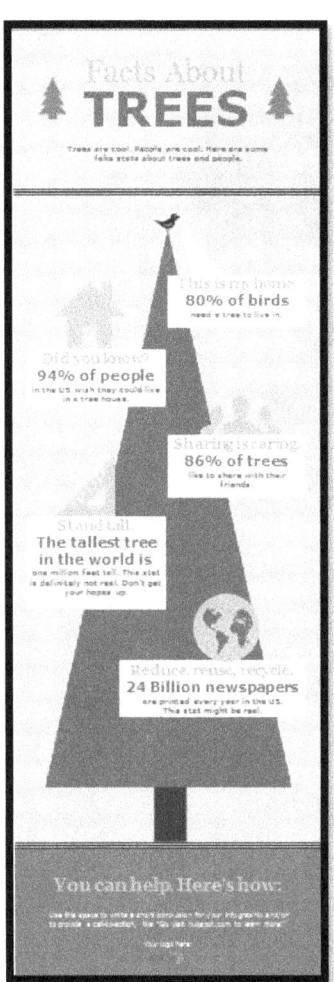 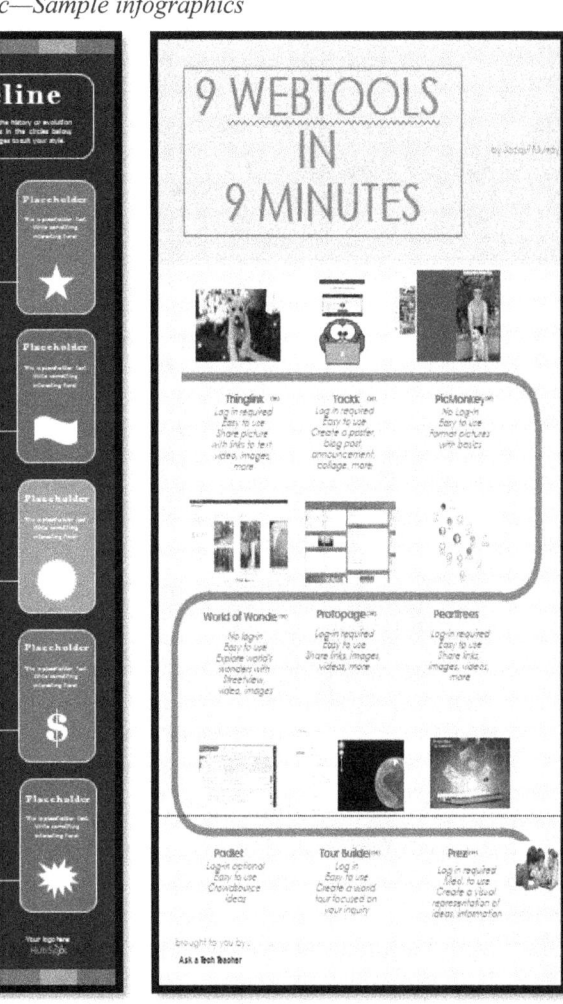

Credit for Figures 104a-b: Hubspot

_____Working in groups, students select a topic that supports class inquiry. Alternatively, all groups could create infographics on the same topic.

_____Data will include information student has learned already on the topic. This is an opportunity to share knowledge, not perform additional research. Exception: Students can take 'a few' minutes to verify data. This could include:

- *facts*
- *figures*
- *essential opinions*
- *organic information*
- *primary sources*

_____In groups, students create their infographic using a template from one of these options or another of your choice (Google for addresses):

- *Canva*
- *Easel.ly*
- *Infogr.am (free)*
- *Piktochart*

Figure 105a-b—Infographic in varied webtools

_____Remind students to provide citations: 1) to give credit, and 2) so classmates can dig deeper into the topic.

_____When done, students share their infographic with class and discuss:

- *the relevance of information*
- *use of multiple sources*
- *selection of credible sources*
- *use of academic and domain-specific language*
- *paraphrased quotes and gave credit where required*

_____Optional: Vote on the most effective in each of these categories with a poll created in Google Forms or another.

_____Continually throughout class, check for understanding.

Class exit ticket: None.

Differentiation

- *Blend this into the 'Internet Search and Research' lesson: Students research a topic and then create an infographic sharing what they've uncovered.*
- *Visit Infographics Archive/ for an archive of infographics.*
- *Instead of an Infographic, students can create a Prezi if they haven't used these before. Goal remains the same: Educate readers visually.*

Lesson #19—Google Earth Lit Trip

Vocabulary	Problem solving	Skills
• Dialogue box • Geek • Lat-long • Overlay • Placemark • Street view • Synopsis • Voice-over	• How do I play a GE tour? (click tour title, not a location in tour) • All locations aren't there (copy-paste from temp folder) • Geography didn't affect this story (really?) • My story isn't about geography or setting (analyze actions, critically consider plot, characters)	GE lit tour Problem solving Keyboarding Digital citizenship Google Earth
Academic Applications Writing, research, literacy, geography	**Materials Required** Backchannel device, novel being read in class, Google Earth or Google Maps	**Standards** CCSS: WHST.9-10.6 NETS: 3c, 3d, 6a-d

Essential Question

How does geography bring learning to life?

Big Idea

Understanding the world's geography helps explain events

Teacher Preparation

- Ensure students have read a book for Lit Trip.
- Ensure required links are on student digital devices.
- Integrate domain-specific vocabulary into lesson.
- Talk with grade-level team so you tie into inquiry.
- Cover tech problems students have difficulty with.
- Know whether you need extra time for this lesson.
- Know which tasks weren't completed last class and whether they are necessary to move forward.

Assessment Strategies

- Completed GE lit trip
- Annotated workbook (if using)
- Worked independently
- Used good keyboarding habits
- Completed warm-up, exit ticket
- Joined classroom conversations
- [tried to] solve own problems
- Decisions followed class rules
- Left room as s/he found it
- Higher order thinking: analysis, evaluation, synthesis
- Habits of mind observed

Steps

Time required: 135 minutes
Class warm-up: Keyboarding on the class typing program, paying attention to posture

_____Required skill level: Google Earth basics.
_____Open backchannel on class screen.
_____Students create a Google Earth (or Google Maps) tour about a book they're reading. Mark locations around the planet and use placemark dialogue boxes to provide detail.
_____If using an iPad, try the Google Earth app but adapt for differences from the software.

_____What do students know about Google Earth from prior years (see *Figures 106a-c*)?

Figure 106a-c—Google Earth projects

_____Share several Google Earth tours created by last year students to review how tours work. Notice 1) tour locations are in the same file folder and, 2) tour goes in order of selections.

_____Student volunteers to review Google Earth toolbar, sidebar, 'My Places', 3D layer, and how to move around the globe Another student explains how to add a location and activate latitude-longitude grid lines. Discuss uses of lats and longs. Zoom in to investigate exact locations of several landmarks. Have a third student show how to measure distance using the ruler.

_____Each student makes a folder under 'Places' with their name. For example: 'Chelsea's Book'.

_____Find geographic location where book starts. Explore with 3D and Street view. Customize a placemark (character or student picture to mark all locations on student tour) and label it with the book title. Provide a synopsis in placemark dialogue. See *Figure 107a* (zoom in if necessary):

Figure 107a—Google Earth placemark; 107b—sample GE tour

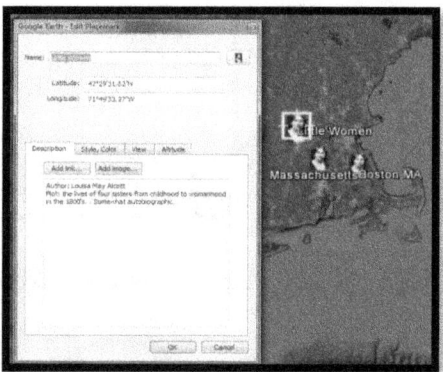 

_____Add five-ten more placemarks that mark high points, important events, significant locations. Tell the story through notes written in placemark dialogue box. Include:

- *a plot summary based on geographic location*
- *a character introduction based on their home or places visited during the story*
- *quotes from book with citations*
- *academic words student didn't know and their meaning (defined by story context)*
- *key concepts about important characters, plot points, settings*
- *insight into effect of geography on story*
- *relevant facts, definitions, concrete details, quotations, examples*
- *other information on characters, plot, setting, story arc, and more where relevant to summarization of story*

_____Be sure all placemarks are saved to the student 'My Tour' folder in the correct order. Show students how to re-order their appearance in the tour.

_____Each class period, back up folder to student digital portfolio. This is critical if school digital device is used by multiple students.

_____By end of the tour, viewers should have an overview of book, characters, setting, plot, events, and how geography impacted the story. See *Figure 107b* for a (very) short example tour.

_____At least three placemarks must include images as well as dialogue.

_____If using the internet, remind students to do so safely and legally, as good digital citizens.

Figure 108a—Placemark with image; 108b—with overlay

_____At least three placemarks must include links to resource sites that support events in the book. This will allow interested readers to dig deeper.

_____Add one image overlay to represent characters in story. See *Figure 108b* for an example.

_____Measure distance between two locations using the Google Earth ruler. This data should be relevant to story and included in placemark dialogue (for example, *how far did a character travel to get to the scene of the crime?*). See *Figure 109* for an example (zoom in if needed).

_____When student thinks they are done, review with a neighbor using rubric at the end of the Lesson. Are all elements included? Is tour clear? Does neighbor understand story? Does tour run well? Plan, revise, edit, and rewrite as needed.

Figure 109—Measure distances in GE

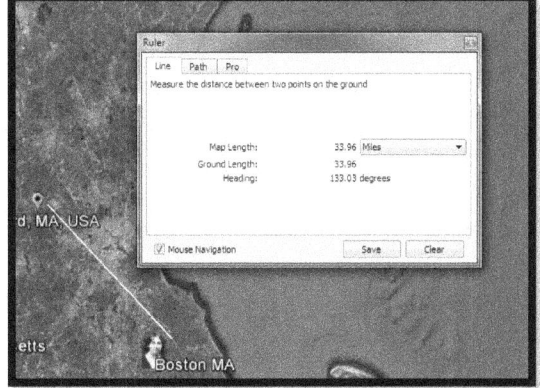

_____Optional: Record tour using GE's 'Record a Tour' tool. You can also add a voice-over.

_____Save/publish/share as is the custom in your school.

_____Embed tour with a reflection to student blog or website. Discuss how geography was critical to story events and how Google Earth provided the right canvas for sharing ideas. How did this digital tool enable a better/stronger/more relevant discussion on issues than word processing or slideshows? Thoughts should be objective, on-point, with precise and domain-specific language appropriate to the task, audience, and purpose.

Class exit ticket: *Watch the tour of several classmates.*

> **Differentiation**
>
> - If possible, use 'Show historic imagery' button on toolbar to go back in time to date of literary piece before creating lit tour.
> - Create a 'Book Reviews' page on class website where students can add a summary of their book and a link to their Lit Tour. This can also include book reviews developed with other web tools and projects in the book. Assign a student to enter due date in class calendar.
> - Early finishers: visit class internet start page for websites that tie into classwork.

Assessment 28—GE Lit Tour rubric

Google Earth Lit Tour Grading Rubric

Your name: _____ Teacher: _____

GE Tour — 10 points
- File folder has student name
- Tour runs
- Recorded tour entered into wiki page
- Sufficient placemarks, in order in tour
- 3 image overlays
- 3 placemarks with images included
- 3 placemarks with links to deeper info

Placemarks — 11 points
- Includes settings in book
- Include info about characters, plot

Each Placemark… — 3 points
- Placed correctly (geographically)
- Labeled correctly (with location name)
- Customized with student picture
- Includes information

Overall Professional Look — 6 points

Lesson #20—Online Image Legalities

Vocabulary	Problem solving	Skills
• Copyright • Creative Commons • Fair use • Filter • Layer • Macro • Transparencies	• Project disappeared (use search) • There's a watermark on picture I picked (Use one not copyrighted) • I found other tools I like (try them!) • This takes a while (it's not a race) • I want to merge two pictures (be a problem solver)	Audio hoaxes Problem solving Keyboarding Digital citizenship Online image legalities
Academic Applications Writing, research	**Materials Required** Backchannel device, image-editing tools, row graphics, links to plagiarism materials—if any	**Standards** CCSS: W.9-10.6 NETS: 2b-c

Essential Question

Why should I learn to create my own unique images rather than use those of others? I'm not creative.

Big Idea

Create images to protect me from plagiarizing others' work.

Teacher Preparation

- Talk with grade-level team so you tie into inquiry.
- Cover tech problems students have difficulty with.
- Ensure required links are on student digital devices.
- Integrate domain-specific vocabulary into lesson.
- Collect words for Speak Like a Geek Board.
- Know whether you need extra time for lesson.
- For general knowledge on plagiarism, read "Plagiarism: What it is and how to identify it" at the end of this lesson.

Assessment Strategies

- Annotated workbook (if using)
- Worked independently
- Completed project
- Used good keyboarding habits
- Completed warm-up, exit ticket
- Joined classroom conversations
- [tried to] solve own problems
- Decisions followed class rules
- Left room as s/he found it
- Higher order thinking: analysis, evaluation, synthesis
- Habits of mind observed

Steps

Time required: **45 minutes**
Class warm-up: **Keyboarding on the class typing program, paying attention to posture**

_____ Required skill level: using online images
_____ Before beginning, put backchannel device onto the class screen to track comments. Show how to access if necessary.
_____ This Lesson is a good prequel to Lesson 21 and 22 on image editing. It reminds students that online images aren't always free and can't always be trusted to be what they appear.
_____ Discuss why make your own artwork. Creativity? Maybe to find exactly what you want?
_____ How about to avoid plagiarizing? Discuss legalities of using creative work from online sources. Discuss when students can and can't use artwork they find online.

_____Review copyright law (discussed in the *Internet Search and Research* lesson). What are the consequences of infringing copyrights? Some people want to share work and collaborate with others. Watch and discuss *Wanna Work Together* about Creative Commons licensing (available on Creative Commons website).

_____Watch and discuss copyright: *Forever Less a Day* (available on YouTube).

_____Discuss how students can find if an image they created is being used online. If they drag-drop it into either of these two websites, it shows all the online sites where it appears:

- *TinEye*
- *Google Images*

Figure 110a-b—Student drawing used without permission

_____*Figure 110a* was drawn by a student and posted to her/his public website to share with family and friends. Without her/his knowledge, it was used forty-seven times (*Figure 110b*), not always in places s/he or her/his parents would approve.

_____What could s/he do? Add a copyright notice to website, announcing that all media contained on the website are protected by copyright laws and cannot be used without permission.

_____Copyrights range from public domain—where creative work can be used without permission or notification—to intensely private—where they are available only to view, on the host website. *Figure 112* is an example of two.

_____When searching for images, adjust the search engine to provide only those that are freely available in the public domain. *Figure 111* shows how to find this option in Google:

Figure 111—Copyright protections on browsers

_____So, besides reasons mentioned above, protection against misusing creative work of others is a significant reason for individual artwork. For the next few weeks, students will be exposed to a variety of methods for creating just that.

Figure 112—Two copyrighted images

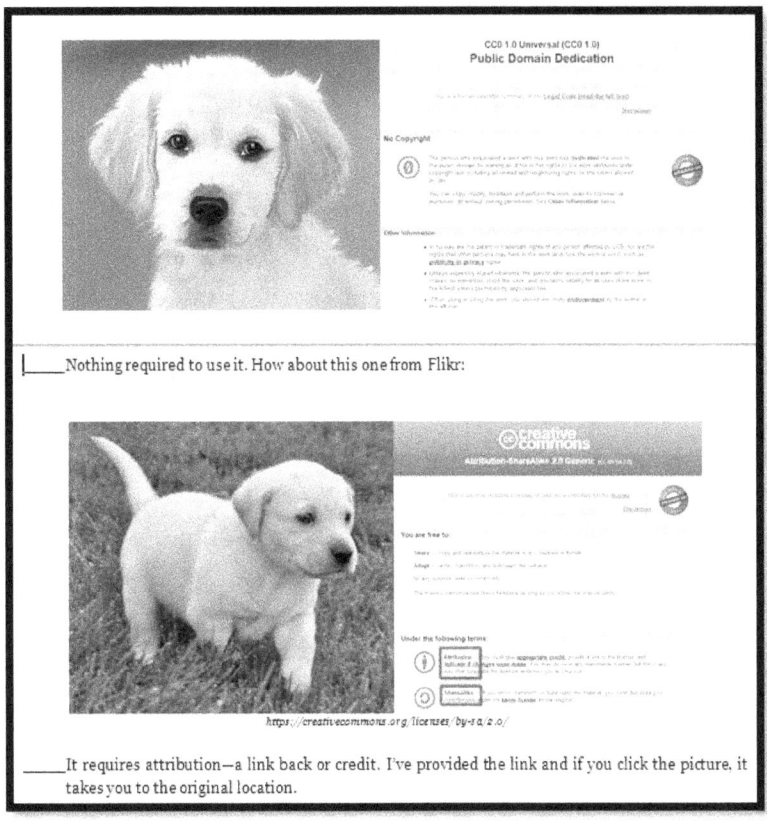

_____ Before finishing with this discussion of copyrights and the law, review the paraphrased law discussed in the lesson on *Digital Citizenship*:

Figure 113—Digital law—rephrased

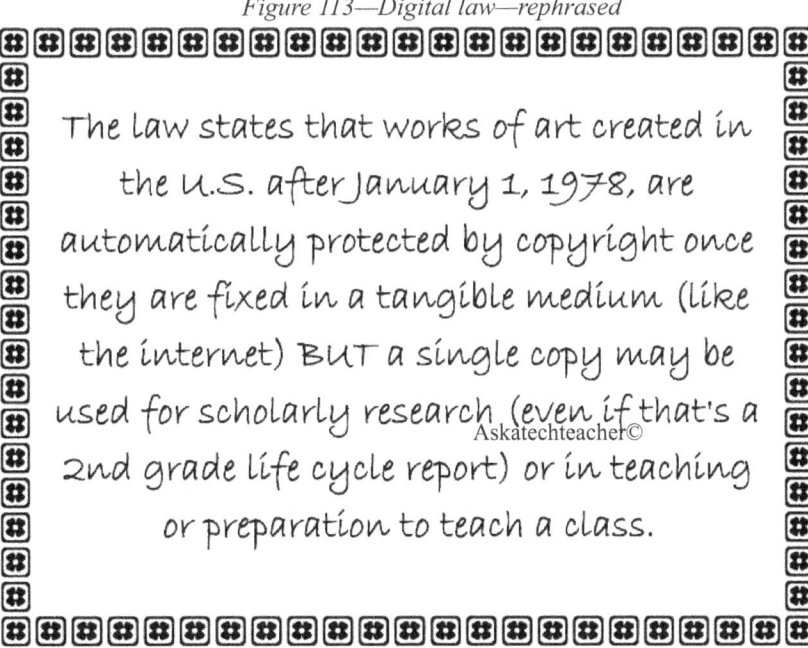

_____Look at *Figure 114*. Did President Roosevelt really ride a moose across a river?

Figure 114—Real or a hoax?

_____In *Figures 115a-b:* Was the tree added to or erased from the original photo?

Figure 115a-b: Add or remove pieces from a photo

_____Discuss as a class whether *Figures 116a-c* are accurate—and how do you know? It's no surprise photos are not accepted as proof in court.

Figure 116a-c—Real or hoax pictures?

_____Show 'War of the Worlds' — a famous video hoax. Discuss how it was confused with reality if listeners missed the first ten minutes.

Class exit ticket: ***Tweet student thoughts about copyrights, use of online images, and how they protect their creative genius.***

Differentiation

- Early finishers: visit class internet start page for websites that tie into classwork.

Article 17—Plagiarism

Plagiarism: What it is and how to identify it

Man is a thinking creature. We like evaluating ideas and sharing thoughts. That's a good thing. The more we collaborate, the smarter we all become.

Implicit in this is that we don't claim someone else's ideas as our own. In fact, it's illegal to do this. Rea

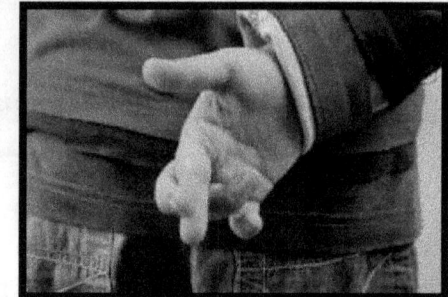

"The law states that works of art created in the US after January 1, 1978, are automatically protected by copyright once they are fixed in a tangible medium (like the Internet). BUT a single copy may be used for scholarly research (even if that's a 2nd grade life cycle report) or in teaching or preparation to teach a class." — Jacqui Murray, Ask a Tech Teacher

When we claim someone else's work as our own, be it text, artwork, movies, music, or any other form of media, it's called **plagiarism**:

"[Plagiarism is the] wrongful appropriation of another author's language, thoughts, ideas, or expressions"

The rules and laws surrounding plagiarism aren't nearly as well-known as those that deal with, say, driving a car or illegally crossing a street. The Josephson Institute Center for Youth Ethics surveyed 43,000 high school students and found that:

- *59% of high school students admitted cheating on a test during the last year. 34% self-reported doing it more than twice.*
- *One out of three high school students admitted that they used the Internet to plagiarize an assignment.*

One note: Laws addressing plagiarizing differ throughout the world. This article deals with commonly-accepted international guidelines and specific rules aligned with the laws of the United States.

Myths about using online material

Lots of adults — including teachers — think they understand the legalities of using only images, videos, audio, and other media forms. Do these sound familiar?

I can copy-paste anything posted to the Internet. Creators know that will happen and are OK with it.
Wrong. Can you grab products from a store shelf just because the clerk is busy? You need to find out what permissions the website allows you when visiting their site.

I can copy-paste anything if I give proper credit.
Wrong again. *Yes* sometimes but *no* other times and you better know the difference. For example, you can't copy Nelson DeMille's latest thriller and post it to your blog and think that's OK because you gave him credit. If you do that, you're infringing on his rights. You can post a small amount of his book but you better

check with his publisher to see what they consider to be a "small amount".

I searched the site and didn't find a copyright so there isn't one.
Wrong. If you can't find the website's media use policy, DON'T use it. Ignorance of the law is no excuse. The courts will not accept an argument that "you tried". Likely places to find media use guidelines are tabs or sections labeled "Privacy", "User terms", "Legal stuff" or links by the picture that say "link credit", "copyright", "rights reserved" "terms and privacy" or anything else that is even close to those terms.

When is it plagiarizing and when isn't it

In general terms, you must cite sources for:

- *facts not commonly known or accepted*
- *exact words and/or unique phrases*
- *reprints of diagrams, illustrations, charts, pictures, or other visual materials*
- *statistics (because these might contradict other statistics so you want to cite the authenticity of your source)*
- *opinions that support research*

...and you **don't** have to cite online material in these instances:

- **No one owns facts.** If it's a fact, like "Mt. Everest is 29,029 feet tall", you can share that without giving credit to anyone.
- **Common knowledge** — *what most people know* is in the public domain so no need to cite. This is information like the location of the Grand Canyon and how many planets are in the Solar System.
- Artwork (writing, pictures, movies, all media) **older than seventy years past the creator's death** is in the public domain (with some exceptions). You can use it without asking permission or providing credit.
- It is generally accepted that you can **share a small amount of someone's creation** without permission. This is why you can quote from a book you read when you review it.

How do you know if you plagiarized?

It seems like an easy question, doesn't it? All creations are automatically copyrighted when created. Novels, artwork, music — all are owned by the creator and you can't use them without permission. So, if you take someone else's work and call it your own, it's plagiarizing.

Specifically, you'll know you plagiarized if:

- you directly copied someone's creative work.
- you changed a few words in someone's work but it's still recognizable. For example:

"Fourscore and seven years ago, our fathers..."

...becomes:

"87 years ago, our predecessors..."

- you rephrased someone's opinions and presented them as your own.
- you purchased a paper and submitted it as your own.
- you copied your own work for a new purpose without confessing to that.

How do others know you plagiarized?

It's a lot easier to recognize plagiarism than most people think — especially those engaging in it. Here are a few ways:

- **changes in their writing voice**. They sound older than their normal writing style.
- **their font changes**. Often what is copied includes different fonts and sizes. It's not as easy as it sounds to normalize that.
- **a quick Google search** of a phrase turns up on Google credited to someone else.
- **the author writes about something they don't understand** or have no reason to know. This is easily checked by asking the purported author a few questions that dig into the topic.

How to cite sources

Lots of people don't want to plagiarize but don't know how to give proper credit. Here are suggestions:

- Use a citation tool like Citation Machine or Easy Bib to correctly format citations with all required information.
- Add citations as endnotes or footnotes.
- Add a citation page to your document.

How to check for plagiarism

Even the best-intentioned writers slip up. We forget to give credit or lose the citation and then don't get around to following up. Here are steps you can follow to find plagiarism in your own work:

- use a program like Turnitin to evaluate whether you pulled more than what was legal from someone else's work. Other plagiarism checkers include Grammarly and Quetext
- read through your document and see if it sounds like you. Are there parts you don't understand (even though you wrote it)? Those are places you may have inadvertently copy-pasted someone else's work.

I know. This is a lot of information with quite a few norms and protocols but becoming proficient in these will make you a better writer and give you a reputation as the author with reliable sources and facts. Whether you're a student, an academic, a journalist, or a parent, that sort of reputation is welcome.

Lesson #21—Image Editing I

Vocabulary	Problem solving	Skills
<ul><li>Filter</li><li>Jpg, tiff, png, gif</li><li>Layer</li><li>Recolor</li><li>Wrap</li></ul>	<ul><li>How do I edit an image (try right click)</li><li>I still can't find it (remember using this tool last year—how did you do it then?)</li><li>I volunteered to demonstrate and can't remember how (ask classmates for help)</li></ul>	Problem solving Keyboarding Digital citizenship Image editing and formatting
Academic Applications Writing, research, images	**Materials Required** keyboard program, row graphic, word processing program, student workbooks (if using)	**Standards** CCSS: W.9-10.8 NETS: 1b, 1d, 6a, 6d

Essential Question

Is there a way to personalize an image to fit a theme?

Big Idea

Most word processing programs include image formatting

Teacher Preparation

- Collect words for Speak Like a Geek (if doing this).
- Talk with grade-level team so you tie into inquiry.
- Ask what tech problems students found difficult.
- Integrate domain-specific tech vocabulary.
- Know whether you need extra time for this lesson.

Assessment Strategies

- Annotated workbook (if using)
- Completed project
- Used good keyboarding habits
- Completed warm-up, exit ticket
- Joined classroom conversations
- [tried to] solve own problems
- Decisions followed class rules
- Left room as s/he found it
- Higher order thinking: analysis, evaluation, synthesis
- Habits of mind observed

Steps

Time required: **45 minutes**
Class warm-up: **Keyboarding on the class typing program, paying attention to posture**

_____ Required skill level: image editing basics
_____ Open a word processing program that includes a basic set of image editing tools. MS Word's tools are robust; Google Doc's not so much, but in this project, it doesn't matter. You want students to see what they can do without leaving their word processing program.
_____ Insert a copyright-free row graphic from Google images. *Figure 117* is an example:

Figure 117—Row graphic for image editing

_____What do students remember about photo editing in Word, Photoshop or another image editing tool? Cropping? Borders? Filters? How have they used these skills in other classes? How might they use them? Where do they see photo editing skills in the world around them? Jog their memory about commercials, legal cases, advertising, and more.

_____Discuss the difference in image file names:

- *jpg*
- *tiff*
- *png*
- *gif*
- *bmp*

_____Discuss the file size of an image. Is 7kb too small? Is 5 MB too big?

_____Ask a student (or several students) to demonstrate how to use the image editing tools available in your class word processing program. This might include:

- *crop*
- *borders*
- *backgrounds*
- *rotate*
- *recolor*
- *wrap*
- *layer another image*
- *add text*

_____Students open a row graphic in their word processing tool, crop each image, and then format each with one of the tools available on the word processing program.

_____Use only tools native to the class word processing program—nothing else. You want students to see what's available within the program, not by leaving it. See samples in *Figures 118*:

Figure 7—Edit image with word processing tool

_____Save/share/publish/print, as is the custom in your school.

_____This can be done in groups or individually. When student(s) finish, share with a neighbor. Do edited images look unique? Creative?

Class exit ticket: *Tweet picture student completed including all image editing tools*

Differentiation

- *Use as summative assessment of skills students already know.*
- *If using Google Docs, show how to access an add-on to get more image editing tools.*
- *Assign a student to enter due date for this project to class calendar.*

Lesson #22—Image Editing II

Vocabulary	Problem solving	Skills
• Anchor points • Auto-correct • Clone • Hue • Layers • Opacity • Pixels • PSD • Saturation • Toggle • Transparency	• Can't edit picture (check layer) • Magic wand doesn't work (is 'add to' selected?) • I can't find the picture (did you save as .psd instead of .jpg?) • What's .psd? • I can't filter part of image (select part first) • Can't find paint brush (under arrow) • Can't edit text (select text layer) • Edits don't look real (edit pixels) • I can't find image (where did you save it)	Advanced image editing skills Cast shadows Problem solving Keyboarding Image editing
Academic Applications Writing, research, art	**Materials Required** Image-editing tool, how-to videos/instructions, theme for projects, before-after pics for auto-correct	**Standards** CCSS: W.9-10.8 NETS: 1b, 1d, 6a, 6d

Essential Question

How do I make original artwork that fulfills my purpose and doesn't plagiarize another's unique and individual work?

Big Idea

I can make original artwork that communicates a message without plagiarizing content from other artists

Teacher Preparation

- Collect words for Speak Like a Geek Board.
- Integrate domain-specific vocabulary into lesson.
- Talk with grade-level team to tie into inquiry.
- Know whether you need extra time for project.
- Know which tasks weren't completed last class and whether they are necessary to move forward.

Assessment Strategies

- Annotated workbook (if using)
- Completed project
- Worked independently
- Completed warm-up, exit ticket
- Joined classroom conversations
- [tried to] solve own problems
- Decisions followed class rules
- Left room as s/he found it
- Higher order thinking: analysis, evaluation, synthesis
- Habits of mind observed

Steps

Time required: **360 minutes**
Class warm-up: **Keyboard on the class typing program, paying attention to posture**

_____Required skill level: graphics, basic image editing.
_____Put backchannel device onto class screen (Twitter, Google form).
_____Introduce the image editor you use in your school. It might be (Google for addresses):

- *Gimp (a free version of Photoshop)*
- *Pixelmator (for Macs)*

- Pixlr (desktop, iPad, web)
- Photoshop Elements

_____If you have iPads or Chromebooks, good online image editors and apps include:

- Adobe Photoshop through Adobe's Creative Cloud
- Adobe Photoshop Express
- SumoPaint (draw only)

_____Whatever you use is fine. The goal of this series of projects is to edit/format/change photos with tools native to your class. Adjust steps/skills to your tool but not in the big idea and overall goal.

_____What is image editing? What are examples?

_____Introduce your school's image editing tool.

_____This lesson uses Photoshop. Adapt the steps to the tool you use including skipping some that aren't available and adding others that are.

_____Photoshop is wildly popular for its versatility in creating professional-looking images.

_____Explain the verb '***photoshopped***'. Discuss Photoshop's impact on society, court cases, and the internet. Discuss why pictures are inadmissible in court: Accomplished editors can 'photoshop' an image to anything they want.

_____Introduce the start screen for your image editor including toolbars, sidebars, layers, and history. Show how selecting a tool on the left side changes the top row of tools (if it does in your tool). Point out tools to be covered and the ones we won't get to this year. Review layout, zoom in on pixels, history, layers, navigator (or their comparable tools in your editor).

_____Let students explore, self-teach, and self-direct their learning with nominal guidance from you.

_____Students will complete up to eight projects, all around one theme. All skills are well within the ability level of High School students. Photoshop and other professional-level image editors can get much more complicated but these are a great start. Projects include:

- Actions
- Auto-correct
- Backgrounds
- Cast shadows
- Clone
- Crop
- Filter
- Hue and Saturation
- Paint
- Summatives: Collage and Photoshop Tennis

Auto-correct

_____Open a picture (provide one you know has a dramatic *before-after*—like *Figures 119a-b*). Duplicate background—remind students to always work on a copy of the background layer.

_____Use 'auto correction tools'.

_____Go to 'History'. Toggle between original picture and corrected version to see difference:

Figure 119a-b—Before and after PS auto-correct

Crop

_____There are three ways to crop:

- **marquis**—*crops as a square or rectangle (Figure 120a)*
- **lasso**—*crops freehand—drag the mouse around what you want to crop (Figure 120b)*
- **magic wand**—*select pixels close in color (Figure 120c)*

Figure 120a-c: 3 ways to crop

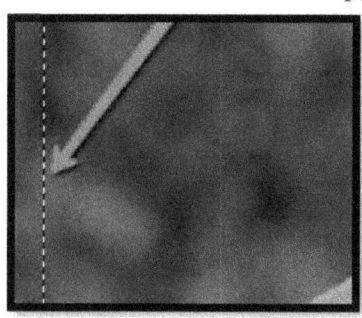  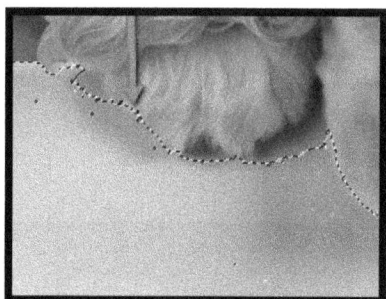

_____Your image editor may have one or all three of these. Try as many as you have, and then drag an image into a new background. *Figures 121a-c* crops a lizard and puts him in the Coliseum. Which cropping tool works best for this situation?

Figure 121a-c—Cropping an image into a new background

_____Use edit-transform-scale to resize picture for correct perspective against background.
_____Save pictures to digital portfolio as a Photoshop .psd and a .jpg. Discuss differences.

Clone

____Discuss cloning, how it's used/abused in the world.
____Open a picture that fits the project theme (I'll use sub-and-polar bear picture).

Figure 122a-b—Cloning within a picture

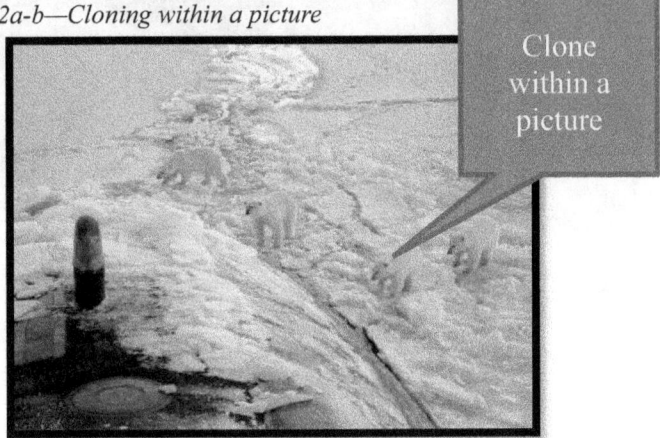

Clone within a picture

____Have students clone an item within the picture. For example, in *Figure 122a*, clone more polar bears to romp on the submarine (*Figure 122b*) or clone ice-snow OVER a polar bear so it disappears. Can you tell which are cloned?
____Remind students to watch the anchor point to see where they're cloning from, so colors match as closely as possible. This is a good opportunity for a discussion on pixels.
____Now clone **between** two pictures (see *Figures 123a* and *123b*). Using the same submarine picture, clone polar bears to a sea cave (in *Figure 123b*): Create anchor point in one picture (*Figure 123a*) and paint with the mouse to clone to second (*Figure 123b*).

Figure 123a and 123b--Cloning

Clone between pictures

____Make sure edge colors are matched to look as natural as possible. These is accomplished by carefully cloning, not rushing: Be patient.
____Save completed pictures to digital portfolios as .psd and .jpg. Remind students what the difference is.
____Save to digital portfolio or a blog post or another format students use to share projects. Include a reflection.

Backgrounds

_____Open a new canvas in the image editor. Today, we create backgrounds using (see *Figure 124*):

- *paint bucket*
- *patterns*
- *styles*
- *gradient*
- *clouds*

_____**First: Paint Bucket**—add a layer over the background layer (never use background). Double click layer name; call it 'paint bucket'. Change foreground and background colors. Select *paint bucket* tool. Make sure 'fill' on top toolbar says 'foreground'. Pour. It will be the foreground color as selected.

_____**Second: Patterns**—add a layer on top. Rename 'patterns'. Select *paint bucket* tool; make sure 'fill' says 'pattern' and select from the dropdown box. Pour.

_____**Third: Styles**—add a layer called 'styles'. Rename. Again, select *paint bucket* tool; select a style (on right toolbar). Pour. Don't like it? Pour another.

_____**Fourth: Gradient**—add a layer called 'Gradient' and rename. Select *gradient* tool nested under *paint bucket*. Drag mouse across the screen.

_____**Fifth: Clouds**—add a layer called 'Clouds' and rename. Select two coordinating (or not) foreground/background colors. Go to *Filter>render>clouds* and fill layer with clouds colored to those colors.

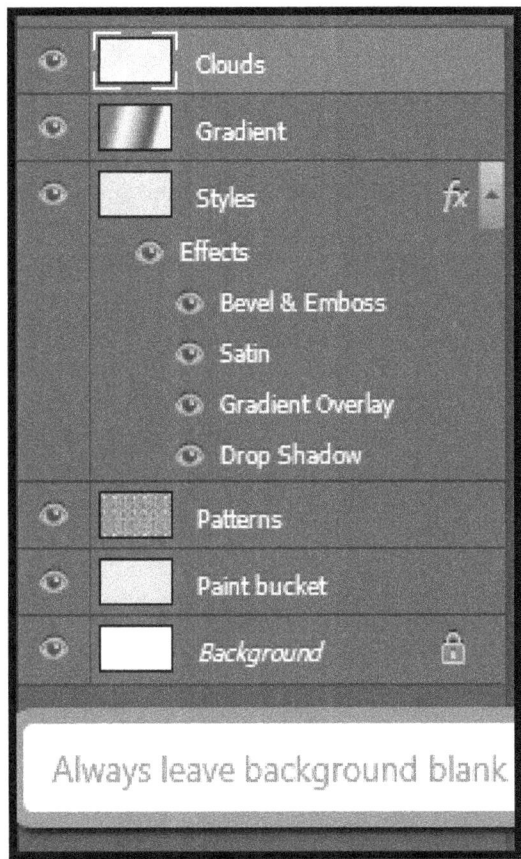

Figure 8—Background layers

_____Drag a favorite background layer to the top of stack. Then, drill through each layer, one at a time, until all five are displayed. This is harder than it sounds as students often forget to switch layers. Remind them to:

- *use marquee tool to select, then delete*
- *make sure you are on correct layer*
- *make sure cutout is sized correctly to display other layers*

_____The finished image will be like *Figure 125a*.

_____If you are pressed for time, you might use just two layers, as shown in *Figure 125b*. Here's how you do this one:

- *open an image in the image editing tool*
- *add a solid color layer on top*
- *use the History Brush to paint back to the original picture*

Figure 125a-b: Drill through background layers

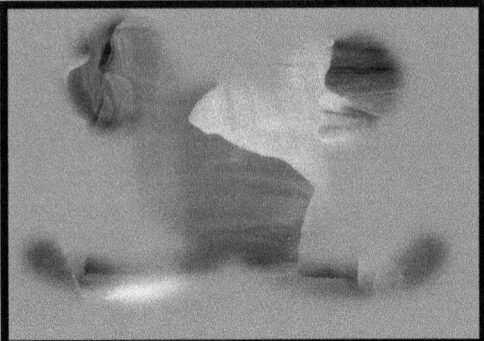

Filter

_____Filters are simple, quick, and will thrill students.

_____Open picture that fits the lesson theme. Duplicate background. **Filter picture** using the many Photoshop filters (see examples in *Figures 126a-b* of elephants). The final image should communicate a feeling that supports the theme.

_____If you can't decide among filters, complete one, then hide the filter by closing the eye (or take a picture if your tool provides the camera function) and try another. Then, pick one you like by hiding/unhiding the filters

_____If you only want to filter part of picture (see large elephant in *Figure 126b*):

- select part of the image (such as the large elephant in the foreground), select the inverse, and filter everything but what you selected OR
- filter the entire picture by selecting the part of the image you don't want filtered and—using the history brush—painting it back to the original picture

_____This is how photographers make one image stand out among many in a photo.

Figure 126a-b—Filters

Hue and Saturation

_____Discuss the meaning of 'hue' and 'saturation'.

_____A popular effect in photography is to change the color emphasis in an image or remove the color entirely. Here's how easily that is done—*Figure 127a* is the original picture:

- go to *Image>Adjustments>Hue&Saturation*
- move *Saturation* and *Hue* slider to new positions and get an image like *Figure 127b*
- move *Saturation* left until color washes out—called *desaturated* (*Figure 127c*)

Figure 127a-c: Changing hue and saturation

_____For fun, pin the History Brush to the original picture and paint over areas you want to bring back to unformatted status:

Figure 128a is the original; 128b is desaturated; 128c is painted back to original

Figure 129a is desaturated; 129b has part painted back to original picture

_____For fun: Students change the color of their favorite car using hue-saturation:

- *copy-paste copyright-free picture of favorite car into PS*

- use Hue/saturation to change color
- use the history brush to paint windshields, rims, license plate, bumpers, and lights back to the original

_____Which is the original picture below—*Figures 130a or 130b*:

Figure 130a-b—*Car color changed with hue-saturation*

Actions

_____An *action* is a series of tasks that take place as the result of a single command. The Photoshop Action tool is on the tiny drop-down menu in the upper right (or with *Alt+F9*).

Figure 131a—*Quadrant colors; 131b—sepia toned*

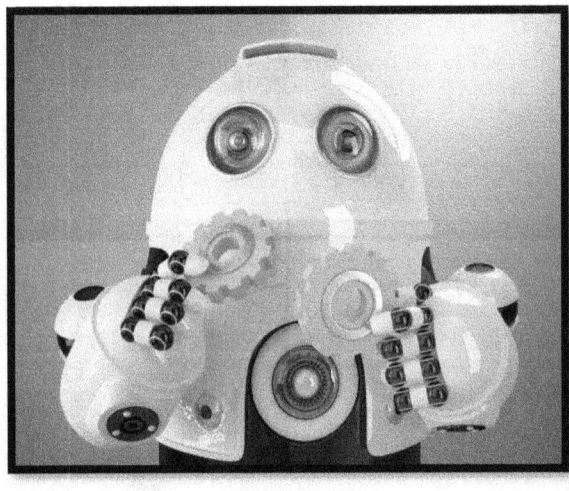 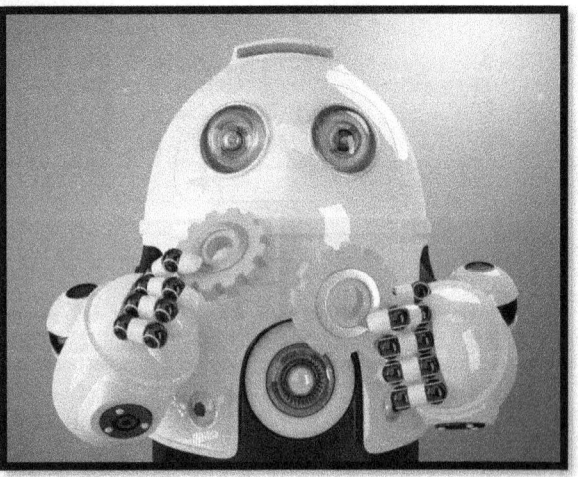

_____Students open a copyright-free picture, and then try different Actions:

- *Quadrant colors*
- *Sepia*
- *Shadow*
- *Water reflection*

_____Use one or more on a picture to communicate whatever idea student feels fits inquiry theme. For example, *Figure 131a* is quadrant color and *Figure 131b* is sepia.

Paint

_____Photoshop is not only for image editing. It is a sophisticated, functional paint program.
_____Open a new blank canvas. In 'new image dialogue box' (*Figure 132*), notice:

- title box—call it 'Paint'
- inches vs. pixels—make it 4x5 inches (pixels are in the drop-down box)
- background contents—make it 'white'
- image size—take note of this

Figure 132—Paint dialogue box

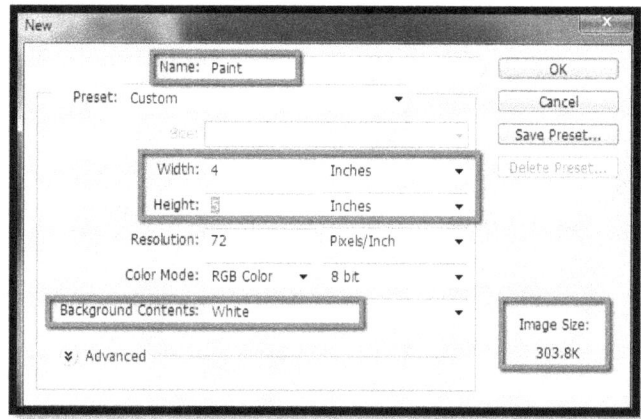

_____Draw a picture. *Figure 133a* is an example of available brushes (yours may be different). *Figures 133b-c* are two drawings students might create:

Figure 133a—Image editing brushes; 133b-c— completed drawings

_____Select brush and size from toolbar. Leave 'opacity' and 'flow' for later.
_____Notice how top toolbar changes with each tool selected in left sidebar:

- *select brush size 20, a traditional brush first, then others*
- *draw a picture that fits inquiry; change the brush and foreground color*
- *go to history—go back in time if necessary*

_____Paint a picture that ties into inquiry. Use text tool for the title. Change the font, size, and shape (be sure you're in Text layer).
_____Save image as a jpg. Notice options available when saving (jpg, PSD, tiff, and more).

Cast Shadows

_____Have students create a 'cast shadow' to support inquiry. Discuss what this means and compare the different types of shadows used in image editing. When ready, create this project:

- *Crop student out of the class picture and add it to a new canvas.*
- *Find a picture that says something about the student—a sports player, a professional, or even an alter-ego. Crop background out and add it to the canvas.*
- *Desaturate/warp until student shadow appears—his/her alter ego— (Figure 134a).*

Figure 134a-c—Cast shadow examples

Summative: Collage

_____Students use pictures created during this lesson for a collage with the addition of text to explain pictures as needed. *Figures 135a-b* are samples. The collage can be created in the image editing tool or another like Canva, PicCollage, and Google Draw (Google for addresses).

Figure 135a-b—Sample collages

_____When done, share it with a partner to see if they can find and recognize every image editing tool used.

_____Print/publish/share as is the custom in your classroom.

Summative: Photoshop Tennis

_____**Photoshop tennis** gets its name from Photoshop but you can use any image editing tool. It is the sequential editing of an image by one member at a time of a team. Players pick a starting image (or you may assign it). One team member alters the image using a skill learned during this unit, labels it with their name and the skill, and then sends the edited image to the next team member. That person does the same—edits, annotates, and passes it on. This continues until all team members have edited the image and all learned skills are represented.

_____Before submitting, the team reviews it for accuracy—that all tools are used, noted, and all team members credited. See *Assessment 30* for an example.

_____This project is not done during class. Members must complete their work outside of class.

_____On the first day, during class, students:

- *break into groups (size varies by the number of skills to be represented)*
- *agree on a starting picture*
- *decide who will do which skill*
- *discuss how the image will be forwarded from student-to-student*
- *decide how to verify as a group the completed image meets all requirements*

Assessment 29—Photoshop Tennis

Class exit ticket: ***Tweet a picture that student formatted using their image editing tool.***

Differentiation

- More how-to Photoshop links can be found on Ask a Tech Teacher's Photoshop resource page.
- Have students volunteer to create and post a how-to screencast on each skill with an example
- Assign a student to enter due dates for image editing projects and summative assessments.

Lesson #23—Webtools

Vocabulary	Problem solving	Skills
• .jpg • Code • Embed • QR code • Screenshot • Snippet	• I can't figure this out (try help files or Google search) • I don't understand program (is it like another you do understand?) • I can't find code (check 'share', 'publish', 'embed')	Problem solving Keyboarding Digital citizenship
Academic Applications Writing, research, publishing	**Materials Required** Backchannel, web tool links, how-to videos and instructions, student workbooks (if using)	**Standards** CCSS: RST.9-10.3-4,7 NETS: 3c, 4a-b, 6b-d

Essential Question

How do I use technology strategically to share ideas?

Big Idea

Technology can be used strategically to communicate ideas AND student must take responsibility for learning.

Teacher Preparation

- Talk with grade-level team so you tie into inquiry.
- Collect words for Speak Like a Geek Board.
- Know whether you need extra time for lesson.
- Integrate domain-specific vocabulary into lesson.
- Ask what tech problems students had difficulty with.
- Ensure required links are on student digital devices.
- Something happen you weren't prepared for? Show how you fix it.
- Know which tasks weren't completed last class and whether they are necessary to move forward.

Assessment Strategies

- *Annotated workbook (if using)*
- *Worked independently*
- *Completed project*
- *Completed warm-up, exit ticket*
- *Joined classroom conversations*
- *[tried to] solve own problems*
- *Decisions followed class rules*
- *Higher order thinking: analysis, evaluation, synthesis*
- *Habits of mind observed*

Steps

Time required: 45 minutes
Class warm-up: Students create groups in preparation for this activity

_____Required skill level: internet basics.
_____Before beginning project, project backchannel device onto the class screen.
_____This project can be done every year to highlight webtools to be used that year or the next. Students use critical-thinking and problem-solving to learn programs and teach them to classmates. There will be lots of positive energy during this lesson.

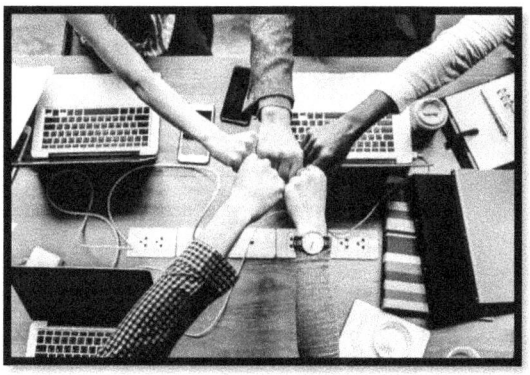

_____Here's how it works. Students work in groups:

- *Learn selected webtool (or one student selected and you approved).*
- *Create a project using that tool that ties into class inquiry.*
- *Teach classmates how to use it. Help them when they have problems and answer their questions. Since this is done in a group, one student may be assigned to present while others troubleshoot.*
- *Optional: Tape presentation and share as a how-to later.*
- *Upload the lesson to student blog or other journal with a reflection.*

_____Helpful resources include:

- *Help files*
- *the webtool website*
- *how-to videos from YouTube*
- *knowledgeable students/adults*

_____Demonstration should include the following:

- *Display the webtool on the class screen while students open it on their devices.*
- *Model its use while other members help classmates with difficulties.*
- *Discuss troubleshooting tips.*
- *Discuss how the tool can be used to address the theme (say, global poverty).*
- *Save project while classmates do the same.*
- *Reflect on it in blog, digital portfolio, or another method selected for students.*

_____Before students begin, discuss digital rights and responsibilities that must be adhered to.
_____Create a list of webtools useful for your student group. *Good idea: Poll teachers to see what tools would be authentic to their inquiry.* Here's a sample list of choices (Google for addresses if not provided):

- *Alice*
- *Scratch*
- *create a QR code*
- *Any brainstorming/mindmapping tool*
- *Wolfram Alpha widgets*

_____They will use one class to prepare. Presentations start next week. Students should work quickly but smart.
_____Review grading details in the *Assessment*.

Class exit ticket: ***Sign up for presentation date and add to class calendar***

Differentiation

- *Have students teach tools to other students in preparation for their class summative project.*

Assessment 30—Webtool presentation

Webtool Presentation Rubric

CATEGORY	Exemplary—4 points	Developing—2 points	Unsatisfactory—0 points	RATING
Knowledge of selected tool 8 points	Shows a clear understanding of tool. Shows evidence of preparation prior to presentation for both teaching and problem-solving for classmates.	Shows unclear understanding of tool. Shows some evidence of preparation for both teaching and problem-solving. Requires teacher assistance more than once.	Shows murky understanding of tool with little evidence of preparation for teaching or problem-solving. Requires substantial assistance from others.	
Ability to teach students 4 points	Demonstrates how to use tool in an authentic, personal and enthusiastic manner. Uses terms class understands. Speaks slowly and clearly so class can complete steps. Provides trouble shooting and problem-solving tips.	Has some difficulty teaching how to use tool. Teaching lacks confidence and doesn't always engage students. Sometimes speaks too quickly for class to follow. Occasionally unable to trouble-shoot or problem-solve.	Has considerable difficulty teaching students. Teaching lacks confidence and doesn't engage students. Unable to trouble-shoot and problem-solve when asked.	
Reflection on use of tool for class theme 4 points	Reminds students how this tool can be used to communicate theme with examples. Fully addresses student questions about how to accomplish this. Displays a thoughtful analysis and includes goals for continued learning.	Doesn't remind students but provides examples. Can address some questions. Reflection is incomplete and shows insufficient original thought and incomplete goals for continued learning.	Reflection doesn't describe tool's use for theme, show little original thought, and does not include goals for continued learning.	
Group Work 4 points	Consistently works toward group goals. Display sensitivity to feelings and values of others.	Sometimes works toward group goals. Not often sensitive to the feelings of others.	Never contributes toward group goals. Is not sensitive to the feelings of others.	

Lesson #24—Webtools: Presentations

Vocabulary	Problem solving	Skills
▪ Academic language ▪ Domain-specific ▪ Embed code ▪ HTML ▪ Multimedia ▪ Webtool	▪ Something happened I don't know how to solve (use problem-solving strategies) ▪ A classmate asked a question I can't answer (do your best) ▪ I can't find embed code (check 'share', 'publish', 'embed')	Webtools Speaking and listening Problem solving Digital citizenship
Academic Applications Any topic	**Materials Required** Presentations, links, student workbooks (if using)	**Standards** CCSS: SL.9-10.4-6 NETS: 6d

Essential Question

How can I communicate effectively with a presentation?

Big Idea

Students present in a thoughtful, clear, responsive manner, adapting as needed for audience feedback

Teacher Preparation

- Know whether you need extra time for lesson.
- Integrate domain-specific vocabulary into lesson.
- Ensure required links are on digital devices.
- Know which tasks weren't completed last class and whether they are necessary to move forward.

Assessment Strategies

- Completed presentation
- Worked independently
- Completed warm-up, exit ticket
- Joined classroom conversations
- [tried to] solve own problems
- Decisions followed class rules
- Left room as s/he found it
- Higher order thinking: analysis, evaluation, synthesis
- Habits of mind observed

Steps

Time required: 180 minutes (45 min./group—30 to present, 15 to work on presentation)
Class warm-up: Prepare for group presentation

_____Required skill level: Webtools lesson; knowledge of screencasts.
_____Expected presentation time: twenty-thirty minutes per group. The balance of a forty-five-minute class is presentation preparation for other students. Groups that have completed their presentation can explore other webtools from the list.
_____Students are expected to use screenshots and screencasts during presentation.
_____Follow speaking/listening rules:

- *come to the presentation prepared*

- *present information with valid reasoning and well-chosen details*
- *include multimedia that clarifies and adds interest*
- *use appropriate eye contact, adequate volume, and clear pronunciation*

_____During presentation:

- *one groupmember will model webtool while other members help classmates with difficulties*
- *discuss troubleshooting tips*
- *discuss how to use tool to address the theme (say, global poverty)*
- *show classmates how to save project by embedding it into digital portfolio or taking a screenshot and uploading that to the digital portfolio*

_____Presentation must show evidence that students:

- *understood procedure for performing task*
- *understood the meaning of symbols, key terms, and could explain them*
- *used academic and domain-specific language*
- *tested instructions before presenting*

_____Audience will:

- *follow rules for collegial discussions*
- *respect all opinions*
- *pose questions that connect ideas or respond to comments*
- *be critical thinkers*
- *use academic and domain-specific language*

_____When the group finishes, they will embed example (or screenshot), directions and reflection to their blog.

_____After students complete the *Assessment* in workbooks (or as a hard copy), take a screenshot and share it with you.

Class exit ticket: ***Comment on the post of presentation group.***

Differentiation

- *Tape presentations and play the video rather than presenting in real-time.*
- *Have classmates assess each other, using Assessment rubric.*

Lesson #25-26—Genius Hour

Vocabulary	Problem solving	Skills
• Benchmark • Extrinsic • Genius Hour • Globalization • Intrinsic • Pitch • Temporal • Videographer	• I don't have a passion (You have interests...they lead to passion) • Just give me a handout (Sorry, we are learning through experience!) • Why do this? (This is the type of learning you will do the rest of your life) • I can't finish in the allotted time (plan your work so you can)	Self-directed investigation Speaking and listening Problem solving Keyboarding Digital citizenship
Academic Applications Writing, research	**Materials Required** Backchannel, Grit rubric, handouts, videos for motivation	**Standards** CCSS: WHST.9-10.7-10 NETS: 1a, 3a-d, 4b, 6d

Essential Question

What would I choose if I could learn anything?

Big Idea

Students dig deeply into a topic that interests them, and create a product or presentation that displays their passion

Teacher Preparation

- Introduce Genius Hour with a video about passions (like TED Talk Science of Motivation).
- Find time for Genius Hour in schedule.
- Something happen you weren't prepared for? Show students how you fix the emergency without a meltdown and with a positive attitude.

Assessment Strategies

- Annotated workbook (if using)
- Worked independently
- Made progress on project
- Used good keyboarding habits
- Joined classroom conversations
- [tried to] solve own problems
- Decisions followed class rules
- Left room as s/he found it
- Higher order thinking: analysis, evaluation, synthesis
- Habits of mind observed

Steps

Time required: 20% of classroom time weekly
Class warm-up: none

This lesson is spread throughout the grading period

_____Required skill level: internet research, presentation tools, optional video devices.
_____Put backchannel device on class screen.
_____Genius Hour gives students 20% of class time to pursue a topic that interests them. It is as loose or structured as you want. This lesson is fairly detailed. Feel free to adapt guidelines to your unique student group.
_____Genius Hour is flexible. Students work on projects multiple times or just once a week.
_____Tie into Math, Science, LA, or Social Studies. Consider co-teaching with these professionals

NEED HELP GETTING READY FOR GENIUS HOUR?

Brainstorm and find inspiration...

10 Things You Love to Do and Learn
10 Things You Are Good At
10 Things You Wonder

adapting goals to their needs. It's also a good fit for technology and digital media.

_____Even if you're not grading this lesson, review rubric at the end of the lesson to explain the intrinsic problem-solving and creative thinking you expect.

_____Each benchmark uses 20% of time (excepting Benchmark 3 and 6—the presentations):

- Benchmark 1: Find your passion
- Benchmark 2: Come up with a project
- Benchmark 3: Project Pitch day
- Benchmark 4: Workday--record your work
- Benchmark 5: Review project with a peer
- Benchmark 6: Class presentations
- Benchmark 7: Evidence of learning

> **Benchmarks**
>
> #1: Find a passion
> #2: Come up with project
> #3: Pitch project
> #4 Research
> #5: Share with classmates
> #6: Present to class
> #7: Assess

_____Part of this project's challenge is working within time constraints. Yes, it would be nice to have endless time to follow a dream, but that rarely happens in life or education. In fact, some colleges build that into their success matrix, throwing more material at the student than s/he can reasonably handle to see how they thrive with stress. Students must budget time to fit schedule:

_____Share strategies to assist students in organizing work, thinking, and prioritizing research.

Figure 136—Genius Hour planning sheet

Action Steps	How?	Timeline	Resources 1. Available 2. Needed	Barriers 1. What? 2. Overcome?	Communication Plan
Step 1:					
Step 2:					
Step 3:					
Step 4:					
Step 5:					
Step 6:					
Step 7:					
Step 8:					
Step 9:					
Step 10:					
Step 11:					
Step 12:					

_____ As students work, fill out *Figure 136* with evidence of progress; submit with the final assessment.
_____ Treat each student uniquely. Their projects and expectations will vary. The lesson goal is to get them excited about learning. In that respect, the Genius Hour can be a transformative tool.
_____ Focus on student growth and engagement instead of the final project.
_____ Allow students to work in pairs, but only for creating the product. The rest is done individually.
_____ You can even decide to "not grade" the final product, and instead focus on the learning path.
_____ In general, discuss what motivates students—what would they learn if they could pick anything.
_____ Done with class discussion? Now students complete the following steps—where relevant, in a collaborative writing tool (like Google Docs). We want to share from the beginning:

- **Step 1:** Interests: What topics, activities, skills would student like to learn more about?

    If student has trouble finding passions, 1) watch previous student projects, or 2) read "Six strategies to find passion" (On A.J. Juliani's website).

    Using a worksheet like *Figure 137*, student lists 64 interests they come up with on the bracket. Individually or with a partner, whittle them down to one:

Figure 137—Find your passion

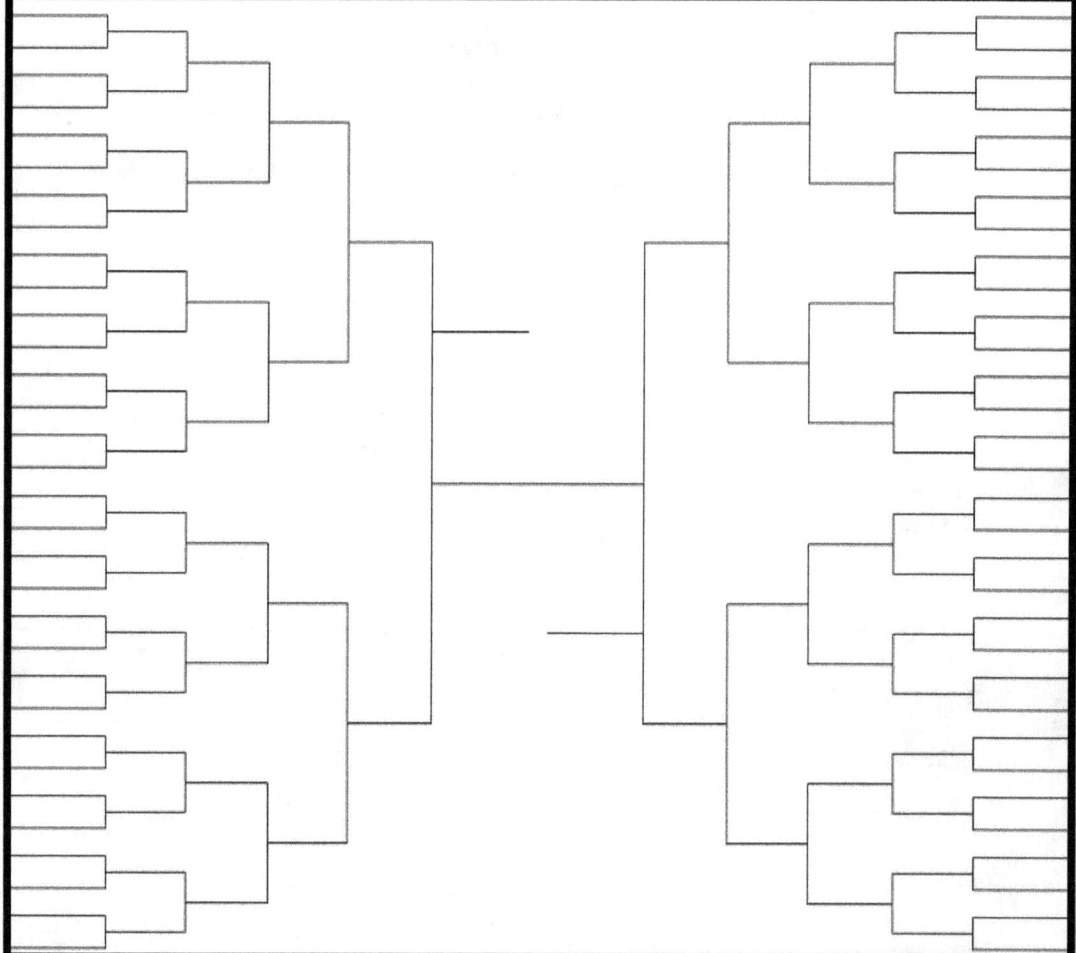

As student works, remember: The chosen topic will fascinate student AND be completed in the time constraints. Do the math with students—how many minutes/hours is 20% of ten hours? Or fifteen hours (How many classes are in your grading cycle?)

- **Step 2:** Made a choice? Write a paragraph of at least five lines on why topic is important to learn and what informed its choice. For example:

    "I would like to learn how to create an app for the iPad because…

    "I would like to study World War II because…

- **Step 3:** Student reviews what they already know about the topic. Write another paragraph of at least five sentences to explain their background knowledge on the topic.

    "I have been studying programming in summer school and learned…

    "My Grandpa was in the Marines in WWII and told me…

- **Step 4:** Read paragraphs from Steps 2/3 to a partner. Elaborate beyond what is written. Ask each other questions to understand topic completely, then write about the conversation:

    "My partner wants to enter a science competition. We discussed…

    Based on discussion, list five questions to guide inquiry. Consider time constraints:

    "Here are my five research questions:

    1. *What are some successful apps?*
    2.

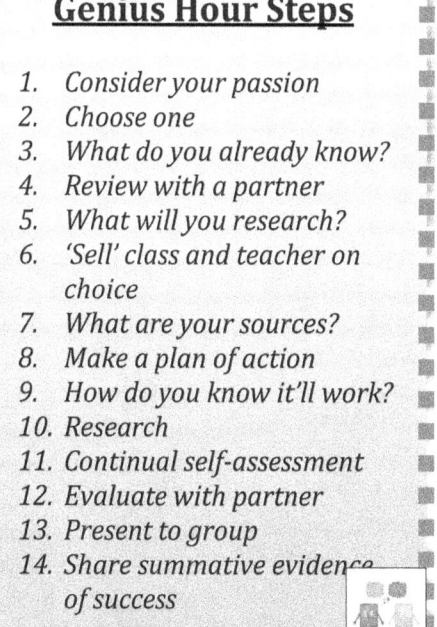

Genius Hour Steps

1. Consider your passion
2. Choose one
3. What do you already know?
4. Review with a partner
5. What will you research?
6. 'Sell' class and teacher on choice
7. What are your sources?
8. Make a plan of action
9. How do you know it'll work?
10. Research
11. Continual self-assessment
12. Evaluate with partner
13. Present to group
14. Share summative evidence of success

- **Step 5:** Each student prepares a quick presentation for Project Pitch Day to 'sell' class on their passion and the importance of spending 20% of their time on this topic. Include:

    - *What will make me successful?*
    - *How will I accomplish my goals?*
    - *How I plan to meet time limits?*

- **Step 6:** With research questions established, develop a list of sources to find answers:

    "Here's where I can find answers:

    1. *My partner has a friend whose Dad creates apps. Interview him.*
    2.

- **Step 7:** Congratulations! Your project is fleshed out! Now make a plan! First: What is most important to learn? Contact someone? Go to library? Internet research? List steps:

    "Here are steps to complete my App:

    1. *Research...*
    2.

    While researching, remember:

    - *summarize key details*
    - *analyze how and why*
    - *cite evidence to support analysis*
    - *visually represent information*
    - *distinguish among facts, judgment based on research, and speculation*
    - *read closely to determine what text says; make logical inferences*
    - *assess how point of view or purpose shapes content*
    - *integrate/evaluate content presented in diverse media*

> **Assessment**
> 1. Pitch
> 2. Genius Hour table
> 3. Ongoing blog updates
> 4. Final presentation
> 5. Anecdotal observation

- **Step 8:** Provide evidence of achieving goals in the following ways:

    - *reflections and comments once a week*
    - *tweets on class stream*
    - *form on Google Apps that is completed weekly*
    - *impromptu videocasts of work which can include interview with student or others*
    - *video journal of progress shared on YouTube (if you have school account), Google Apps, or other*
    - *any student-generated self-assessment method*

- **Step 9:** Collect relevant information from multiple sources. Assess credibility and accuracy of each source—see *Internet Search* lesson—and avoid plagiarism by giving credit as needed. Integrate information into a bigger picture.

- **Step 10:** When done researching, share the project with a classmate 1) in person, or 2) via a virtual meeting. Do they understand? Do they feel the excitement? Then, share with the teacher. Based on feedback, plan/revise/edit/rewrite. Add details or a new approach if called for.

- **Step 11:** In a class presentation, share passion. Student has flexibility on the approach they use (slideshow, video, screencast, or another), but whatever it is must communicate their excitement and show evidence of what they've learned. It shouldn't be the same method used in pitch. Use academic and domain-specific vocabulary in presentation making sure that meaning is clarified by context and other clues.

- **Step 12:** Evaluate how the desired results were achieved with the following evidence:

    - *completed Genius Hour Project table*
    - *'Sales' Pitch to classmates*
    - *progress reports via blogs*
    - *final class presentation*
    - *anecdotal observation of student work*

_____Throughout class, check for understanding.

Class exit ticket: **None**

Differentiation

- Have students share projects with other classes doing a Genius Hour.
- Invite parents to watch presentations. Or take the best presentations to the next school board meeting!
- Have students create online assessments at beginning and end of project with Google Forms to gauge interest in subject.
- Have student create his/her own rubrics and forms for self-assessment.
- Assign a student to enter dates into class calendar for Genius Hour due date.

Assessment 31—Genius Hour rubric

Genius Hour Rubric

We started Genius Hour with the hopes of giving each of you the opportunity to explore your true passions in life. I hope your final presentations show an intrinsic motivation to better yourself and become a life-long learner.

	20	**19-16**	**15-13**	**12-10**	**9-0**
Creativity	Demonstrates a high level of curiosity and offers a unique perspective on topic. Final product is distinct from other projects	Demonstrates a solid level of curiosity and offers a unique perspective on the topic. Final product is distinct from other projects.	Demonstrates some curiosity and offers a different perspective on topic. Final product is like other projects.	Demonstrates marginal curiosity and offers a similar perspective on topic. Final product is like other projects.	
Organization	Created a well-developed action plan, kept deadlines throughout process. Independently able to figure out what needed to be done and in what order.	Created a well-developed action plan, finished deadlines throughout process. Able to figure out what needed to be done in what order with some help.	Created action plan and completed deadlines by presentation. Able to figure out what needed to be done and in what order with a lot of help.	Had help creating action plan and rushed to meet deadlines. Figured out what needed to be done and in what order with a lot of help.	
Productivity	Showed a strong and efficient use of time and resources	Showed efficient use of time and resources	Not always prepared and wasted time.	Rarely prepared and consistently wasted time.	
Grit/Hustle	Demonstrated ability to overcome obstacles and distractions. Never let setbacks get in way of accomplishing goals.	Demonstrated ability to overcome most obstacles and distractions. Rarely let setbacks get in way of accomplishing goals.	Demonstrated ability to overcome some obstacles and distractions. Sometimes setbacks hindered accomplishment of goals.	Had difficulty overcoming most obstacles and distractions. Allowed setbacks to get in way of accomplishing goals.	
Presentation	Showed strong passion and sense of purpose. Conveyed successes and failures to class.	Showed passion and sense of purpose. Conveyed both successes and failures to class.	Showed sense of purpose. Conveyed some successes and failure to class.	Purpose was unclear. Failed to convey successes and failure to class.	

Askatechteacher©

Lesson #27-28—Coding

Vocabulary	Problem solving	Skills
• Debug • Hotkey • Hour of code • If-then • Macro • Sequence • Shortkey • Symbolism • Variables	• I don't know how to program (experiment; be a risk-taker) • I don't like coding (why?) • Start-up screen is confusing (watch the video) • My partner does lots of the work (OK if you do your part also) • I tried to debug my program, but it didn't work (start at beginning)	App creation Problem solving Digital citizenship Coding Hour of Code
Academic Applications Math, problem solving, critical thinking	**Materials Required** App links, digital phone (or mock-up), student workbooks (if using)	**Standards** CCSS: Stds. for Math. Practice NETS: 4a-b, 5c-d

Essential Question

How do I use a program I've never seen before?

Big Idea

By thinking critically and using information from other parts of my life, I can create something new and useful

Teacher Preparation

- Ensure all required links are available.
- Integrate domain-specific vocabulary into lesson.
- Collect words for Speak Like a Geek Board.
- Ask what tech problems students had difficulty with.

Assessment Strategies

- Worked independently
- Completed the app
- Used good keyboarding habits
- Completed exit ticket
- Joined classroom conversations
- [tried to] solve own problems
- Decisions followed class rules
- Left room as s/he found it
- Higher order thinking: analysis, evaluation, synthesis
- Habits of mind observed

Steps

Time required: 75 minutes in one sitting; multiple classes for some projects
Class warm-up: None

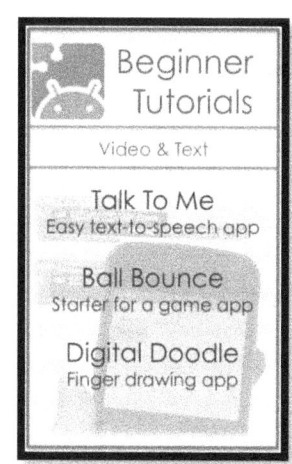

_____ Required skill level: coding basics
_____ Discuss critical thinking and problem solving. Does this apply to, say, games students play?
_____ The reason educators embrace coding is simple: **It teaches thinking.** Discuss fundamental programming concepts:

- *abstraction and symbolism—variables are common in math, but also in a student's education. Tools, toolbars, images—these all represent something bigger.*
- *creativity—think outside the box; find unique solutions*

- *if-then thinking—actions have consequences*
- *debugging—write-edit-rewrite; problem-solve; when you make a mistake, don't call an expert. Look at what happened step by step and fix where it went wrong.*
- *logic—think through a problem, understand the predictability of movement*

_____Most people—students and adults—think programming looks like *Figure 138a* when it actually looks like *Figure 138b*:

Figure 138a-b—What programming feels like vs. what it is

_____Do students remember *Figure 139a-e* coding activities from previous years (if you studied coding in prior years)?

Figure 139a-e—Coding from previous years

  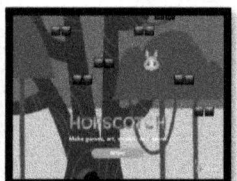  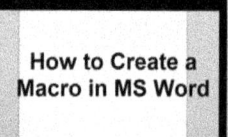

_____December will host the **Hour of Code**, a one-hour introduction to programming and why students should love it. It's designed to demystify "code" and show that anyone can learn to be a maker, a creator, and an innovator.
_____This unit may be done individually or in small groups.
_____This year, students will create an app. Students will not be able to complete the app during the Hour of Code, but they'll get a start.
_____If necessary, explain to students what an 'app' is.
_____Why build an app:

- apps teach real-world skills—design, marketing, video production, project management, presentation skills, special media use
- the process teaches

    o programming
    o creativity
    o innovation
    o critical thinking

    o problem solving
    o communication and collaboration
    o decision making
    o technology operations and concepts

High School Technology Curriculum Book 1: Teacher Manual

_____For this project, follow the videos and directions included in MIT's App Inventor and create one (or all) beginning level apps such as:

- *TalkToMe Text-to-speech app*
- *Extended TalkToMe—shake the phone!*
- *BallBounce Game app*
- *Digital Doodle drawing app*

_____Show the process on the class screen while students follow on their digital devices.

_____If you prefer, try one of these sites to guide app invention (Google for addresses):

- *Game Salad – shows how to build a game or an app*
- *Apps Geyser*
- *TinyTap App – simpler than others*

Class exit ticket: **Share a screenshot of the student work on Twitter or blog**

Differentiation

- *Post project due date to class calendar.*
- *Early finishers: visit other coding websites.*

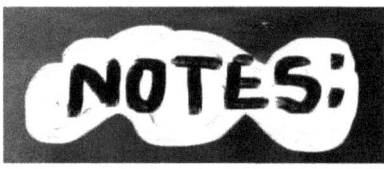

___
___
___
___
___
___
___
___

Lesson #29—Write an Ebook

Vocabulary	Problem solving	Skills
• Back-up • GHO • Novella • Point of view • Prologue • Rhetoric • Setting • Theme	• I forgot to attend GHO (is it taped?) • I started my novel in Word, but Word isn't on all computers (import to Google Docs) • I can't think of what else to say (get help from group) • I'm not comfortable evaluating writing of classmates (use a checklist—be objective) • I don't want to sell book (discuss options)	Write an ebook Problem solving Keyboarding Digital citizenship
Academic Applications Writing, research	**Materials Required** parent permission for GHO	**Standards** CCSS: W.9-10.5-7,10 NETS: 1b, 6b, 6d

Essential Question

I'm just a kid. How can I write a book?

Big Idea

With proper planning, any student can write a book.

Teacher Preparation

- Parent permission slips for GHO (if necessary).
- Ask what tech problems students had.
- Integrate domain-specific vocabulary into lesson.
- Know whether you need extra time for lesson.

Assessment Strategies

- Worked independently
- Used good keyboarding habits
- Completed exit ticket
- Joined classroom conversations
- [tried to] solve own problems
- Decisions followed class rules
- Higher order thinking: analysis, evaluation, synthesis
- Habits of mind observed

Steps

Time required: 90 minutes a week, every week of the semester or grading period
Class warm-up: Meet in critique group to discuss topics

This project is completed over a period of months as an ongoing exercise to practice writing skills.

_____Required skill level: Passion for writing.
_____Before beginning, put backchannel device on class screen.
_____Students will write an ebook working in a critique group with four-five classmates. Each week, students complete one of the steps required to complete the book, and then meet with their critique group virtually (say, via Google Hangouts) to discuss.
_____The critique group will serve as mentor and coach. For example, if the assignment is to establish a theme (as in

#3 below), each student will bring **their theme** to critique group and share, be critiqued, and comment on the ideas of others:

- *Prepare by reading groupmates' work.*
- *Use evidence to evaluate classmate's point of view.*
- *Build on others' ideas and express own clearly and persuasively.*

_____During critique sessions, through classmate stories, students are exposed to all types of writing (as required in high school) and open-mindedly evaluate them.

_____Once planning steps are completed (Prologue – Step 5), students will write their story.

_____About once a month, students will reflect on their story—what was easy, hard, did they have writer's block, and was research required. This can be done in blogs, Discussion Boards, or even a Twitter feed.

_____About once a week, students comment on the written reflections of at least three classmates.

_____Before beginning, discuss 1) difference between an amateur and professional writer, 2) what it means to be 'published', and 3) publication options (see **7: Publish!**).

Prologue: Discuss young authors, i.e.:

_____Alexandra Adornetto—published *Halo* at 18.
_____Christopher Paolini—published *Eragon* at age 16
_____Steph Bowe—published *Girl Saves Boy* at age 16.
_____Cayla Kluver—published *Legacy* at age 16

1: **Make decisions about how to tell story**

_____1st or 3rd person? Discuss and research.
_____Present or past tense—discuss and research.
_____Author's voice—discuss and research.
_____Genre—history, science fiction, YA? Discuss and research.
_____Topic—how do you pick a topic?

- What are you passionate about?
- What do you have experience in/with?

_____Be prepared to discuss these weekly with critique group.

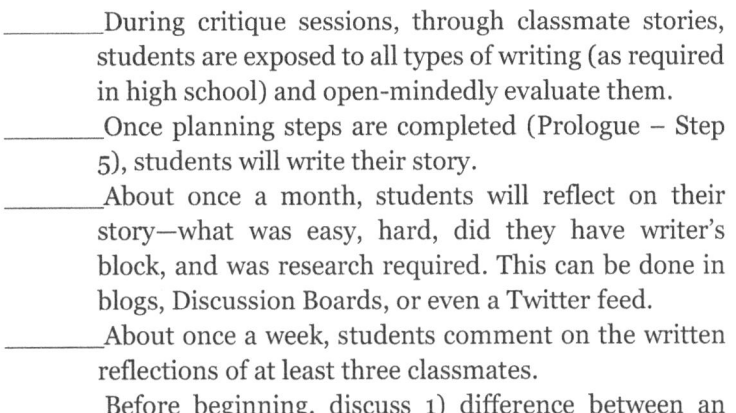

How to Write an Ebook

1. Research
2. Decide POV
3. Decide voice
4. Decide genre
5. Decide theme
6. Decide topic
7. Brainstorm content with writing group
8. Flesh out characters
9. Plot action
10. Research settings
11. Sketch out chapters
12. Write book
13. Review as you write
14. Publish!

2: **Brainstorm content**

_____Where does the story occur? What fits story's characters, theme, and goals?

_____Each student shares a one-paragraph summary of their story with their critique group. This reads like the inside flap of a novel—quick introduction to characters, plot, setting, and why readers should be interested. Each groupmember reads all summaries to prepare for meeting.
_____At virtual meeting, each student makes suggestions based on evidence and textual information.

3: What is the theme?

_____What is a 'theme'? Why is it important? Review several books students have read and discuss the impact of 'theme' on story's success.
_____Determine theme of student story and discuss how it will be conveyed to the critique group.
_____When discussing, cite evidence.

4: Heroes, villains, plot, and where it happens

_____Based on the theme, determine characters, how they deliver the story, general story arc (plot), and setting.
_____Make sure characters grow from their experiences.
_____Discuss character sketches, story arc, settings with critique group. Pay attention to:

- how the plot unfolds
- how the characters change as the plot moves toward resolution
- whether this is a character- or plot-driven story (explain)

_____When discussing, groupmembers cite evidence to support analysis.

5: Sketch out at least ten chapters of the book.

_____Chapters continually increase reader interest:

- What problem creates a crisis?
- What plot points make the story increasingly complex and interesting?
- What major conflicts and resolutions develop?
- What is the final critical conflict/crisis?

_____Share outline with the teacher.
_____When discussing, cite evidence to support.

Great Writing Quotes

A book is proof humans are capable of magic. –Carl Sagan

I'm a writer. Anything you say or do may appear in a story. – Anonymous

All good writing is like swimming under water and holding your breath. –F. Scott Fitzgerald

There is nothing to writing. All you do is sit at a typewriter and bleed. –Ernest Hemingway

Writing is easy. All you do is cross out the wrong words. —Mark Twain

The road to hell is paved with adverbs. –Stephen King

Why don't you write books people can read? —Nora Joyce to her husband James

The true writer has nothing to say. What counts is the way he says it. —Alain Robbe-Grillet

It takes a heap of sense to write good nonsense—Mark Twain

It's difficult switching gears because characters have very different voices and very different ways of thinking. –George RR Martin

Write every day. –advice of all serious writers

6: Write the book

_____ Write in any word processing program (Google Docs, Word, Notes, or another).
_____ Write 1000 words at a sitting—two-three pages. Let the words tumble out based on the outline and research. Don't edit until the end. Each novel must be 15,000 words (technically a novella).
_____ Use proper writing conventions, descriptive details, and well-structured event sequences.
_____ Use domain-specific and academic language in story.
_____ Use narrative techniques, such as dialogue, pacing, and description to develop experiences, events, and characters.
_____ Use transition words to signal shifts from one-time frame or setting to another.
_____ Provide a conclusion that follows from events.
_____ Develop and strengthen writing by planning, revising, editing, rewriting, or trying a new approach, based on collaboration and feedback from critique group.
_____ Research where necessary; draw on several sources and refocus when appropriate.
_____ Hints for writing:

- *Write every day even if you don't want to. Write, throw it out if no good, but write.*
- *Read—a lot. Especially in your genre.*
- *Experience life—so you can write about it. Notice the world around you. Think how you could write it.*

_____ As student works, share their draft novella with critique group:

- *Does it demonstrate command of grammar and spelling?*
- *Are sentence patterns varied for interest and style?*
- *Is style and tone consistent?*
- *Does plot unfold in episodes?*
- *What details carry theme?*
- *How do characters respond as the plot moves forward?*
- *Are word meanings clear based on context?*
- *How is point of view developed? Is it effective? Why?*
- *Does story engage and orient reader by establishing a context, introducing narrator/characters, and organizing events to unfold naturally and logically?*
- *Does story use narrative techniques such as dialogue, pacing, and description, to develop experiences, events, and characters?*
- *Does story use transition words, phrases, and clauses to convey sequence and signal shifts from one-time frame or setting to another?*
- *Does conclusion follow from events?*

_____ Remind students to back up their work:

- *on a flash drive*

- on hard drive
- in cloud
- by emailing a copy of the draft to themselves every time they work on it

Class exit ticket: **Tweet weekly on class Twitter account on individual progress. Use a #hashtag like #MrCgradeebook.**

Differentiation

- Compare Mark Twain's quote about the use of the word 'very' ("Substitute 'damn' every time you're inclined to write 'very;' your editor will delete it and the writing will be just as it should be") and George RR Martin's (author of "Game of Thrones") quote including 'very' three times. What do students think about that? BTW, be ready to swap Twain's D word for a more school-friendly one if necessary.
- Compare and contrast two student novellas, including what they "see" and "hear" when reading text to what they perceive when they listen or watch.
- Compare and contrast student novellas in different genres.
- This activity may be used for Genius Hour.
- Assign a student to enter virtual meeting times, publication dates, and more.

Lesson #30—Publish an Ebook

Vocabulary	Problem solving	Skills
• Agent • Ebook • Kindle • Novella • Publisher • Share	• I'm not comfortable evaluating class-mate writing (use a checklist) • Can't get my book ready on time (discuss with GHO group how to do this) • I lost my document (did you back up?) • I don't want to sell book (discuss options)	Publish an ebook Videography Problem solving Keyboarding Digital citizenship
Academic Applications Writing, videography, collaboration, sharing	**Materials Required** parent permission slips for GHO, back-up for novellas (cloud, flash drive, other)	**Standards** CCSS: W.9-10.5-7,10 NETS: 6d

Essential Question

I'm just a kid. How can I publish a book?

Big Idea

With proper planning, organization, and creativity, any student can publish a book.

Teacher Preparation

- Know which tasks weren't completed last class and whether they are necessary to move forward.
- Ensure all required links are on student digital devices.
- Integrate domain-specific tech vocabulary into lesson.
- Know whether you need extra time to complete this lesson with your student group.

Assessment Strategies

- Worked independently
- Used good keyboarding habits
- Completed warm-up, exit ticket
- Joined classroom conversations
- [tried to] solve own problems
- Higher order thinking: analysis, evaluation, synthesis
- Habits of mind observed

Steps

Time required: 90 minutes at the end of the semester or grading period—following prior 'Write an Ebook' lesson

Class warm-up: Keyboarding on the class typing program, paying attention to posture

_____Required skill level: completed an ebook in previous lesson (or another activity)

7: **Publish!**

_____Publish student ebooks through:

- iBooks
- class Kindle account
- PDFs read through Kindle or iBooks on iPads, netbooks, Chromebooks, desktop computers, other digital devices

Make a Book Trailer

_____Introduce student ebooks and inspire enthusiasm with a book trailer.
_____Discuss the meaning of 'book trailer'.
_____Show students samples like these:

- *Tuesdays with Morrie—available on SchoolTube*
- *The Vampire Diaries—available on SchoolTube*
- *A Summer of Kings – available on YouTube*

_____Tools for book trailers include:

- Animoto
- a slideshow program (convert slideshow to video)
- iMovie (or another movie maker tool)

Class exit ticket: **Tweet a link to student trailer and a quick synopsis.**

Differentiation

- Cost of publishing? Fund it with Kickstarter as this class did. Tie in with discussion on economics and money.
- Early finishers: visit class internet start page for websites that tie into classwork.

_____
_____
_____
_____

Lesson #31—The Debate: Research

Vocabulary	Problem solving	Skills
• Argument • Conjecture • Evidence • Opinion • Perspective • Persuasive writing • Point of view • Rebuttal	• I can't speak in front of people (this is a good project for practicing) • Why can't I use my opinion (you can if it's based on fact and evidence) • I don't like trying to talk people into my opinion (share evidence) • I can't counter one of the arguments (chat with teammates)	Debate Research skills Digital citizenship Compare-contrast Problem solving
Academic Applications research	**Materials Required** Backchannel devices, examples of debates, assessment rubrics	**Standards** CCSS: SL.9-10.1a-d NETS: 5a-d, 6d, 7b-d

Essential Question

How do I evaluate evidence to support my point of view?

Big Idea

Perspective taking is critical to understanding issues

Teacher Preparation

- Talk with grade-level team so you tie into inquiry.
- Ask what tech problems students found difficult.
- Ensure required links are available.
- Know if you need extra time to complete lesson.

Assessment Strategies

- Worked well in a group
- Completed warm-up, exit ticket
- Joined classroom conversations
- [tried to] solve own problems
- Decisions followed class rules
- Left room as s/he found it
- Higher order thinking: analysis, evaluation, synthesis
- Habits of mind observed

Steps

Time required: 90 minutes to prepare for debate presentations
Class warm-up: break into debate groups as assigned by teacher or selected by students

_____Required skill level: Understand online research; passion for thinking.
_____Before beginning, put backchannel device onto the class screen (Padlet, class Twitter account, Google Forms).
_____Debating makes research, listening, presenting, and learning fun.
_____Throughout the Common Core standards, you see words like *interpret, argument,* and *analyze*. College and career-ready students are expected to **make and justify their point through argumentation**.
_____The college and career-ready student will, among other things:

... without significant scaffolding, comprehend and evaluate complex texts across a range of types and disciplines, and construct effective

arguments and convey intricate or multifaceted information.

_____Show two examples of debates:

- *Boston University—on YouTube*
- *World University Final—on YouTube*
- *Presidential Debate*
- *college debate team—on YouTube*

_____Look for speaking style (formal), evidence presented to support claims, organization of information, and vocabulary used.

_____Debates help students grasp critical thinking and presentation skills, including:

- *abstract thinking*
- *analytical thinking*
- *citizenship/ethics/etiquette*
- *clarity*
- *critical thinking*
- *distinguishing fact from opinion*
- *establishing/defending point of view*
- *identifying bias*
- *language usage*
- *organization*
- *perspective-taking*
- *persuasion*
- *public speaking*
- *teamwork*
- *thinking on their feet—if evidence is refuted, students must 'get back into game'*
- *using research authentically*

> **Students who are College-Career Ready**
>
> ...demonstrate independence.
>
> ...delineate and evaluate the argument and specific claims, including validity of reasoning as well as relevance and sufficiency of evidence.
>
> ...evaluate intricate arguments and...surmount challenges posed by complex texts
>
> —Common Core

_____Working in groups, students research opposite sides of an issue and then debate it in front of class. They tie arguments to class reading, general knowledge, as well as evidence from research. They take questions.

_____Listeners must ask evidence-based questions with the goal of finding information that will convince them which side is right.

_____Students break into two-four-person teams. Offer a list of topics related to their studies or current events. Divide into 'pro' and 'con'.

_____Explain that some students might be debating positions opposite to their beliefs. 'Perspective taking' is an important skill to learn.

_____Give students time to research, but not too much. Expect them to read closely, work quickly, and

> ... evaluate the argument and specific claims, assessing whether the reasoning is valid and the evidence is relevant and sufficient; identify false statements and fallacious reasoning.
>
> —Common Core

_____make decisions based on their knowledge of reliable websites.

_____When students use the internet, remind them of their rights and responsibilities (see Lesson on *Digital Citizenship*). How can students make sure what they find is reliable and trustworthy?

_____Students work to "...*construct viable arguments and critique the reasoning of others...*" The goal is that, during the debate, they can (Common Core):

- *introduce claim*
- *support claim with clear reasons and relevant evidence*
- *use words, phrases, and clauses to clarify the relationship between claim and reasons*
- *establish and maintain a formal style*
- *provide a concluding statement that follows from the argument presented*
- *demonstrate command of speaking conventions*

_____Additionally, student groups are expected to:

- *develop three reasons for and three against the topic, and how to refute each*
- *develop a response to points expected from the other team. Teams can't simply spiel off pros and cons. They must connect to opponent's arguments.*

_____Team must conjecture opposition arguments and responses so they are prepared.

_____Team members assume responsibility for researching topics. Once resources are collected, they present to group for discussion. Group will decide if and how they should be used.

_____Use notetaking tools to collect and share information.

_____Teacher is *facilitator*—assisting students to understand team roles, maintain focus, and brainstorm research topics.

_____Prior to debate, students review debate evaluation rubric.

Class exit ticket: ***Tweet a summary of team position on the topic.***

Differentiation

- *Assign a student to enter debate dates into online calendar.*
- *Early finishers: Work with team on preparation for presentation.*

Lesson #32—The Debate: Presentation

Vocabulary	Problem solving	Skills
• Argument • Bias • Conjecture • Evidence • Opinion • Perspective • Persuasive writing • Point of view • Rebuttal	• I can't find anything on topic (work with your team) • I can't speak in front of people (practice) • Why can't I use my opinion (you can if it's based on fact and evidence) • I don't like trying to talk people into my opinion (share evidence) • I can't counter one of the arguments (chat with teammates)	Debate presentation Speaking and listening Problem solving Digital citizenship
Academic Applications	**Materials Required**	**Standards**
Most academic topics	Two long tables, mic, video equipment, assessment rubrics, student workbooks (if using)	CCSS: SL.9-10.1a-d NETS: 6d

Essential Question

How do I evaluate evidence to support my point of view?

Big Idea

Perspective taking is critical to understanding issues

Teacher Preparation

- Know which tasks weren't completed last class and whether they are necessary to move forward.
- Ask what tech problems students need help with.
- Know if you need extra time to complete lesson.

Assessment Strategies

- Worked well as part of team
- Gave debate presentation
- Completed warm-up
- Joined classroom conversations
- [tried to] solve own problems
- Decisions followed class rules
- Higher order thinking: analysis, evaluation, synthesis
- Habits of mind observed

Steps

Time required: 45 minutes per debate
Class warm-up: Prepared debate materials if a presenter, assessment rubrics if audience

_____Required skill level: Prior lesson on Debate.
_____During debate, students:

- organize reasons and evidence clearly
- support claim(s) with clear reasons and relevant evidence, using credible sources and demonstrating understanding of the topic
- use words, phrases, and clauses to clarify the relationships among claim(s)
- establish and maintain a formal style
- provide a concluding statement that follows from argument presented

_____Students who are NOT presenting will grade their classmates using *Assessment* below. In 'Comments' box, they will provide evidence to support score.

Assessment 32—Debate evaluation

Debate members: _____ **Did this side win:** _____

Criteria	1-10	Comments
Appearance of Team		
Opening statements were well organized, not read (from memory) with evidentiary references		
Team members addressed remarks to audience, speaking loud enough for all to hear		
Team members participated equally		
Rebuttal was specific to arguments in opening statement		
Answers to audience questions were well thought out		
Respect was shown throughout for opposing team. (No name calling, interruptions, etc.)		
Effective use of evidence to support point of view		
Used academic and domain-specific vocabulary where required		
Demonstrated command of language conventions		
TOTAL POINTS	/100	

_____ Over a period of classes, students:

- debate each other in front of classmates, parents, teachers—-you decide—presenting both sides of the argument
- use evidence to support claims; provide evidence without reading from notes
- provide attribution of claims as required
- use academic and domain-specific vocabulary facilely
- become comfortable sharing debates on the class website/blog with interested parties

_____ Listeners must be prepared to ask evidence-based questions. Debaters must use evidence to convince listener. Both sides challenge information and demand proof.

_____ Listeners grade teams. Complete one rubric for each side of debate.

_____ Standard debate format is:

6 minute Presentation - Pro	2 minute Response – Pro
6 minute Presentation - Con	2 minute Response - Con
5 minute Work Period	1 minute Work Period
4 minute Rebuttal - Pro	1 minute Position Summary - Pro or Con
4 minute Rebuttal - Con	1 minute Position Summary - Pro or Con
3 minute Work Period	5 minute Tally Ballots/Announce Winner

_____Collect rubrics after each debate and tabulate. This can be done with hard copies or the assessment in student workbooks (saved as a screenshot and shared).
_____Include a rubric from yourself and other teachers that are participating.
_____Decide how to award winners—school ceremony, in class, public announcement.
_____Have students share their thoughts via a blog post or class Twitter feed. Thoughts should be objective, on-point, with domain-specific language appropriate to task, audience, and purpose.

Class exit ticket: ***Tweet a summary to compare-contrast the positions of two teams.***

Differentiation

- Have students stage a famous debate, like Lincoln-Douglas or Southern cessation from the union, as part of inquiry into those topics.
- If this is election time, debate presidential or local politics.
- Virtually debate another school.

Index

academic slideshows, 160
Acrobat, 35
Adobe Slate, 159, 160
Adobe Voice, 159
Alice, 198
Animation, 164, 165
Animoto, 89, 107, 207, 219
Annotating PDFs, 33
Annotation Tool, 8, 35
App creation, 210
argument, 138
Articles, 12
ASCII Art, 90
Ask a Tech Teacher, 9
Assessment, 5, 15, 30, 78, 79, 80, 81, 108, 196
Autosum, 134
Avatars, 33, 36
backchannel, 167
Backchannel device, 33, 93, 109, 147, 171, 175, 203
Back-up, 24
Banzai, 144, 145
benchmark, 77
Best Practices, 10
Blank keyboard quiz, 78, 81
Blog grading rubric, 52
Blogging, 33, 37, 58, 59, 63, 202, 203
Calendar, 115, 130, 133, 152
Canva, 118, 120, 129, 170, 194
Cartoons, 109, 110
Cast shadows, 185, 186, 194
cell phones, 64
Charts, 139
Chromebook, 9, 34, 35, 77, 78, 82, 105, 107, 135
Chromebook blank keyboard, 82
Class Calendar, 38
Class Internet Start Page, 35, 39
class rules, 25
Class warm-up, 24, 33, 62, 73, 93, 104, 109, 115, 127, 134, 144, 147, 151, 158, 165, 167, 171, 175, 183, 185, 197, 201, 203, 210, 213, 218, 220, 223
class website, 40
Clone, 188
Cloud, 41
Coding, 11, 12, 210, 211
Columns, 171
Comics, 11, 12, 109, 110
Common Core, 4, 5, 10, 31, 37, 58, 100
Compare-contrast, 25, 104, 105, 116, 117, 128, 136, 220
Composer, 197
Composition, 210
Content Standards, 33, 62, 73
Copyright, 10, 28, 54, 66, 147, 175, 176
cover page, 129

cracking, 65
Creative Commons, 64, 176
Critical-thinking, 197
Crop, 187
Cyberbullying, 63
Data, 73
Debate, 11, 12, 148, 220, 221, 223, 224
Decoding vocab, 33
desktop, 190
Diagram, 134
differentiation, 5, 8
Digital citizenship, 24, 62, 73, 93, 104, 109, 115, 127, 134, 144, 147, 151, 158, 167, 171, 175, 183, 185, 197, 201, 203, 210, 213, 218, 220, 223
Digital Communications, 63
digital devices, 9
Digital footprint, 64
Digital Law, 64
digital lockers, 41
Digital notetaking, 33, 40
Digital Portfolio, 54
digital portfolios, 35, 41
Digital Privacy, 65
Digital rights and responsibilities, 65
Discussion Board, 42
Domain, 147
Dropbox, 41
Drop-box, 41
DTP, 136
Electronic communication, 63
email, 27, 42
embed, 202
essential question, 5
Evidence Board, 24, 33, 35, 43, 104
Excel, 135, 137, 140
Exit Tickets, 5, 30
extensions, 147, 149
Fair use, 65, 66, 176
Filter, 190
Financial literacy, 144
flaming, 66
Flier, 129
Flipboard, 123
Formative assessments, 7, 1407
Formatting, 115, 127
formulas, 136, 171
Games, 90
GE lit tour, 171
Genius Hour, 11, 12, 203, 204, 205, 208, 209
Gimp, 186
Gmail, 42
Google Apps, 41, 44
Google Calendar, 38, 152
Google Docs, 107, 118, 120

Google Earth, 11, 12, 151, 153, 156, 171, 172, 173, 174
Google Earth Board, 153, 156
Google Earth tour, 156
Google Forms, 30, 92, 152
Google Maps, 171
Google search, 6, 8
Grammar, 69, 137, 164
Graph, 134, 139, 140
Graphic organizers, 168
Graphics, 159
Habits of Mind, 8, 28, 29
hacking, 65
Haiku Deck, 159
Hardware, 47, 48
hits 148
home row, 76
Homework, 26, 42, 76
Hour of Code, 211
https 66
Hue and Saturation, 186, 191
hunt 'n peck, 74
iAnnotate, 8, 35
IB, 28, 29
image copyrights, 65
image editing, 175, 183, 184, 185, 186, 190, 193, 194, 195, 196
image editor, 186, 189, 195
Images, 13
iMovie, 219
Important Keys Quiz, 78
Infographics, 11, 12, 167, 168, 169
Inquiry, 7, 9, 90
internet images, 169
Internet safety, 66, 148
Internet Search, 148
Internet Start Page, 56
iPad, 34, 36, 49, 77, 78, 91, 97, 105, 106, 107, 106, 111, 118, 120, 129, 158, 171, 186, 206
Keyboard Curriculum, 79
Keyboarding, 9, 25, 32, 33, 62, 73, 79, 89, 93, 104, 109, 115, 127, 134, 144, 147, 151, 158, 165, 167, 171, 175, 183, 185, 197, 201, 203, 213, 218, 220, 223
Keyboarding Challenge, 79, 88
Kindle, 218
Lab Manners, 27
learning styles, 168
line graph, 140
Linoit, 30, 155
LiveBinders, 39
Mac, 35, 105, 118, 120, 135
macro, 183
Magazine, 117, 120, 121, 122, 126, 129
Math, 12, 92, 93, 100, 134, 136, 137, 144, 204, 210
mathematically proficient, 138
menu, 24
MIT's App Inventor, 212

models, 135
mouse, 32, 34, 187, 189
MS Publisher, 118, 120, 129
MS Word, 107
Mulligan Rule, 76
Netiquette Rules, 66
newsletter, 117, 118, 119
Notability, 35
Notable, 8
Online Reputations, 65
outlining, 38, 106, 109
Padlet, 30, 36, 56, 57, 96, 109, 134, 147, 151, 152, 155, 213, 220
Paint, 193
passwords, 66
PC, 104
PDF annotation, 33
photo editing, 184, 186
Photoshop, 186, 195, 196
Photoshop Tennis, 186, 195
Piktochart, 167, 169, 170
Pixelmator, 186
Pixlr, 186
Placeholder, 115, 127
Plagiarism, 65
Polls, 30
Posters, 127, 129
posture, 32, 74
PowerPoint, 105, 116, 118, 128, 159, 160, 186
Presentations, 89, 164, 172
Problem solving, 24, 33, 62, 73, 93, 94, 97, 104, 109, 115, 127, 134, 144, 147, 151, 158, 165, 167, 171, 175, 183, 185, 197, 201, 203, 210, 213, 218, 220, 223
Problem Solving Board, 93, 95, 96, 97, 98, 153
Protopage, 39, 57
Public domain, 64, 65, 66, 176
Publish an ebook, 218
Publisher, 118
quotes, 94
QWERTY, 76
Reliable Websites, 149
repeated reasoning, 139
research, 156
Right-click, 24
rights and responsibilities, 66
risk takers, 8
Rows, 171
rubric, 35, 38, 45, 97, 119, 120, 123, 125, 126, 130, 132, 133, 152, 161, 164, 166, 173, 174, 203, 204, 209, 222, 224, 225
Scoop It, 123
Scope and Sequence, 25
Scratch, 198
screen, 115
screencasts, 44, 96, 104, 105, 107, 201, 207
Screenshots, 11, 44, 104
Search/Research, 12

sequencing, 108
Serialized novel, 109, 113, 114
sharing, 31, 58, 62, 128, 197, 213, 218
shortkeys, 77, 90, 93, 95
Sign-up Genius, 152
Slideshow, 162, 164, 165, 166
smartphone, 8
Social Media, 62, 67
software, 9
spam, 43
Speak Like a Geek, 25, 62, 73, 104, 109, 115, 127, 134, 144, 147, 153, 154, 157, 158, 175, 183, 185, 197, 210
Speaking and Listening, 12
speed quiz, 78
spelling, 111
Spreadsheet Skills, 135, 136, 141
Standards for Mathematical Practice, 100
Stock Market Game, 144, 145
Storyboard, 104, 111, 158, 160, 163, 164
Student blogging agreement, 51
student digital workbooks, 7
Student website, 45
Student workbooks, 9, 35
SumoPaint, 186
Surface tablet, 36, 105
syllabus, 25
Symbaloo, 39, 56
table, 108
Teacher Training, 92
Teacher Web,, 41
Technology Curriculum, 5
Text box, 115, 127
texting, 43, 63, 64, 70
timeline, 121, 122
TinEye, 176
Transition, 165

Twitter, 11, 12, 26, 32, 33, 36, 37, 41, 67, 68, 69, 70, 109, 104, 109, 112, 113, 134, 147, 151, 155, 185, 212, 213, 214, 217, 220, 225
Twitter Novel, 112
Type to Learn, 77
TypingTest.com, 78
Video, 107
Videography, 218
virtual wall, 25, 30, 36, 155
visual organizer, 168
Vocabulary, 24, 31, 33, 46, 62, 73, 93, 104, 109, 115, 127, 134, 144, 147, 151, 158, 165, 167, 171, 175, 183, 185, 197, 201, 203, 210, 213, 218, 220, 223
Vocabulary Wall, 155
VoiceThread, 108
Web-based Tools, 7, 11, 12
website address, 149
Website grading rubric, 53
Webtools, 201
widget, 198
Windows, 35, 36, 105
Wix, 45
Word, 31, 107, 118, 140
Word processing, 40, 90, 109, 104, 107, 108, 109, 128, 159
Wordpress, 45
workbook, 137
worksheet, 137
Wrap, 158
Write an ebook, 213
Writing, 11, 12, 33, 52, 53, 54, 69, 70, 73, 104, 109, 110, 113, 115, 119, 127, 171, 175, 183, 185, 197, 203, 213, 218, 220
writing skills, 68, 70
YouTube, 107, 198
Zoho Docs, 135

Which book	Price (print/digital/Combo)
K-8th Tech Curriculum (each)	$25.99-32.99 + p&h
K-8 Combo (all 9 textbooks)	$210-450 + p&h
K-8 Student workbooks (per grade)	$199 and up; license for room/school/district)
HS Technology Curriculum Bk. 1-3	$25.99 and up
35 K-6 Inquiry-based Projects	$31.99/25.99/52.18 + p&h
55 Tech Projects—Vol I, II, Combo	$18.99 /$35.38–digital only (free shipping)
K-8 Keyboard Curriculum—3 options	$20 and up + p&h
K-8 Digital Citizenship Curriculum	$29.95/25.99/50.38 + p&h
CCSS—Math, Language, Reading, Writing	$26.99 ea./80 for 4–digital only
K-5 Common Core Projects	$29.95/23.99/48.55 + p&h
Themed webinars	$8-30
PD classes (online—for groups)	$795
Tech camp for kids	$179 + p&h
College credit classes (online)	$497 and up
Digital Citizenship certificate class	Starts at $29.99
Mentoring (30 min. minimum)	$50/session
Consulting/seminars	Call or email for prices
169 Tech Tips from Classroom	$9.99 (digital only)
PBL lessons—singles	$1.99 and up
Bundles of lesson plans	$4.99 and up (digital only)
Tech Ed Scope and Sequence	$9.99 and up (digital only, Word format)
New Teacher Survival Kit	$285-620+ p&h
Homeschool Tech Survival Kit	$99 + p&h
Classroom tech poster bundles	Start at $9.99

Free sample? Visit Structured Learning LLC website
Prices subject to change
Email Zeke.rowe@structuredlearning.net
Pay via PayPal, Credit Card, Amazon, TPT, school district PO

www.ingramcontent.com/pod-product-compliance
Lightning Source LLC
Chambersburg PA
CBHW080224170426
43192CB00015B/2741